JUVENILE JUSTICE
AN AUSTRALIAN PERSPECTIVE

Chris Cunneen and Rob White

Melbourne

OXFORD UNIVERSITY PRESS

Oxford   Auckland   New York

OXFORD UNIVERSITY PRESS AUSTRALIA

Oxford   New York
Athens   Auckland   Bangkok   Bombay
Calcutta   Cape Town   Dar es Salaam   Delhi
Florence   Hong Kong   Istanbul   Karachi
Kuala Lumpur   Madras   Madrid   Melbourne
Mexico City   Nairobi   Paris   Singapore
Taipei   Tokyo   Toronto

and associated companies in
Berlin   Ibadan

OXFORD is a trade mark of Oxford University Press

National Library of Australia
Cataloguing-in-Publication data:

Cunneen, Chris (Christopher), 1953–   .
    Juvenile justice: an Australian perspective.

    Bibliography.
    Includes index.
    ISBN 0 19 553613 4.

    1. Juvenile justice, Administration of – Australia.
    2. Juvenile delinquency – Australia.   3. Juvenile detention –
    Austraila. I. White, R. D. (Robert Douglas), 1956–   .
    II. Title.

364.360994

Edited by Janet Mackenzie
Indexed by Trischa Baker
Cover design by Steve Randles
Text design by Guy Mirabella
Typeset by Syarikat Seng Teik Sdn. Bhd., Malaysia.
Printed by McPherson's Printing Group, Australia.
Published by Oxford University Press,
253 Normanby Road, South Melbourne, Australia

contents

tables and charts

Tables

Charts

acknowledgements

The authors would like to thank their colleagues and office staff in the Institute of Criminology, Sydney University Law School, and the Department of Criminology at Melbourne University for their support during the writing of the book. Research assistance for sections of the book was provided by Jon Morrow with the support of a Legal Scholarship Research Grant from the NSW Law Foundation and the Sydney University Law School. Special acknowledgement is made of the Human Rights and Equal Opportunity Commission and the Queensland Anti-Discrimination Commission which provided office space for Chris Cunneen in Cairns during study leave in the latter part of 1994. Jim Brooks, the Regional Director of the commission, was particularly helpful. Finally, thanks to Jill Lane from Oxford University Press for her mixture of perseverance and patience.

The authors are grateful for permission to reproduce the poem 'Hate' by C.B. from M. Searles and G. Goodfellow (eds) *Heroes and Villains: An Anthology of Poems by Young People in Detention* (Adelaide, 1994), funded by the South Australian Crime Prevention Strategy and the Department for Family and Community Services.

introduction

Young offenders and juvenile crime have a high public profile in Australia today. Indeed, in most advanced industrialised countries the same heightened awareness of youth issues, fuelled by extensive media hype surrounding youthful deviance and anti-social behaviour, is apparent. Electoral campaigns centring on 'get tough' policies and general public concern over juvenile offending will not abate in the foreseeable future. This is especially so because the conditions linked to the generation of youth crime (such as poverty and homelessness) and the official responses to crime (favouring a coercive and disciplining approach rather than social justice) do not appear likely to change significantly in the next few years, if at all. In this context, it is even more important, therefore, that we develop strategies and programs relating to juvenile justice issues which are based upon informed opinion rather than conjecture, exaggeration and stereotype.

This book is about the people and institutions involved with juvenile justice in Australia. While the material in the book concentrates on Australian facts and figures, histories and examples, we hope that the broad conceptual and empirical descriptions will be of use and interest to readers beyond these shores as well. For the issues, theories and social conflicts with which we deal are grounded in general economic and social conditions which share important commonalities with countries such as Canada, the United States, New Zealand and the United Kingdom. Certainly the general processes and issues we describe are in many ways applicable to more than just the Australian domestic context.

Our intention in writing the book was to provide an introduction to the main concepts and issues in juvenile justice, and to provide a consolidated overview of the dynamics of youth crime and the institutions of social control. Given the need for considered debate and thoughtful policy formulation, we wanted to prepare a book which dealt with all facets of the juvenile justice process in a manner which is both simple and descriptive, yet critical. In other words, we thought it was important to undertake a book that provides basic information across a broad range of areas, but which also raises questions about the actual workings of the juvenile justice system and, indeed, which might challenge some of the ways in which we think about juvenile justice issues.

We have attempted to provide a general and comprehensive review of juvenile justice. However, we do not pretend that we have been able to deal adequately with all of the dimensions and issues surrounding it. For example, in Australia there are some eight different jurisdictions, besides the federal government, which in some way impinge upon juvenile justice. A full overview of all legislation, all programs and all statistical collections in each State, territory and federal jurisdiction would be an enormous task, and somewhat questionable in utility, given the rapidly changing legal and administrative landscapes in each. Nevertheless, we can provide broad sketches of the existing systems, and expose the main principles which guide the systems around the country.

In a similar vein, the book does not purport to provide an in-depth exploration and analysis of each conceptual argument and empirical debate in the field of criminology as these pertain to juvenile justice. Again, our approach has been to lay the theoretical and political groundwork whereby the issues we do identify may be elaborated and critically evaluated in substantive detail elsewhere.

We view this book as being introductory in nature, and in particular designed for student use. But we also see it as an important reference for youth and community workers, justice department officials, members of the police, criminologists and other social scientists, social workers, and young people themselves who want to find out more about parts of the system, and important social issues, about which they do not have adequate information.

THE BOOK IN OUTLINE

The book is divided into three parts. Part I, 'History and Theory', provides a historical and theoretical overview of the development of juvenile justice. This section of the book is necessarily international in flavour. This is because the historical changes which gave birth to 'juveniles' and to 'juvenile justice' institutions were not unique to Australia. The advent of industrial capitalism was to transform basic human relationships in profound ways, and the transformations occurring culturally and in social institutions had a dramatic impact on the position of young people generally in countries such as Great Britain, the United States and Australia. Not surprisingly, the institutional changes wrought by industrial capitalism were accompanied by new forms of state intervention in the lives of young people, including young offenders. As we show, the development of specifically youth-oriented institutions in this country paralleled, and occasionally led or followed, similar developments in comparable countries overseas.

Our understanding of the nature of juvenile justice, and its institutions, is inextricably bound up with our explanation for the causes of juvenile crime.

Certainly the most influential perspectives in criminology have been those associated with 'classical' and 'positivist' explanations of crime. It is important, therefore, that we have some idea of the origins and basic propositions of these traditional perspectives on crime, especially since they have shaped and continue to shape the basic institutions and ideas of our contemporary criminal justice system.

Twentieth-century criminology has largely focused at a theoretical level on juvenile offending. This too has had major implications for the types of state intervention, and methods of responding to youth crime, which have emerged since the beginning of the century. Mainstream theoretical perspectives have tended to be more sociological in nature, to explore the impact of social background, social opportunity and labelling processes on the making of a juvenile offender.

Finally, there is a range of theories which challenge the mainstream orthodoxies of much contemporary thinking about juvenile justice issues. These range from theories of the Left (such as Marxism and feminism) to perspectives associated with the far Right (such as libertarianism and authoritarian populism). The discussions of theory highlight the fact that how we think about young people, and crime, is ultimately a political process imbued with value judgement, ideology and ethical principles.

Part II, 'The Dynamics of Juvenile Justice', examines the nature of contemporary juvenile crime from several different angles. For example, it is important to establish the factual basis of what we are talking about by presenting and critically analysing the statistical indicators available on the extent and composition of youth crime. There is a range of official and unofficial ways to 'measure' youth crime, none of which is completely satisfactory, but none of which is completely untrue or useless either. The media images of crime are, however, very problematic. And they can have a major impact on public policy, depending upon how politicians use and misuse media portrayals of youth crime trends. This is a matter of particular concern.

If we are to adequately examine the nature of youth offending, it is essential to acknowledge the influence of class, indigenous status and gender on the manner in which young people are actually processed by the system. To do this, we explore the differential position of young people in the spheres of production (paid work) and consumption (buying things), the alienating experiences which some young people have of school, and the attempts by the state to manage and contain a large and growing marginalised youth population. The relationship between class and community resources, including public spaces, is an important consideration in any account of juvenile justice institutions.

One of the major deficiencies in many discussions of juvenile justice is the lack of adequate consideration of the fact that a disproportionate number of institutionalised young offenders are indigenous young people. The impact of colonisation and post-colonial interventions has had and continues to have an enormous effect on young Aboriginal and Torres Strait Islanders. To understand the injustices of 'justice' it is necessary to examine such things as the transition of indigenous people from welfare recipients to criminals. High rates of contact, incarceration and deaths in custody are phenomena which need to be explained and acted upon; they do not fit simply or neatly into traditional or mainstream theoretical frameworks on causes and responses to offending.

Similarly, the gendered nature of juvenile justice has begun to receive greater attention in recent years. The relatively low number of young women involved with the formal criminal justice system has been used to rationalise major silences in academic study of juvenile justice on gender issues. Today, feminist writers in particular have presented a number of important insights into the unequal treatment meted out to boys and girls by the system, and analysed the manner in which a male-dominated social system manifests itself in areas such as criminal justice. In addition to questions such as the sexualisation of offences as these pertain to young women, attention is also being devoted to unravelling the manner in which 'femininity' and 'masculinity' can be used conceptually to explain the social processes underlying juvenile justice.

The final part of the book, Part III, 'The State, Punishment and Crime Prevention', looks more closely at the responses of the state to juvenile offending. It is important to begin with an overview of the key institutions and key players, and to understand the broad legislative framework of juvenile justice. The 'law' is not something which young people simply break: it also incorporates a wide range of institutional structures, different jurisdictional responsibilities, and particular ways of dealing with young people in society.

A central figure in the lives of many young people, especially those who contravene the law, is the police officer. The police have many different tasks to perform, and several alternative methods and strategies with which to perform these tasks. The nature, extent and type of intervention by the police in relation to young people is tremendously important in shaping the 'criminal career' or otherwise of young offenders. Issues of youth rights, police accountability and the potentials of community policing are, therefore, crucial to an appreciation of the dilemmas and conflicts involving police–youth relations.

Young offenders who have been charged with an offence must at some stage enter into the criminal justice system. An important part of this system is the court. How courts make their decisions, and the principles upon which they operate in terms of sentencing options, reflect the special position of young people in our society. So too do the experiences that young people have of the 'law' and of the courtroom. The use of detention is the most intrusive sanction available to the court. If incarceration is to be used, then a number of issues must be considered regarding the consequences of imprisonment for the young person and for society at large.

Finally, it must be recognised that the majority of young offenders do not end up in court, or in prison. There is a wide variety of community-based programs which are designed to divert young people from committing crime in the first place, and to keep them out of the formal criminal justice system if they have done so. Preventive measures aim to reduce crime rates through a number of alternative, and at times competing, social means. Other programs attempt to deal with young offenders by providing less formal forums in which to mete out punishment or provide restitution to victims. Even where sentenced in a court, the young offender may be placed back into the 'community' via some type of probationary or community service order. The relationship between formal state intervention and the extensive range of community-based informal programs warrants our close attention.

As the above summary indicates, we have tried to provide a wide-ranging survey of most parts of the juvenile justice system, the main theories which underpin policy development in this area, and the issues and perspectives necessary to a critical appraisal of key questions in the juvenile justice area. It is our hope that the reader will be informed, and provoked, by the descriptions and analyses provided in this book.

Crucially, we hope that the reader will be better equipped to intervene constructively and actively in juvenile justice debates and reform as a result of reading this book. If knowledge is power, then we hope that, in its own modest way, this book will empower those who wish to create a more humane and socially just system of juvenile justice in Australia.

history and theory

1 the development of juvenile justice

To understand the contemporary debates about juvenile justice and the nature of juvenile crime, it is important to think about issues relating to history and theory. Have juveniles always been involved in crime, or is it a modern phenomenon? How have our thoughts about young people and crime changed? Has the place of young people in society changed?

First, it is necessary to realise that the categories of 'youth', 'adolescent' and 'juvenile' are not universal, nor are they necessarily used consistently within a society. It is important to know where particular ideas about young people came from and how they developed. The social construction of youth is neither a natural nor neutral process, nor is it divorced from wider social, political and economic developments.

Secondly, notions of juvenile delinquency both depend on and recreate particular ideas about young people as a separate and socially definable group. Put simply, there can be no theory of juvenile offending without a concept of juvenile. For example, often in public usage and academic study the word 'youth' has implicitly, if not explicitly, referred primarily to young men. Much of the concern with youth questions has consistently ignored the experiences of young women, or relegated these to secondary importance because of sexist definitions and conceptions of the 'real world' (see McRobbie & Garber 1976; Brake 1985).

Thirdly, the systems developed for dealing with juvenile delinquency and crime are created and developed in particular historical contexts. A considered understanding of the historical development of juvenile justice is important because of the level of mythology surrounding juvenile offending. Pearson (1983) in particular has analysed the way notions of 'hooliganism' have taken on a symbolic and mythological quality. He has analysed the way in which 'causes' of juvenile crime constantly find their way into public rhetoric and reappear at particular historical moments. Such sentiments usually involve the presumed loss of authority and order. Pearson summarised the stereotype as follows.

The family no longer holds its proper place and parents have abandoned their responsibilities. In the classroom where once the tidy scholars applied themselves diligently in their neat rows of desks, there is a carnival of disrespect. The police and magistrates have had their hands tied by the interference of sentimentalists and dogooders (Pearson 1983: 3).

These common themes of loss of authority in the key institutions—the family, education and law enforcement—constantly re-emerge, along with claims that permissiveness has increased the levels of juvenile violence and lowered the standards of public behaviour. Within this scenario, the solutions which are proposed are often equally simple: greater levels of intervention by state agencies armed with more punitive powers.

The concept of juvenile delinquency dates from the beginning of the nineteenth century. According to Bernard (1992) one of the first uses of the term was in the *Report of the Committee for Investigating the Causes of the Alarming Increase of Juvenile Delinquency in the Metropolis*, published in London in 1816. The *concept* of juvenile delinquency is historically contingent. In other words, the concept developed at a particular moment in history. Several commentators have also argued that the *phenomenon* of juvenile crime is also contingent. Indeed Ferdinand (1989) provocatively asks, 'Which came first: juvenile delinquency or juvenile justice?' In our view, both arise simultaneously. The phenomenon of juvenile delinquency appears to be specifically modern. Some commentators have argued that it occurs with the transition from rural to urban societies and is associated with five factors: the breakdown of traditional mechanisms of social control; urbanisation; industrialisation; population growth; and juvenile justice mechanisms which systematically detect juvenile offending (Bernard 1992: 43–4). While these factors are important, it is our view that the class-based nature of juvenile justice needs to be recognised. The transformations to which Bernard refers occurred with the development of industrial capitalism which created an urbanised working class. It was the youth of this newly-formed class who were the targets of new systems of dealing with young people. In addition, the systems of control which were introduced into colonies like Australia were imposed in a society which was also in the process of dispossessing an indigenous minority. The treatment of indigenous young people became an important component in the development of juvenile justice in Australia.

The key period in understanding the development of a separate system for dealing with juvenile offenders was the second half of the nineteenth century. This was also an important period for the construction of other age-based differences involving young people, including restrictions on child labour and the introduction of compulsory schooling. The state also began to intervene actively in the provision of 'welfare' for the children of the 'perishing classes'. In practice these various measures were closely interlinked. For example, in the same year that the Public Schools Act was passed in New South Wales (1866), the Reformatory Schools Act (for young people convicted of criminal offences) and the Industrial Schools Act and Workhouse Act (for vagrant children) were passed. Specifically, in Australia the first moves to identify and recognise the category of 'young offenders' occurred with the development of institutions for dealing with neglected and destitute children. The major legal change in Australia during the period was the modification of court procedures to allow for juveniles to be dealt with summarily (that is, to have their less serious charges determined by a magistrate) (Seymour 1988: 3). More broadly, juvenile justice was an element in the expansion of state control and regulation during the later part of the nineteenth and the early twentieth centuries.

EARLY NINETEENTH-CENTURY DEVELOPMENTS

There were a number of similarities in the methods developed for dealing with juveniles across various nations, including Australia, the USA and Britain. As we have already suggested, a reason for these similarities is the economic, social and political transformations which were occurring at the time.

Until the early nineteenth century, children were expected to enter the adult world at a young age. Child labour was still regarded as universal. For instance in the early part of the nineteenth century, some 80 per cent of workers in English cotton mills were children (Morris & Giller 1987: 4). Similarly, the criminal justice system did little to formally separate children from adults. There was no separate legal category of 'juvenile offender'. At common law, the age of criminal responsibility was seven years. For children between the ages of seven and fourteen years, there was a presumption that they were incapable of committing an offence (*doli incapax*). However, this presumption was rebuttable in court by showing that the child knew the difference between right and wrong, and knew the act to be wrong. It is not clear whether rules relating to the age of criminal responsibility were effective in practice. Accurate knowledge of children's ages might not have been available; magistrates may have been ignorant of the law. In either case, children under the age of seven were incarcerated. In Victoria in the mid-1860s, children as young as six could be found in Pentridge gaol (Seymour 1988: 6).

In terms of punishment, adults and juveniles were treated the same: deterrence was the main object. An English judge, after sentencing a ten-year-old to death, stated that the child was a 'proper subject for capital punishment and ought to suffer'. On one day in 1815, five children between eight and twelve were hanged for petty larceny (Morris & Giller 1987: 6). Similarly, in Australia youth were executed, flogged, and sentenced to road gangs, transportation and imprisonment (Seymour 1988: 8–9).

However, there is some argument over the extent to which children were regularly treated the same as adults. The youth of the offender was sometimes held to be a mitigating factor in sentencing. Platt (1977) suggests that in cases relating to capital punishment, the prosecution refused to charge, juries refused to convict, and pardons were more frequently given. Notions of 'contamination' were also important in arguments concerning the separation of juveniles from adult offenders in prison. In 1836 in England the report of the Inspector of Prisons noted that 'the boy [*sic*] is thrown among veterans in guilt . . . and his vicious propensities cherished and inflamed . . . He enters the prison a child in years, and not infrequently also in crime; but he leaves it with a knowledge in the ways of wickedness' (cited in Morris & Giller 1987: 8). In Australia there were attempts to keep children separate from adults even where they were held in the same gaol. Some magistrates attempted to avoid the use of imprisonment for young people by discharging first offenders; using conditional discharges by placing children in the care of parents or institutions; or using conditional pardons (Seymour 1988: 9). These practices modified an otherwise draconian code. The swelling size of the prison population in England during the mid-nineteenth century also prompted reform (May 1981).

In the United States, the first juvenile institutions were houses of refuge such as the New York House of Refuge. The refuge was established in 1825 after numerous reports drew attention to the fact that the penitentiaries contained no separate facilities for juveniles. However, it appears that few of the youth sent to the refuge would have gone to the penitentiary in any case. Many were there for vagrancy. The 'placing out' system for juveniles developed about the same time, whereby youth were sent to work on farms (Bernard 1992).

There was a sense of crisis in the early nineteenth century concerning social issues like urbanisation, industrialisation, the growth of trade unions and working-class militancy, along with concerns about pauperism, vagrancy and juvenile crime. And there were also changes in the way crime was being conceptualised. As we discuss at greater length in the following chapter, classical criminology had seen crime as an outcome of free will, and the role of punishment was deterrence. However, by the early nineteenth century there was the growth of classificatory systems of criminal causation related to the rise of positivist criminology (see Chapter 2). For example, the 1816 committee's report into juvenile delinquency in London stated that the main causes were improper conduct of parents; the want of education; and the want of suitable employment. The committee also identified problems with the severity of the criminal code and the defective state of the police. In other words, the responsibility for juvenile offending was not necessarily seen as solely that of the young person (Morris & Giller 1987: 16).

The growth in the collection of criminal statistics facilitated a focus on juveniles. By the mid-nineteenth century, criminal statistics in England and Wales were showing that the 15–20-year-old age group was over-represented in offending figures (Morris & Giller 1987: 7). Thus the development of statistics, combined with other disciplines, allowed for the discovery of a 'new problem'.

Contemporary religious views also fitted well with the notion that delinquency was the result of social and moral conditions rather than innate depravity. There was then an increased focus on the physical conditions of the poor as well as the view that working-class families were ineffective and unreliable in their parenting.

POOR OR CRIMINAL?

The first steps in Australia towards creating a separate system for juveniles arose as a result of the problem of dealing with young people who were arriving as transported convicts. From the late eighteenth century various schemes involving apprenticeships were utilised. Indeed the first 'special institution' for juveniles was barracks for the training of convict boys under sixteen years of age.

Orphan schools were also established from the early 1800s to deal with destitute children. The origins of the child welfare system in Australia included the establishment of the Female Orphan School (1801); the Male Orphan School (1819); the Benevolent Asylum (1821) for 'destitute, unfortunate, needy families'; the Female School of Industry (1826); the Roman Catholic Orphan School (1837); and the Destitute Children's Asylum (1852). Both the Female and Male Orphan Schools adopted the policy of apprenticing children out to work. Legislative changes in New South Wales beginning in 1828 and 1834 enabled magistrates to place orphans as apprentices. Further legislative changes occurred until the late 1850s which expanded the category of children who could be bound over as apprentices (Seymour 1988: 21–3). There was overlap between the processes of criminalisation and the development of specific welfare institutions. A child in poverty could be dealt with under vagrancy laws and potentially imprisoned, or the child could be treated as destitute and kept in a welfare institution. In this sense, it is possible to see the development of different strategies to deal with issues essentially related to poverty and young people. There are important questions raised here about discretion and decision-making powers. Certainly, part of the method of dealing with poverty was reflected in class notions of the 'deserving' and 'undeserving' poor. Although the poor lived under similar material conditions, a distinction was made between the deserving and undeserving on the basis of behaviour, attitudes and respectability. The welfare and charitable institutions were there to assist those defined as the deserving poor; the others were treated as criminal. It appears that many of the children sent to gaol in Australia were there as a result of vagrancy charges. A large proportion of the 230 children under fourteen years of age sent to prison in Victoria during 1860 and 1861 had been sentenced for vagrancy (Seymour 1988: 18–19). Thus they were imprisoned for the crime of poverty rather than for the commission of any substantive offence.

REFORMATORIES AND INDUSTRIAL SCHOOLS

During the mid-nineteenth century there were two fundamental moves towards the establishment of a separate system for dealing with juveniles. One was to change the role of the magistrate's court in relation to hearing offences against juveniles; the other was to establish reformatories and industrial schools.

In Britain, the first parliamentary bills to alter procedures for dealing with juveniles were debated in 1821, 1829 and 1837. However, it was not until 1847 that the Juvenile Offenders Act was passed. The legislation increased the powers of magistrates to hear summarily larceny and theft offences committed by persons under the age of fourteen. In Australia the method of dealing with 'young offenders' began to change with the introduction of an 'Act to provide for the care and education of infants who may be convicted of felony or misdemeanour' (13 Vict. No. 21) in 1849. The legislation dealt with young people to the age of nineteen and allowed the court to apprentice young offenders. A more significant legislative change was the introduction of an 'Act for the more speedy trial and punishment of Juvenile Offenders' (14 Vict. No. 2) in 1850. The act extended the summary jurisdiction to young people under the age of fourteen charged with larceny (theft) and associated offences. The legislation also allowed for different and lesser penalties to be applied to juveniles convicted of larceny. The legislation began the process of the development of children's courts in Australia; it created both different procedures for dealing with young people and different penalties for offences.

The establishment of reformatories represented a major change in the dealing with young people. In Britain, the statutory recognition of reformatory and industrial schools for the 'dangerous' and 'perishing' classes occurred with the *Youthful Offenders Act 1854* and the *Industrial Schools Act 1857* respectively. Similarly, reformatories developed in the US in the middle of the nineteenth century. In Australia, amidst concern about destitute children and criticism of the lack of alternatives to imprisonment for young offenders, industrial and reformatory school acts were passed in most States between 1863 and 1874.

English reformers like Mary Carpenter were influential in developing new methods of dealing with young people. They saw discipline through punishment as ineffective; rather, they sought fundamental and lasting rehabilitation through inner change of the young person. The issue of training and reform was essentially one of effectiveness rather than benevolence. It demonstrated the fundamental shift away from deterrent rationales for punishment. Carpenter noted that reform occurred 'only when the child's soul is touched, when he yields from the heart'. Carpenter played a leading role in the movement, particularly with her book *Reformatory Schools for the Children of the Perishing and Dangerous Classes and for Juvenile Offenders*, published in 1851. Carpenter's work made a distinction between the establishment of reformatory schools for delinquents (of the 'dangerous classes') and industrial schools for the poor (the pre-delinquent of the 'perishing classes'). However, both regimes stressed religious instruction, elementary education and industrial training.

The Australian legislation contained definitions of the situations in which 'neglected' children could be placed in institutions. For example the *Neglected and Criminal Children's Act 1864* (Vic.), Section 13 defined a neglected child as any child found begging or receiving alms; 'wandering about' or having no home or visible means of subsistence; or any child 'whose parent represents that he is unable to control such child'. In some cases, the legislation simply recast the existing vagrancy definitions as being applicable to children, but it also added new definitions which were the forerunner of modern notions of 'uncontrollability'. The legislation in Victoria, Queensland and New South Wales also provided for the establishment of industrial schools for those young people defined as neglected (Seymour 1988: 37–43).

In addition, the new legislation provided for special procedures for dealing with young offenders. In Victoria, Queensland and South Australia, a child convicted of an offence could be sent to a reformatory school *regardless* of the seriousness of the offence. In New South Wales, a young person who had been convicted of an offence that was punishable by fourteen or more days' imprisonment could be committed to a reformatory. These changes represented an important shift in the sentencing of young people through the separation of the nature of the offence from the penalty imposed, and a new focus on the offender rather than the offence.

Although the system established two groups of neglected children and young offenders, in reality there was a blurring of distinctions. In most Australian States, young offenders could be sent to industrial schools by the court under certain circumstances. Amendments to legislation during the 1870s further blurred the distinctions, when courts were empowered to send neglected children to reformatories if they had been leading an 'immoral or depraved life'. In addition, neglected children could be transferred administratively to the reformatory system if they were a management problem.

The new legislation also empowered courts to commit young people for extended periods of time. This power expressed the ideology that young people were being committed for training and education. Offenders were to be committed for lengthy periods regardless of the seriousness of the crime. As a result, the normal tariff considerations in sentencing were not seen as part of the law governing juveniles (Seymour 1988: 48–9).

A further factor which was important in terms of the development of the juvenile justice system was that release from institutions was determined by the administration rather than the court. Additionally, the conditions of release (on licence, etc.) were also determined by the administration. This administrative discretion was legitimated by the ideology which saw the system as operating in the child's interest.

The use of reformatories and industrial schools in Britain was similar to Australia. The offence was often irrelevant to committal. Reformatories encouraged early intervention unrelated to the nature of the juvenile's offence, and about half the juveniles sent to reformatories were sent there on their first conviction. In addition, reform was based on discipline through work. Yet the 'work' was not training or skills acquisition, but laborious and monotonous work designed to produce individuals who would be disciplined for any menial job (Morris & Giller 1987: 24–7).

In the United States, there were important legal challenges concerning the placement of young people in houses of refuge, reformatories and industrial schools. The Pennsylvania Supreme Court determined the Crouse case in 1838. The girl, Mary Anne Crouse, had not committed a criminal offence but was seen to be in danger of growing up to be a pauper. She was committed to a house of refuge. The court decided that holding Crouse in the house of refuge was legal because the young person was being helped and not punished. The state was assuming the role of *parens patriae* whereby it was acting in the role of the child's parents who were seen to be incapable of fulfilling that task. Further, because Crouse was being helped and not punished, there was no need for the protections of formal due process (such as presumption of innocence, proven guilty of an offence beyond reasonable doubt, etc.) (see Bernard 1992: 68–70). The Crouse case was important as the first American legal challenge to the practice of committing young people to houses of refuge and reformatories although they had committed no criminal offence.

In the O'Connell case, determined in the Illinois Supreme Court in 1870, the court rejected the *parens patriae* argument (the court acting in the best interests of the child and protecting the child) and ordered the release of O'Connell from the Chicago Reform School. The court heard of the harsh conditions in the reform school and found that O'Connell was being punished, not helped. The court was of the view that O'Connell was being imprisoned although he had not committed any criminal offence. The O'Connell decision influenced the establishment of the juvenile court in Chicago in 1899. The establishment of the juvenile court allowed the O'Connell decision to be circumvented through new definitions of delinquency (Bernard 1992: 70–3).

The rationale for the establishment of the reformatories was that they would provide a special form of prison discipline for young people. They were to transform delinquents into law-abiding citizens. According to Platt (1977), the reformatory plan was designed to teach the value of adjustment, private enterprise, thrift and self-reliance. Like Mary Carpenter's aim to 'touch the soul', the reformatory masters sought to 'revolutionise . . . the entire being' (Platt, 1977: 52). This transformation involved a different mode of punishment and can be contextualised within broader changes occurring in punishment during the second half of the nineteenth century. By the end of the century this shift in focus had moved from the belief that a criminal should be punished according to the severity of the offence to a view that the offender should receive treatment. Treatment was to be based on the diagnosis of the person's pathological condition. Treatment also enabled the expansion and diversification of penal sanctions. According to Garland, this development marked the beginning of a new mode of sentencing which claimed to treat offenders according to their specific characteristics or needs, and not according to a scheme of presumed equality (Garland 1985: 28, Foucault 1977).

THE REALITY OF LIFE IN THE SCHOOLS

If so much faith was placed in the development of these new methods of control and reformation, it is fair to ask what the outcomes were. Although a separate penal system was established for young people, in some areas children were still imprisoned with adults. In the United States, the reformatories themselves were described as 'overcrowded, poorly equipped, badly situated and more like a prison than a school' (Platt 1977: 146). In England, the reality of the reformatory schools was similarly far from the rhetoric. According to Harris and Webb (1987: 14), there were serious problems in the recruitment of suitable staff; punishments were severe, including solitary confinement, bread and water, and whipping. These punishments mirrored the adult system. In addition, early attempts to separate juveniles from adult offenders were not successful. The prison hulks (boats) used for young people were in worse condition than those for adults.

In Australia, hulks were used as reformatories in Victoria, South Australia, Queensland and New South Wales. There was a series of official investigations into conditions in the reformatories and industrial schools during the 1870s and 1880s. The inquiries in South Australia, New South Wales, Victoria and Tasmania painted a picture of the institutions as brutal gaols (Seymour 1988: 58–61).

Reformatories and industrial schools were often combined, thus further undermining the distinction between 'neglected' young people and young offenders. Indeed, the criteria for referral to reformatory and industrial schools were vague:

- *The perishing classes:* Regarded as the pre-delinquent, they were seen as the legitimate object of the state's intervention. They were young people who had 'not yet fallen' into crime but because of poverty were likely to do so.
- *The dangerous classes:* Young people who had already committed offences and received the 'prison brand'.

The actual mixing of welfare and criminal cases within the systems of detention became a hallmark of dealing with young people brought into the juvenile justice system until well into the contemporary period.

Many young people were sent to reformatories for minor offences. Seymour gives examples of young people being given long committals, such as a nine-year-old boy in South Australia being sent to a reformatory for six years for stealing six apples (Seymour 1988: 56). One outcome was that institutions provided for the detention of young people who would not previously have been imprisoned.

In Britain, it has been suggested that the 'institutions constituted a major extension of control over the young, while simultaneously offering the apparent possibility of mass reformation and the near elimination of juvenile crime' (Harris & Webb 1987: 11). Certainly, it appears the reformatories attracted a new clientele. More juveniles were brought into the juvenile justice system and were sent reformatories. In England between 1865 and 1873, some 26,326 juveniles were sent to reformatory or industrial schools. In addition juveniles spent longer incarcerated: instead of an average three months' imprisonment, they spent two to five years in reformatories (Morris & Giller 1987: 24–7).

We can summarise the effects of the changes brought about by the introduction of the reformatory and industrial schools as:

- separate procedures for dealing with young people for some offences
- different penalties for some offences for juveniles compared to adults
- different and separate penal regime for juveniles
- different criteria for intervention between juveniles and adults
- overlap between welfare and criminal intervention
- high levels of administrative discretion over those young people within the juvenile penal regime
- extended and indeterminate committals
- adult sentencing tariffs no longer seen as relevant to juveniles
- earlier committal intervention for minor offences
- more young people incarcerated than previously.

It was within the context of these changes that the development of specialist Children's Courts took place. We deal with this issue below.

THE JUVENILE COURT

The new juvenile courts which developed at the end of the nineteenth century were based on the notion of *parens patriae*. The concept had originally referred to the protection of property rights of juveniles and others who were legally incompetent. However, it came to refer to the responsibility of the juvenile courts and the state to act in the best interests of the child.

As one early-twentieth-century British commentator put it, the doctrine of *parens patriae* allowed the court 'to get away from the notion that the child is to be dealt with as a criminal; to save it from the brand of criminality, the brand that sticks to it for life' (cited in Morris & Giller 1987: 12).

Children's Courts were established at roughly the same time in Britain, the United States and Australia during the last decades of the nineteenth century and the early years of the twentieth century. The powers of the court varied from State to State and country to country.

In the United States, the Illinois *Juvenile Court Act 1899* established the juvenile court with the power to determine the legal status of 'troublesome' or 'pre-delinquent' children. The courts were able to investigate a variety of behaviour. Statutory definitions of delinquency included acts that would be criminal if committed by adults; acts that violated country, town, or municipal ordinances; and violations of vaguely defined catch-alls—such as vicious or immoral behaviour, incorrigibility, truancy, profane or indecent language, growing up in idleness, or living with any vicious or disreputable person (Platt 1977: 138).

The concept of *parens patriae* authorised the courts to use wide discretion in resolving the problems of young people. A child was not accused of a crime, but offered assistance and guidance. Intervention was not supposed to carry the stigma of a criminal record, and hearings were conducted in relative privacy with informal proceedings.

The legislation introduced in Illinois was well received by the judiciary and legal profession and became the foundation for other US States. Juvenile courts were established in Wisconsin and New York in 1901, and in Ohio and Maryland in 1902. By 1928 all but two US States had adopted a juvenile court system. Canada adopted legislation in 1908.

The first annual reports from the Cook County juvenile court in Chicago indicated that public order offences and school truancy were the majority of charges that led to the 'delinquency' cases dealt with by the court (Platt 1977: 140). Failure to conform to the new forms of social control such as compulsory education was clearly an important source of delinquency classifications.

In England by the end of the nineteenth century, some towns such as Manchester and Birmingham had begun to operate separate juvenile courts. Separate courts were established throughout England and Wales after the *Children Act 1908* was introduced. The legislation gave the courts both criminal jurisdiction over criminal matters and civil jurisdiction in relation to welfare matters. According to Harris and Webb, 'it made the juvenile court itself a locus for conflict and confusion, a vehicle for the simultaneous welfarization of delinquency and the juridicization of need' (1987:9). This legislation also contained a variety of provisions, of which those dealing with a separate juvenile court were only one part. Other sections dealt with the prevention of cruelty to children and prohibitions on begging and prostitution. At around the same time there was the statutory creation of probation and preventive detention.

In Australia, the major reason given for the establishment of Children's Courts was to ensure that young people were tried separately from adults and were not subject to the harmful effects of contamination and stigma—particularly where the young person was before the court on neglect matters. Australian legislation establishing separate courts was introduced as follows:

- South Australia: *State Children Act 1895*
- New South Wales: *Neglected Children and Juvenile Offenders Act 1905*
- Victoria: *Children's Court Act 1906*
- Queensland: *Children's Court Act 1907*
- Western Australia: *State Children Act 1907*
- Tasmania: *The Children's Charter 1918*.

The legislation was based on child-saving rhetoric similar to that in the United States. The courts were to be parental and informal, with correction administered in a 'fatherly manner' (Seymour 1988: 70–1). Magistrates were to be specially selected, trained and qualified to deal with young people, and probation officers were to play a special role in supervising young people and preparing background reports.

The legislation establishing Children's Courts in Australia gave jurisdiction to the courts over both criminal matters (juvenile offending) and welfare matters (neglected children and young people). The Children's Courts also had exclusive jurisdiction, which meant that other lower courts could not hear cases involving children. The legislation also stipulated that the Children's Court had to sit separately to the other courts, and that special magistrates had to be appointed. In practice, though, most magistrates were simply designated as children's magistrates, and only in the major cities did anything like special courts exist (Seymour 1988: 96).

There were important variations between jurisdictions concerning the extent to which the juvenile court differed from the adult criminal courts. For instance, the Children's Court in Australia was not as different from the adult courts as was the case in the United States. There the young person appeared in the court as a result of a delinquency petition, and the court had to determine whether the child was delinquent, not whether they had committed a particular offence. In contrast, in Australia the court had to determine whether the young person had committed an offence, at least in regard to criminal matters. In relation to neglect matters, the court had to be shown that the child or young person was neglected within the terms of the legislation.

The development of probation was also an important adjunct to the new Children's Courts. Probation pre-dated the courts and had arisen from voluntary charitable and religious work. In the United States, members of the Board of State Charities attended court hearings involving children. As a result, about one-third of the children were placed on probation under the supervision of the members. In Britain the First Offenders Act was passed in 1887, which allowed the supervision of minor first offenders by 'missionaries' and voluntary workers. Similarly, in Australia the courts had offered conditional discharges to offenders and this had been referred to as probation. However, the development of separate courts for young people had the effect of leading to a more systematic use of probation. In various parts of Australia, the Children's Court legislation allowed for release on probation. Initially, honorary probation officers were attached to the Children's Courts with the function of preparing background reports and conducting supervision. At least in the specialist Children's Courts, the use of probation became an important sentencing option for the courts.

JUDICIAL THERAPISTS

The Children's Courts encouraged minimum procedural formality and a greater dependency on new personnel such as probation officers. Judges were encouraged to look at the character and social background of the delinquents. In this sense the movement has been described as anti-legal (Platt 1977: 141). Furthermore, the court's intervention was justified where no offence had actually been committed but where the young person was causing problems for someone in authority: parent, teacher, or social worker. In Australian jurisdictions, such matters could come before the courts in the form of a range of welfare complaints or status offences such as uncontrollability, exposure to moral danger, or truancy.

One way of conceptualising the relationship between the Children's Court, its ancillary staff and the young person has been through notions of the 'therapeutic' state. Some commentators have argued that the 'role model for juvenile court judges was doctor-counselor rather than lawyer. Judicial therapists were expected to establish a one-to-one relationship with delinquents' (Platt

1977: 142). Donzelot (1979) has also argued that the advent of the juvenile court changed the relationship of the family to outside agencies. He argues that the family became subject to a 'tutelary complex' whereby a number of agencies, including juvenile justice, reduced the autonomy of the family and instead established the family as a site of intervention. In Donzelot's terms, the transition has been from government of the family to government through the family. With the development of a separate system for dealing with young people, families can be more closely policed (in the broadest sense of the term) and recalcitrant children removed.

During the late nineteenth century there were specific intellectual developments which impacted on the construction of a notion of juvenile delinquency and facilitated specific forms of intervention. The new forms of knowledge gave the promise and legitimacy of scientific neutrality reinforcing the benevolent intentions of the court. The discourse of reformation included a range of new disciplines, such as child psychiatry, psychology and paediatrics. These forms of intervention were also connected to the new categorisation of young people as 'adolescent'—a term thought to have been created by G. Stanley Hall in his book *Adolescence* published in the late nineteenth century (Morris & Giller 1987: 4). The development of social and psychological theories specified that the particular age group was thought to be vulnerable and unstable. These intellectual developments were linked to and justified the introduction of 'a deluge of protective legislation' (Gillis 1981: 133).

There was also a shift in attitudes towards penality. The scientific discourses on behaviour supported the move to impose long-term 'training' through indeterminate (open-ended, with no fixed term) sentences for young people. The growth of positivist criminology in the later part of the nineteenth century also provided an intellectual framework which facilitated separate treatment for juveniles with the emphasis on classification and psychology of the offender (Morris & Giller 1987: 18).

The therapeutic nature of intervention is also reflected in the development of the notion that justice is to be personalised in terms of its style as well as its outcomes. At the time the new juvenile court buildings were opened in Chicago in 1907, it was claimed that

> the hearings will be held in a room fitted up as a parlour rather than a court, around a table instead of a bench . . . The hearings will be in the nature of a family conference, in which the endeavour will be to impress the child with the fact that his own good is sought alone (cited in Platt 1977: 143).

Similar arguments were put forward in Australia for the construction of separate facilities for the hearings of the Children's Court. In reality, though, most matters were determined in the physical surroundings of the local magistrate's court.

GENDERED APPROACHES

From the earliest developments of separate systems for dealing with young people, there appear to have been specific differences in the treatment of young men and young women. Schlossman and Wallace (1978) note that in the United States, young women were focused upon because of their sexuality. The 'immoral conduct' of girls was broadly defined and they were subjected to physical examinations to determine whether they had been sexually active. Schlossman and Wallace also found that girls were given longer sentences in the reformatories.

Similar issues have been raised in Australia. Jaggs (1986: 62) noted that in Victoria 'girls' larceny and other offences gave cause for concern, but general "wildness" and sexual misbehaviour gave more, since they breached strongly held views on female purity'. Girls who misbehaved were thought to be worse than boys and more difficult to reform. As a result, longer periods of incarceration seemed appropriate for young women.

A study of Parramatta Industrial School for Girls also argued that the focus of the school was on the moral reconstruction of the young women sent there. The training focused on domestic skills and moral purity. At least until the early twentieth century, the regime was harsh, with no personal possessions, no privacy, two outside visits per year, and no outside authority to whom the girls could appeal. Punishments included caning ('thrashing' or 'whipping'), head shaving, standing out (standing outside perfectly still for a number of hours), and isolation (Willis 1980: 184–8).

By the early twentieth century, legislation also began to specfically refer to young women and their behaviour. Thus the New South Wales *Neglected Children and Juvenile Offenders Act 1905* had specific provisions which related to girls and young women under the neglect category. Girls and young women (aged five to sixteen) could be charged with neglect if they were found soliciting men or otherwise behaving in an indecent manner (Willis 1980: 185). There were no equivalent provisions relating to males.

POLICE, LAW AND JUVENILE DELINQUENCY

The development of new methods of dealing with young people went hand in hand with developments in the recorded incidence of essentially new categories of minor juvenile crime. An analysis by Gillis (1975) of Oxford Police Court records between 1895 and 1914 showed that juvenile crime was apparently increasing at a faster rate than adult crime. These figures seemed to support fears about rising juvenile crime. However, a closer examination of the pattern of offending showed uneven distribution across various offences. The major increases were in minor summary and public order offences such as drunken-

ness, gambling, malicious mischief, loitering, wilful damage, begging, dangerous play, and discharge of fireworks. The analysis of a more serious offence,
theft, showed that it was associated with minor items (fruit, vegetables, toys,
sweets, cigarettes, etc.).

It would appear that two broad categories of offences were important.
Young people were brought before the courts for public order offences related
to leisure activities in public, and for property offences associated with economic need. Humphries (1981) has argued, on the basis of oral histories, that
many offences can be viewed as expressions of 'social crime'. The concept of
social crime encompasses 'the innumerable minor crimes against property committed by working class children and youth that were condoned by large sections of both the youth and parent cultures as legitimate despite their illegality'
(Humphries 1981: 151). Many property crimes were necessitated and justified
by extreme poverty and the struggle for survival. The most common form of
property theft, which was seen as a customary right among working-class
communities, involved supplementing the family's food and fuel supply. In
England, the single most important category of juvenile crime during the early
twentieth century was 'simple and minor larceny' which 'comprised taking coal
from pitheads, chumps of wood from timber yards and vegetables from farmer's
fields, poaching rabbits and so on' (Humphries 1981: 151). The actual nature
of social crime was complex and it varied significantly between different areas,
depending on opportunities offered by the local economy and the nature of
local traditions.

Various government studies at the time suggested that petty crime was most
common among unskilled, unemployed and sole-parent families, and that older
children in the family were more likely to be delinquent. The dominant
criminological classifications of juvenile delinquency during the late nineteenth
century and early twentieth century saw juvenile crime as associated with weak-
ness of character, ignorance, irrationality, or some other form of pathology. The
explanations relied on biological and psychological interpretations such as
'primitive impulses'. However, Humphries has argued that such explanations
ignored the significance of poverty, inequality and class conflict as significant
factors in crime. The domestic economy of the working-class household provided a rational set of motives, where the eldest children committed offences to
help support the family. In other words, there was a moral economy operating
which valued family support more greatly than compliance with the law.

Offences related to public order tended to involve arrests of young people in
groups of two or more, and sometimes as many as ten or fifteen. Charges relating to property damage, mischief and dangerous play could involve many young
people and derive from particular policing activities. Gillis states:

Sliding on bridges, throwing rocks and playing street football were typical activities which led to the arrest of large groups. This would seem to suggest that there was a tendency on the part of the public and the police to attribute anti-social intents to boys collectively, thus raising the rate of recorded offences . . . (1975: 103).

The surveillance of public space and the ability to arrest young people raise the issue of developments in policing—particularly with a focus on the class and leisure activities of working-class young people. Gillis argues that, ironically, the collective behaviour of youth had actually improved by the later part of the nineteenth century. Thus, increased arrest rates were likely to have been a function of a number of factors, including law enforcement practices, new legislation, and the growth of a range of organisations (such as the Boy Scouts) with the intent to modify the behaviour of young people.

Police functions and practices were altering. The late nineteenth century saw expanded, reorganised and increasingly professional police forces. Police had responsibilities in relation to young people which extended beyond the notion of criminality to one of monitoring the social life of young people. Police were involved as welfare agents, truant officers and moral guardians (Finnane 1994: 7). In New South Wales in the 1890s, the police took on the role of regulating truants. Official arrest figures from the nineteenth century in Australia showed a primary concern with petty crime and public order; however, welfare complaints such as neglect or uncontrollability were also important. Girls were increasingly represented in welfare complaints, such as uncontrollability (Finnane 1994).

The different sentencing regimes for juveniles convicted of larceny, and the extension of the magistrates' jurisdiction resulted in more juveniles being prosecuted by police. In other words, the net was made wider because more juveniles were brought before the courts as a result of the seemingly beneficial reform (Seymour 1988: 33). Special laws were developed during the 1870s and 1880s which were specifically aimed at young people's behaviour. In legislation such as the Tasmanian *Juvenile Offenders Act 1875*, specific juvenile behaviour, such as indecent exposure, assault, obscene language, throwing stones, obstructing a railway and vandalism, could be dealt with in the magistrate's court.

There was also a move away from the old police practice of dealing with juvenile offenders on the spot. Corporal punishment by police was viewed as inappropriate, particularly by organisations such as the National Society for the Prevention of Cruelty to Children. One effect of reducing the use of arbitrary punishment was that the police made more use of the courts (Gillis 1975). Indeed, in New South Wales the establishment of the Children's Court and legislation related to neglected children was recognised by its architects as facilitating police intervention (Finnane 1994: 17). Information available from the Sydney Children's Court was seen to support greater intervention, particularly in relation to public behaviour. In 1911 about one-third of all the offences determined in the Sydney Children's Court related to riotous behaviour, throwing stones, playing games, 'boarding or quitting tram in motion' and 'bathing in view' (Seymour 1988: 104). Similar evidence from Western Australia also suggests prosecutions for very minor offences, such as breaking branches from trees and kicking footballs in a park. Seymour argues that minor incidents such as these would probably not have been brought before magistrates prior to the advent of the Children's Court, and it seems likely that the net was widened, with greater level of prosecutions for minor offences (Seymour 1988: 109).

Schools and youth organisations also had the indirect effect of causing more young people to appear before the courts as they defined and attempted to control the public behaviour, work activities and leisure of young people. Their influence was extended through social changes, such as the provision of compulsory education, and legislation, such as the English *Prevention of Cruelty and Protection of Children Act 1889*. There was also a range of reformative organisations, such as the Salvation Army, Boy Scouts, Boys' Brigades, Young Men's Christian Associations (YMCA) and Young Women's Christian Associations (YWCA), which were engaged in activities aimed at altering the public and private behaviour of young people. 'Keeping them off the streets' became a shorthand way of describing this function (Maunders 1984; Gillis 1975). The school itself also became a site of discipline and the law. One school's punishment book for 1905 showed that almost a third of the punishments related to extra-curricular activities (Gillis 1975: 118).

One outcome of the changes in legislation, the spread of schooling and youth organisations was that clearer distinctions between 'rough' and 'respectable' working-class youth were established. Certainly, police perceptions of male youth were defined in terms of class and sex. 'Such perceptions did not necessarily mean that police would deferentially side with the wishes of social elites against the alleged depredations of working class youth. But they did work with social distinctions which pitted the respectable against the rough' (Finnane 1994: 13).

The new and expanding jurisdiction specifically dealing with young people allowed greater regulation. New offences were created and welfare provisions were developed. There were new methods of surveillance and new bureaucratic structures for enforcing social regulation. Certainly there is widespread empirical evidence to suggest that increased numbers of young people were dealt with formally.

CONCLUSION

The changes which occurred with the introduction of specific measures to deal with young people brought before the courts can be understood within the context of broad changes occurring in terms of state intervention. Education acts compelled children between certain ages to attend school. Legislation regulating labour prohibited children of certain ages from working. The period of dependency of children was extended. In relation to welfare, there was a transformation from reliance on private philanthropic organisations to the assumption of the responsibility for the provision of welfare by the state.

State intervention changed the overall position of young people in Australia during the late nineteenth and early twentieth centuries. New forms of regulation related to education, work and leisure. Increased police surveillance, the development of the Children's Court, alterations to the penal regime for young people, and the growth of new professions were all part of this broader change. There was also greater regulation in family relations, including guardianship laws. It is clear that the law was used to enforce standards and obligations on parents. Compulsory education is one example. In England there were 86,149 prosecutions of parents under the 1870 Education Act in one year alone (Morris & Giller 1987: 22).

Historians and criminologists have debated how the effects of the establishment of a separate legal regime for dealing with young people should be conceptualised. These debates are not of purely academic interest because they also illuminate current issues relevant to juvenile justice.

One way of conceptualising the period of changing policy is to view it in terms of progress. A separate Children's Court and separate penal system are seen as an humanitarian advance on former methods of dealing with young people. These liberal or 'Whig' histories are often criticised for their teleological or evolutionary view of the past: that is the past is seen as inevitably and progressively leading to the present. An often implicit assumption is that, because the present is the outcome of progressive steps in the past, the present system is the most advanced in terms of development.

In the 1960s and early 1970s these views of the past were subjected to intense criticism. The institutions of juvenile justice were seen as a mechanism of social control, and criticised for being inefficient, brutal, mismanaged and corrupt. A key component of the critique was that the new systems of regulation increased the levels of surveillance and 'subjected more and more juveniles to arbitrary and degrading punishments' (Platt 1977: xvii). In some of these 'social control' approaches, the issue of class was seen as important. Social control mechanisms were seen to be extending control over the working class— particularly young people. Implicit in these approaches is the view that state institutions are a form of regulation by one class over another.

Some writers have stressed the incorporation of a political economy approach which argues that the developments in juvenile justice were not isolated nor autonomous. Broader economic and social reforms were occurring which were opposed to laissez-faire capitalism, and there was an increased role for state institutions in economic regulation. The new political economy was characterised by long-range planning and bureaucratic routine (Platt 1977: xix). These conceptual changes related to scientific management in industry; to intelligence testing in education; and to classifications and treatment in criminal justice.

Australian historians of child welfare and juvenile justice like Van Krieken (1991) have argued that it is important to understand how the working class used the new institutions to their own advantage. Class was important, but the new institutions were not merely repressive. Complaints about young people might arise from family members, neighbours or the public and not simply derive from police or institutional surveillance.

Van Krieken argues that there was a division between the respectable and non-respectable sections of the working class. The respectable working class and sections of the labour movement supported some aspects of the new institutions, such as compulsory education. They might well have supported new standards of public propriety and morality against what they saw to be the behaviour of the non-respectable urban poor. According to Van Krieken, we need to consider how working-class people accepted certain standards in their own interests and were not simply passive victims of new levels of state intervention.

However we conceptualise the changes, it is clear there were fundamental shifts during the late nineteenth and early twentieth centuries in the relationship between young people and the law. There was a separate method of punishment for young people, including new penal institutions and greater surveillance at home and in the community through probation officers. Separate sentencing regimes were established, including the use of indeterminate sentencing. Separate Children's Courts were established, not only to determine criminal matters but also to assess neglect and welfare matters. Particular practices were also seen as appropriate in dealing with young people before the courts, particularly the use of social background reports. Partly as a response to changes in legislation and developments in policing, and partly as a result of the existence of separate Children's Courts, there was an increase in the number of young people prosecuted and brought formally into the justice system. Finally, there were gendered approaches to the application of the new forms of controlling young people.

These changes in policy need to be contextualised within the theoretical developments in criminology. We have referred on a number of occasions in this chapter to developments in classification, new disciplines, and changes in thinking about young people. In the following chapters we explore the developments of criminological theory and various explanations for juvenile offending.

2 traditional criminological theory

The study of crime is essentially a study of society. That is, how we define and view crime is itself shaped by our conceptions of what kind of society we live in, and what sort of society we would like to see. The selection of criminological issues, topics and problems which we feel to be important is partly determined, therefore, by our own location in society—our class and ethnic background, our sex, whether we are an established Australian or a recent migrant, our language, age, ability, etc.—and the concerns which most impinge upon us as active social beings. Such issues are also highly influenced by the images and perspectives put forward by, and for, the dominant institutions in society—the media, schools and families.

The study of crime is also a study of explanations and causes. Theories of 'criminogenesis' or 'causes of crime' emphasise many different reasons for committing criminal offences or engaging in deviant behaviour. Some theories challenge how we define 'crime' and 'delinquency', arguing that there is no essential definition or reality of crime. The focus of the many different theories varies considerably. Some concentrate on examining the criminal act; some, the offender. Others see crime as a social process; still others look at it in terms of power relations.

The manner in which causes are represented has major implications for strategies of crime prevention and crime control. Again, depending upon the theory adopted, the 'solution' may be seen in terms of punishment, treatment or rehabilitation of offenders; restitution involving victims and offenders; or major structural change requiring transformations in the nature of our basic social institutions. Specific theories, therefore, arise from specific ways of viewing crime, the role of criminal justice institutions, and the appropriate strategies for grappling with criminal and deviant behaviour.

This chapter begins by briefly exploring some of the general differences between criminological theories. Such theories often vary according to the *level of analysis* at which they are pitched, and in terms of the *political perspective* with which they are most closely identified. Following this, the chapter outlines the two most important perspectives of traditional criminology—the **classical** and

positivist conceptions of crime, criminal behaviour and crime control. While each theoretical approach tends to centre on the individual, they provide diametrically opposed views as to where the offender fits within the broader criminological explanation.

GAINING PERSPECTIVE

Criminological theory can be presented in abstract fashion as discrete perspectives or approaches. Each approach or paradigm attempts to understand a particular phenomenon by asking certain types of questions, using certain concepts, and constructing a certain type of framework of analysis and explanation. In practice, it is rare to find government departments or academic criminologists relying solely or exclusively on any one criminological framework or approach. Often, wide-ranging ideas and concepts are combined in different ways in the course of developing policy, or in the study of a specific empirical problem.

For sake of presentation, it is nevertheless useful to present **ideal types** of the various theoretical strands within criminology. The use of ideal types provides a means by which we can clarify main ideas and identify important differences between the broad approaches adopted in the field. An ideal type does not exist in the real world. Rather, the intention is to abstract from concrete situations the key elements or components of a particular theory or social institution, and possibly to exaggerate these elements, in order to highlight the general tendency or themes of the particular perspective (see Freund 1969). An ideal type is an analytical tool, not a moral statement of what ought to be. It refers to a process of picking up different aspects of social phenomena and combining them into a **typical** model or example. For instance, an ideal bureaucracy would include impartial and impersonal merit and promotion structures, set rules and regulations, a hierarchical chain of command, and so on. We know, however, that people who work in bureaucracies are not always promoted on the basis of the qualifications; nor is decision-making always rational. But by constructing a model of a typical bureaucracy we are able to compare how different organisations actually are structured and how they actually work in the real world.

If we are to construct ideal types in relation to criminological theory, then it is useful to identify the central focus of theory, and the level of analysis and explanation at which the theory is pitched. As Chart 2.1 indicates, there are three broad levels of criminological explanation: the individual, the situational, and the structural. Criminology theories tend to locate their main explanation for criminal behaviour or criminality at one of these levels. Occasionally, a theory attempts to combine all three levels in order to provide a more sophisticated and comprehensive picture of crime and criminality.

The level of analysis chosen determines how crime and the offender are viewed, and how the criminal justice system should be organised. For example, a biological positivist approach which looks at characteristics of the individual offender (e.g., their genetic make-up) sees crime as stemming from the specific personal attributes of the individual. A situational perspective, on the other hand, might consider the interaction between police and young people on the street, and argue that 'crime' is defined in the process of specific interactions, behaviours and attitudes. From a structural perspective, the issue might be seen in terms of the relationship between poverty and crime, that is, the elements of social life which underpin particular courses of action. The biological, the situational and the structural approaches would each advocate quite different policies because of their particular perspectives. The vantage point from which one examines crime—from a focus on personal characteristics through to societal institutions—thus shapes the ways in which one thinks about and acts upon criminal justice matters.

Chart 2.1 Levels of criminological analysis

Level	Comments
Individual	The focus is on the personal or individual characteristics of the offender or victim. Study considers, for example, the influence of appearance, dress and public image on the nature of crime causation or victimisation (e.g., tattoos or earrings as indicators of a 'criminal' attitude in men). This level of analysis tends to look to psychological or biological factors which are said to have an important determining role in why certain individuals engage in criminal activity. The key concern is with explaining crime or deviant behaviour in terms of the choices or characteristics of the individual person.
Situational	The site of analysis is the immediate situation or circumstances within which criminal activity or deviant behaviour occurs. Attention is directed to the specific factors which may contribute to an event occurring, such as how the participants define the situation, how different people are labelled by others in the criminal justice system, the opportunities available for the commission of certain types of offences, and so on. A key concern is the nature of the interaction between different players within the system, the effect of local environmental factors on the nature of this interaction, and the influence of group behaviour on social activity.
Social structural	This approach tends to look at crime in terms of broader social relationships, and the major social institutions, of the society as a whole. The analysis makes reference to the relationship between classes, sexes, different ethnic and 'racial' groups, the employed and unemployed, and various other social divisions in society. It also investigates the operation of specific institutions, such as education, the family, work and the legal system, in constructing and responding to crime and deviant behaviour.

The different levels of analysis apparent in criminology also reflect the diverse disciplines which have contributed to the study of crime over many years. Researchers, scholars and writers in areas such as biological science, psychology, philosophy, law, sociology, forensic medicine, political economy, education, history and cultural studies have all contributed to the multi-disciplinary nature of criminology. Each discipline uses its own concepts, debates and methods when examining a criminological issue or problem. This means that within criminology there is a natural diversity of viewpoints as different writers and researchers see the world through very different analytical spectacles. Such differences are reflected in the adoption of a wide range of techniques and methodologies in the study of crime. These include historical records, surveys, participant observation, interviews, evaluation of official statistics, study of policy documents, and discourse analysis.

Differences in the broad level of analysis, and in specific discipline-related perspectives, can also be linked, to some extent, to differences in the political framework of the writer. Chart 2.2 outlines three general perspectives on the nature of society: the conservative, the liberal and the radical. It is a truism that any particular criminological theory does not exist in a political vacuum—each is tied to a wider social and philosophical view of society. The motivation, conceptual development, methodological tools and social values associated with a specific approach are usually intertwined with one of the three broad political perspectives outlined in the table. If we acknowledge the centrality of 'politics' in criminological analysis, then we must accept that there is no such thing as value-free criminology. Values of the Right (conservative), Left (radical) and centre (liberal) are embedded in the criminological enterprise.

A further aspect relating to the politics of criminological theory is that the dominant paradigm or approach adopted by governments, and represented in criminological circles (professional journals, conferences), varies over time. That is, there are always competing general perspectives within criminology, but in different periods, particular perspectives are ascendant over others. For example, the conservative perspectives (usually associated with classical and positivist views, and theories which centre on punishment and control strategies) held considerable sway at the level of policy formulation and action in the 1950s. By the late 1960s, the liberal perspective (centring on labelling and efforts at rehabilitation) influenced much of the reform activity related to the criminal justice system. By the mid-1980s and into the 1990s there had been a swing back to the Right, with strident calls for the adoption of tougher measures to deal with issues of 'law and order'. Simultaneous with the more conservative push at the level of policy were both liberal and radical critiques of the effectiveness and fairness of such measures. Criminological theory is thus always related to

Chart 2.2 Political perspectives

Perspective	Comments
Conservative	A conservative perspective on society tends to support the legitimacy of the status quo, i.e., it generally accepts the way things are, traditional ways of doing things and traditional social relationships. Conservatives believe dissenters should be made to conform to the status quo. They believe that there is a 'core value system' to which everyone in society should conform. The function of the main institutions is to preserve the dominant system of order for the good of society generally. The values and institutions of society should apply equally to all people, regardless of social background or historical developments.
Liberal	A liberal perspective on society accepts the basic limits of the status quo, but encourages small-scale changes in societal institutions. This approach tends to avoid questions relating to the whole structure of society. Instead, it emphasises the need for action on particular limited 'social problems'. Specific problems such as sexism, racism, poverty and so on can be resolved without fundamental changes to the economic or social structure. Rather, policies and programs can be developed to reform existing institutions and day-to-day interactions. Problems tend to be studied in terms of their impact on individuals ('the poor' as the focus of research) and the disadvantage suffered by these individuals or groups.
Radical	The radical perspective on society questions the legitimacy of the status quo. It looks at society as whole (as the conservative perspective does), but sees 'social conflict' as the central concern. Society is seen to be divided on the basis of class, gender, ethnicity, 'race' and so on. The key issue is who holds the power and resources in any particular community. The focus of the radical perspective is fundamental change to the existing social order. Specific issues, such as poverty, are explained in relational terms (e.g., relationship between the rich and poor), and the solution is to deal with the structural imbalances and inequalities that lead to the problem (of poverty) in the first place.

specific historical contexts, specific material conditions, and specific political struggles.

The objectives and methods of analysis used in criminology reflect certain underlying ideas and concerns of the writer. In reading criminological material, then, it is important to examine the assumptions of the writers, the key concepts they use, and the methods or arguments used to support their theories, in order to identify their conceptions of society and of human nature, and the kinds of reforms or institutions that they ultimately support. It is also important to identify the silences in a particular theory or tradition. That is, what questions are not being asked, and why not? Finally, it is crucial to consider the social relevance of the theory or perspective. What does it tell us about our society, and the direction that our society is or ought to be taking? Fundamentally, the study of crime involves the values and opinions of the criminologist, as students of crime must understand if they are to develop an informed view of the issues.

CLASSICAL THEORY AND THE CRIMINAL ACT

The intellectual and social climate within which various criminological theories emerge is an important part of understanding the development of traditional, mainstream and alternative perspectives within criminology.

The emergence of the classical theory coincided with major changes occurring in Europe over a period of several centuries to the eighteenth century. More specifically, a revolution was happening in the basic structures of society in a literal and direct sense of the word. From the creation of the United States to the bloody terror of the French Revolution, major shifts and transformations were taking place in all spheres of life—economic, social and political. Over several centuries there occurred a transition from one mode of production, feudalism, to another mode of production, capitalism. The former traditional ruling classes (the landed aristocracy) were being challenged by an emergent ruling class (the monied capitalists), and this was reflected in substantial changes in the nature of the law.

From the age of mercantile capitalism onwards there was a steady push to reconceptualise and legally entrench bourgeois property rights over and above customary social obligations (Fine 1984). Whereas the ownership of property (especially land) had been linked to certain social responsibilities (e.g., in time of famine to provide a share of community goods to the poor), property was now deemed to be absolutely and exclusively in the hands of the individual. Any obligations to help the poor were simultaneously transferred from private hands to the state. The commodification of the countryside—in the form of the selling of game for luxury markets, market prices for grain, and mass-production of wool—were part of the breakdown of the traditional feudal order and the beginnings of a system founded upon the notion of private rights to property. The notion of 'individual rights' became a catch-cry of the age. The new class, the bourgeoisie, called for the universalisation of rights (at the least to those who had wealth and property), as opposed to the prevailing rule based upon hereditary privilege.

Under feudalism, there was an absence of formal legal status that was common to all. Rights were instead tied up with an individual's particular social status, such as their class, religion, gender, rank in society, and extent of property holdings. With the rise of capitalism came claims that all should have equal rights. This argument was extended to the law and courts in particular, as well as to general political processes. Accordingly, rather than being subject to arbitrary judgements and a justice system based upon different rights for different classes of people, there developed the idea that all social attributes (e.g., class, rank, property holdings) should be ignored once one has entered the court. People would thus be transformed into abstract legal subjects who were to be treated equally in the eyes of the court (O'Malley 1983).

In addition to major changes in the conception of legal rights and the legal subject of the law, there were major changes in the administration of the law as well. Typically, feudal law in England had been localised, and thus irregular, unsystematic, unpredictable, and closely linked to personalised and patriarchal forms of justice administration. In short, the law operated on the personal whim of the decision-makers, who happened to be local landowners, rather than on any systematic principles of justice. For economic reasons (long-term planning purposes) as well as political reasons (the location of decision-making power) a new form of law evolved: it was bureaucratic (rather than personalised), and it provided a more systematic and impersonal method of administration. In essence, the state emerged as a distinct public authority, as a guarantor of equality under the law in relation to freedom, rights and obligations. The divine rule of kings and queens had now given way to the **rule of law**.

The shifts in conceptions of rights and of who should be subject to the law were closely associated with parallel developments in the area of work. No longer tied by tradition or custom to the land, peasants now had a legal right to freely sell their labour. Political economists, such as Adam Smith (1776), were to argue that competition was the lifeblood of an economy, fuelled by the division of labour, and motivated by people's interests in property and their personal welfare. It was in this context of major social, economic and political change that the classical school of criminology was born.

Classical theorists essentially conceive of humans as self-interested and self-seeking. They assume that all people are essentially equal in the eyes of the law, and that each person has an equal capacity to reason (Taylor, Walton & Young 1973). The classical theory rests upon the notion of a **social contract**. That is, there is an implied consensus between individuals and the state, whereby individuals give up certain rights to the state; in return, rights and security of person and property are protected from other individuals, and from the state itself. The assumption behind the social contract is that the rights of each person will be protected against the corruption and excesses of institutions and other individuals by virtue of a systematic, predictable and regular system of law. The rule of law in effect means that everyone is to be treated equally, without fear or favour, and regardless of social background in the courts of law. It also means that those who make the laws are bound by those laws.

There are three basic elements in classical theory.

- All of us as individuals are self-interested at heart.
- All of us as individuals are implicated in a social contract with the state

which protects us from the self-interested behaviour and actions of others.
• All of us are essentially equal in legal status and in our capacity to reason.

In the classical tradition, the purpose of **punishment** within the law is to deter individuals from impinging upon and violating the rights and interests of others. All of us as individuals are seen to have an equal capacity to reason, and hence are deemed responsible for our own actions. The classical view is that there is a consensus among members of a society regarding the desirability of a social contract which denotes the relationship between the state and individual. Since individuals are viewed as having equal power to reason and to support a rational system based upon reason (i.e., the social contract), then any laws and rules developed under this system are seen to be reasonable and binding upon all. Thus, rule is by consensus, which in turn is rationally established. An individual who engages in crime either acts irrationally or makes a bad choice.

Classicism locates the source of criminality within the rational, reasoning **individual**. It is a matter of choice and intent on the part of the offender. Related to this is the notion that each individual should be made familiar with the law, and with its punishments, so that a correct choice in terms of behaviour is made. Punishment is intended to deter the individual from choosing wrongly in their immediate and future activities, through the threat of possible pain (i.e., penalty). Individuals are to be held responsible for their actions.

The classical conception of human nature, one based upon the idea of self-interest, revolves around the idea of a **pleasure–pain calculus**. Crime is seen in relation to a presumed universal tendency in human beings to seek pleasure and to avoid pain. The decision on whether or not to engage in crime is a matter of weighing up these two principles. According to Bentham (cited in Gottfredson & Hirschi 1990), decisions regarding different behaviours are determined according to whether or not the consequences are pleasurable or painful. There may be physical limitations to action, and religious and moral sanctions pertaining to specific activities, but it is the criminal law which prescribes whether behaviour is criminal or non-criminal. In order to deal with behaviour which has been subject to political sanction in the form of the law, crime control needs continually to adjust the certainty and severity of state penalties in accordance with the pleasure–pain calculus.

The classical system was intended to be more humane than one based upon social vengeance, while still maintaining a strong element of deterrence. In the words of Beccaria (1767: 43):

> The end of punishment, therefore, is no other, than to prevent the criminal from doing further injury to society, and to prevent others from committing the like offence. Such punishments, therefore, and such a mode of inflicting them, ought to be chosen, as will make the strongest and most lasting impressions on the minds of others, with the least torment to the body of the criminal.

Constructed in this way, the purpose of punishment is linked to notions of prevention of crime. It offers painful disincentives for criminal activity and establishes certainty in the applications of the law against convicted criminals.

Classical criminal policy focuses primarily on the **criminal act** and suggests equal punishments for equal crimes. Again, the emphasis is on equal treatment because of the presumption of equal rationality, and the necessity of equality in legal proceedings. The punishment is meant to fit the crime. Through punishment, it was thought that the offending individual would come to see obeying the law as the most rational of choices. For the sake of equality, penalties should be fixed prior to sentencing, and be administered in accordance with the actual offence which had been committed (rather than any prior offences, or speculation regarding the commission of offences in the future).

In summary, the classical school of criminology emphasises choice, responsibility and intent. As such, it is a **voluntaristic** conception of crime, which locates the reasons for crime within the individual social actor. There is a stress upon equality before the law, and in the equal capacity of people to reason and make choices. Crime is seen as a violation of the legal consensus, which itself is seen to reflect the social contract. The law should be codified, neutral and impartial. Punishment is intended to deter individuals according to pleasure–pain principles. The main stress is on the criminal act, and the application of laws equally and systematically in relation to this act.

The main problem of the classical theory is that it tends to ignore individual differences between criminal actors. It assumes that everyone is a rational actor capable of exercising free choice. Practically speaking, however, it was soon recognised that some categories of people—the aged, the young, people with mental illness or intellectually disabled—do not have the same capacities as others. Thus they should be singled out as possessing diminished responsibility for their actions. More generally, classicism has been criticised for assuming equality for all, yet this is clearly not the case in a society riven by deep social divisions and inequalities (Young 1981). The location of crime causation within the individual, via the exercise of free will or choice, was also criticised by another emerging school of criminology, namely, the positivists.

POSITIVISM AND THE CRIMINAL OFFENDER

The advent of positivism as a major perspective is associated with significant changes occurring in European society in the nineteenth century. Positivism represents a radical shift away from classicist principles, with a very different view of society and human nature. It arose in a period characterised by the further movement forward of the Industrial Revolution. This was a new phase of productive innovation, organisation and technological development. It was accompanied by the further concentration of mobile villagers and peasants into the city, the creation of factories, and the introduction of new systems of energy production (e.g., steam engine), communication and transport. Changes in the means of production were accompanied by significant changes in social and political life. In particular, the combination of urbanisation, mass production and 'free labour' meant that there emerged a whole new class, the working class, which very quickly saw itself in opposition to the now established ruling class, the capitalist class.

The rise of the proletariat as a distinct and growing class was accompanied by conflict over the nature of their work and the ownership and control of production in society. In theory, in a capitalist free market, workers were free to sell their labour as they wished. In practice, the asymmetrical or unbalanced relationship between employers and employees was generally marked by different levels of exploitation of the workers. The extent of the exploitation was highlighted in fictional accounts of city and working life, as in the stories of Charles Dickens: his *Oliver Twist* deals with aspects of child labour and criminal exploitation of children. The proletariat was not a passive force in society, however. Workers began to organise themselves politically and industrially, in the form of unions, working-class organisations, alternative presses, and through various socialist, anarchist and labour parties. Armed struggle also featured in the class conflict, most notably in France in 1848 and in the Paris Commune of 1871, when workers took over Paris and put it under the democratic control of the proletariat.

Against this backdrop of profound technological, industrial and politial change, new theories regarding human nature and societal development were emerging. Theories of 'stages of civilisation' were to the fore, and were in part influenced by the impact of Darwin's theory of evolution which drew upon the biological sciences. Biology featured in many a theory of 'race' and society, particularly in the context of justifying further expansionary efforts of the European powers. The carving up of the globe via imperialist and colonial economic, political and military coercion was accompanied by 'scientific' discussion of biology, superiority and supposed white supremacy. Questions of racism were intertwined with notions of biological determinism. In the grand societal scheme of things, Europeans saw themselves as being at the top of the 'civilisation' and 'race' hierarchies. The new criminology also reflected these hierarchies.

The visible presence of class conflict and social misery, the rise of scientific interest and industrial innovation, and the idea of evolution and stages in human development were all to influence the establishment of positivism as an approach. Positivism is founded upon the belief that society is progressing ever forward, and that the social scientist can study society, provide a more accurate understanding of how society works, and ultimately provide a rational means of guidance to overcome various social ills and problems. It is oriented toward a positive intervention in social life. The positivist approach manifested itself in the second half of the nineteenth century with the coming to power and influence of the professions (medical practitioners, psychiatric workers, welfare agencies) and a steady increase of 'expert' intervention in all aspects of social life, but particularly in the area of parenting and child-rearing.

The positivist approach is heavily influenced by certain assumptions regarding the applicability of 'natural science' methods to the study of society (Benton 1977). Certainly it was no longer the case that appeal to divine authority, revelation, faith or simple opinion would be adequate to decide major social questions. Instead, the positivist appealed to scientific criteria, based upon logic and empirical evidence, and the notion of 'objectivity' in the study of society. Social scientists were seen as neutral observers of social reality, their job being to merely record the 'facts' as they exist and not to let their own values intrude upon the scientific process. Again borrowing from the natural sciences, early positivists viewed society as an organism, made of up various components working together in order to ensure the proper functioning of the system as a whole.

The application of positivist methods in criminology is identified with two different traditions (Gibbons 1979). In the late nineteenth century, the Italian Lombroso was engaged in a form of criminal anthropology; meanwhile, his medical and criminal justice colleagues in England were concerned with matters of a medico-legal and psychiatric nature.

Lombroso developed the notion that we could isolate discrete types of human individuals and classify them. His concern was with a general theory of crime. Influenced by the theories of evolution and civilisation, Lombroso in his early writings classified individuals into broad groupings, such as the 'genius', the 'insane', the 'epileptoid', the 'criminal'. Each classification represented individuals exhibiting traits roughly corresponding to various stages in the evolutionary process. In effect, Lombroso advanced the idea that there was such a thing as a **born criminal**.

The second early strand of positivism came out of England. This tradition was associated with the work of doctors, psychiatrists and people working within the prison system. Like Lombroso, they discovered differences in individuals, but they also discovered that there was a whole range of offenders who were not entirely responsible for their actions. This approach was therapeutically oriented. It was based upon a classification system which discussed the condition separately from the individual in whom the condition was manifest. For Lombroso, the criminal was born criminal, and thus appeared to be doomed from the outset. According to the therapeutic approach, however, an offender who is exhibiting conditions of criminality can be treated. It was left to the experts to determine the nature of the problem and then to devise an appropriate cure.

In contrast to classical thinking, the hallmark of positivism is that behaviour is **determined**, in the sense that individual behaviour is shaped by factors such as physiology, personality, social upbringing, and so on. It is further asserted that offenders vary, that individual differences exist between offenders, and that these in turn must be acknowledged and classified or measured in some way. The focus is on individuals, who are seen to require treatment, since they are not necessarily responsible for their criminality. The role of the practitioner is to identify the specific determining factors with regard to a particular offender, and then to treat the offender or correct the problem in some way.

Another major difference between classicism and positivism relates to their views of crime. Classicists espouse a strictly legal definition of crime, one where 'crime' includes only that activity which has transgressed the legal order as evidenced in the conviction of the offender. In contrast, positivists assert that there is a moral consensus in society which can be described and quantified, and which can be violated without necessarily being detected or processed formally in the criminal justice system. The concept here is that in measuring crime one can be guided by the notion of **natural crime**. While the law represents and crystallises the moral consensus of a society, and crime can be seen as behaviour which contravenes the moral consensus, not all perpetrators of crime are pulled into the criminal justice system.

Given this wider definition of crime, latter-day positivists have argued that more crime exists in society than is shown in official statistics. In measuring the extent of crime, techniques such as large-scale questionnaires, interviews and other types of measuring instruments are used. The issue then becomes the effectiveness of the social contract. The solution suggested by some positivists is that we need to intervene outside the formal legal system itself, especially since behaviour is determined in nature. Hence, a proactive approach may be called for, one which attempts to identify the 'hidden' crimes which are occurring, and which also attempts to prevent the commission of offences by early intervention in people's lives, before a crime is actually committed.

Three premises underpin the 'scientific' approach as conceived by positivists (see Taylor, Walton & Young 1973).

- That through various measurement techniques (e.g., genetic tests, use of surveys) we can classify and quantify human experiences and behaviours. Having done this, we can then make predictions about human activity, insofar as social phenomena are seen to obey general laws of operation.
- That the measurement and classification process, and interpretation of results, is essentially an 'objective' process. The social scientist is considered to be 'value-free' and hence devoid of value judgement. The idea is that the world exists 'out there', it has an external reality, and the scientist records empirical 'facts'.

- That the activities and behaviour of, particularly 'deviant', individuals are governed by factors that are largely outside their individual control. The social scientist's role is to identify the causal determinants of behaviour, and to establish the reasons why individual offenders act as they do.

Positivists concentrate on **the offender** and the characteristics of the offender. Individual offenders are the subject of attention insofar as they need to be diagnosed, classified, and treated. If we accept this view—that people are determined by forces outside their consciousness and therefore outside their control—the implication, of course, is that the individual is not responsible for crime. This type of reasoning places a lot of power in the hands of the 'expert' whose job it is to diagnose, classify, and ultimately prescribe treatment for the individual.

A central idea of positivism is that when a person is sentenced, they are sentenced to receive help. The idea is to **treat the criminal**, not the crime. The concept of treatment differs from the classical emphasis on punishment when it comes to the operation of the criminal justice system. For example, it translates into an argument in favour of indeterminate sentences. The criminal act is downplayed in favour of a concentration on the offender. Since each individual offender is different from the others, treatment must be individualised. The length of sentence in custody therefore depends upon one's diagnosis and classification (severe or minor problem, dangerous or not dangerous) rather than simply the content of the criminal act that was committed. As we saw in Chapter 1, these ideas had particular application to young people.

Positivism is an overarching perspective, and thus within this general orientation there are numerous different studies and explanations. The three main strands of positivism include the biological, the psychological and the sociological. Although positivism embraces a diverse range of ideas, techniques and concepts specific to particular disciplines, a central proposition is that a moral consensus exists in society in relation to what constitutes deviant and normal behaviour. Our concern in this chapter is with positivist approaches which see behavioural problems in terms of an **individual pathology** or deficiency. These approaches can be summarised in terms of three main tendencies in research: those which focus on biological factors, those which concentrate on psychological factors, and those which present bio-social explanations for crime.

Biological Explanations

There are two broad strands within this type of explanatory framework. One argues that, in essence, the criminal is **born**. Criminality and criminal behaviour are thus primarily attributable to inherited predispositions. The other strand argues that biological factors are crucial in determining behaviour, but they may stem from the environment rather than simply be inherited. In this framework, criminals are **made** as a result of environmental factors which affect their biological functioning.

Internal factors

Here are some examples of the first strand, in which crime is seen as the result of something essential to the nature of the individual.

- Lombroso discussed the notion of an 'atavistic criminal', that is, a born criminal who was a reversion to an earlier evolutionary period or earlier levels of organic development. He claimed that criminals could be recognised by a series of physical stigmata, such as abnormal dentition, large ears, extra fingers or toes, eye defects, and even tattoos (see Taylor, Walton & Young 1973).
- Sheldon (1940) was concerned with body types and their influence on personality. He argued that there are three basic somotypes: endomorphic (soft and round), mesomorphic (hard and round), and ectomorphic (fragile and thin). Each body type was associated with a particular personality type, and the mesomorphic in particular tended to possess an aggressive and active disposition most closely linked to criminal behaviour.
- Some argue that our genetic make-up directly affects things such as our intellect and inherited temperamental traits, and thus puts us at risk of engaging in criminal behaviour (Fishbein 1990). Genetic differences are thus linked to particular behavioural patterns. To avoid the reproduction of criminal behaviour, the human reproduction process must be examined, as in the case of the eugenics movement of the first half of this century (Bessant 1991).

External factors

The following examples of the second strand, where crime is seen as a result of external or treatable biological factors, are drawn from Fishbein (1990):

- The presence of biochemical differences—linked to certain hormones, neurotransmitters, peptides, toxins and metabolic processes—is seen to affect people's general state of aggressiveness or iritability. For example, studies of pre-menstrual tension or pre-menstrual syndrome (PMS) attempt to associate criminal behaviour with changes in hormonal activity. The existence of high lead levels in a local environment, especially in regard to children, is seen to have an adverse effect on their development, and ultimately on their propensity to engage in crime.
- Psychophysiological variables, relating to such things as heart rate, blood pressure, brain waves, arousal and attention levels, are seen to been associated with cognitive and neuropsychological impairment. One consequence of this, for example, is the ways in which endomorphines and overall levels of

arousal demand more and more risky forms of activity, including criminal behaviour. In a nutshell, what gets the adrenalin pumping?

- Psychopharmacological inducements, such as cocaine, alchohol, PCP and amphetamines are a further influence on behaviour. It is suggested here that these kinds of external factors propel or facilitate the commission of crimes by those under their influence.

In each of these areas of study and research it is broadly possible for some kind of biological 'corrective' to be developed to prevent criminal behaviour occurring. This can take the form of removing the source of the problem (e.g., removing lead from one's living environment, banning alcohol sales), or regulating the biochemical and physiological operations of the body through appropriate treatment (e.g., drugs which restore hormonal equilibrium or ensure a regular heart rate).

Psychological Explanations

Psychological explanations of crime are based upon analyses of the minds of individuals and of various personality or behavioural traits which propel some people into committing crime. These people may lack some kind of internal regulatory form of self-control, or patterns of early socialisation may have negatively affected their social development.

Psychological approaches include those which focus on 'personality types', and which present typologies of the abnormalities in the psychological structure of individuals (e.g., over-aggressive, highly strung). The formation of particular personality types is often linked to certain biological predispositions as well as developmental experiences. Another kind of approach is the psychoanalytic, which turns attention to the unconscious mind and the way in which experience shapes and is shaped by processes beyond those which are consciously apparent to the subject (see Gibbons 1977).

A psychiatric theory of deviant behaviour is based on the assumption that certain childhood experiences have an effect that transcends all other social and cultural experiences (Clinard 1974). Such explanations adopt a medical model in which deviancy or criminality is seen to reside within the maladjusted individual. All of us are seen to have inherited universal needs, such as the need for emotional security. The deprivation of these needs during childhood leads to the formation of particular personality patterns in later life, and especially those personality types associated with deviant or criminal behaviour. Family experiences thus determine later behaviour. Ultimately, the development of certain behaviour is seen as a means of dealing with particular personal traits such as aggression, emotional insecurity or feelings of inadequacy (which were generated by unmet needs during childhood).

Bio-social Explanations

More sophisticated biological and psychological accounts of criminality accept that behaviour is in fact subject to both biological and environmental influences. It is a case of nature plus nurture, rather than one or the other. It is argued that human beings have a 'conditional free will', that is, that there is individual choice within a set, yet to some degree changeable, range of possibilities (Fishbein 1990).

For example, Eysenck (1984) put forward the argument that behaviour can be explained as resulting from a combination of biological and environmental influences. His study analysed crime in terms of two broad processes of development.

- *The differential ability to be conditioned:* Genetic inheritance affects one's ability to be conditioned. That is, the sensitivity of the autonomic nervous system which one has genetically inherited will determine whether one is an extrovert or an introvert, and thus how well one is able to be conditioned in society.
- *The differential quality of conditioning:* Family conditioning makes use of a range of techniques, some of which are more efficacious than others. That is, the way in which a child is reared will have an impact upon the child's subsequent behaviour.

The argument is that a combination of biological potentials set through inheritance, interacting with environmental potentials shaped by parenting practices, determine the overall propensity to commit crime. Human behaviour thus contains both a biological and a social element.

In summary, the positivist perspective in criminology emphasises the role of external and internal determinants of crime and criminality. People do not choose to engage in deviant or criminal behaviour; they are locked into such behaviour by a wide range of biological and/or psychological influences beyond their immediate control. The stress is on 'individual differences' between people, and on the necessity to pinpoint the main factor or factors which have given rise to the criminality. This is to be done through testing, diagnosis, classification and treatment, all of which are centred upon individual traits and needs as perceived by the expert professional.

One problem with the individual-focused type of positivism discussed here is that it puts an inordinate amount of power into the hands of a few 'experts' who may argue for ever greater levels of intervention in the lives of citizens generally. For example, in order to deal adequately with the 'predisposition to crime' (based upon biological or psychological indicators), ideally intervention should take place before the crime or deviant act is actually committed. How early are we to intervene to 'change' someone? Who is going to do this? Should we 'treat' people when in fact no crime or breaking of the law has occurred? Further questions can be asked with regard to whose 'norms' and 'values' we are to measure people's behaviour against, the social impact of attempting to mould each individual into a form of passive conformity, and the way in which racist and sexist assumptions have been built into 'scientific' study of biological difference and social behaviour.

CONCLUSION

The classical theory in criminology emerged in the period of transition from feudalism to capitalism. The ideological or philosophical basis of the theory was heavily influenced by the prevailing 'rights' discourse which emphasised the notion of a free and equal individual who possessed the ability to make rational choices. Rational choices are said to be made in accordance with the hedonistic principles of pain–pleasure; hence, punishment (which obviously produces pain) is regarded as a necessary means of deterrence, to ensure that irrational choices are not made. Although developed initially in the eighteenth century, many of the key elements of classical conceptions of the law, crime and punishment remain at the heart of the contemporary criminal justice system. In Chapter 11, for example, we discuss how issues of proportionality, responsibility and deterrence still impact on the sentencing of young people.

The emergence of positivist criminology is closely associated with a concern to develop a 'scientific' approach to the study of society and social behaviour. It is a criminology immersed in concerns about empirical quantification and grounded methodology. The theoretical basis of this perspective is one which privileges 'difference' over 'sameness'. That is, each individual is seen to be unique and to undergo experiences which are not equal at the level of practice and biography. Crime is seen as a matter of individual pathology (sickness, deficiency). As such, the task of the criminal justice system is to heal the person or fix the problem through a process of treatment and rehabilitation. Again, elements of positivism are apparent in the contemporary criminal justice system. Historically, notions of rehabilitation have been an important part of the development of juvenile justice. They are still an important part of sentencing young people today.

Chart 2.3 provides a summary of the main elements within the two traditional criminological theories which we have discussed in this chapter. It is important that we recognise both the differences and the similarities of the theories. Each demands a high level of involvement on the part of the state in the life of the offender, but each constructs the nature of criminality in very different ways. Both the classical and the positivist approach locate crime in terms of individual attributes, whether with respect to 'rationality' or 'pathology'. Similarly, each builds upon a consensus view of society, one which implies that the laws and informal norms and mores reflect a majority opinion and the interests of society as a whole. Crime is a given. That is, it exists as a relatively uncontentious category, although its extent and distribution may be subject to debate (depending upon whether it is defined simply as a violation of law, or includes reference to violation of the general consensus regarding acceptable behaviour). The 'remedy' in each case is to deal with the individual directly—either to coerce the individual back into rational decision-making, or to cure the individual of their predisposing tendency to commit deviant acts. In the end, the objective is to reintegrate the offender into the consensus. This can be achieved either through the threat and experience of punishment, or by the intervention of expert assistance to resocialise and rehabilitate the individual.

Chart 2.3 Traditional criminological theory

Issue	Classical position	Positivist position
Definition of crime	Legal • violation of law • rights and social contract	Natural • violation of social consensus • conformity and deviance
Focus of analysis	The criminal act • specific offence	The offender • characteristics of offender
Cause of crime	Rationality • individual choice • irrational decisions	Pathology • individual deficiency • no choice
Nature of offender	Voluntaristic • free-will, self-interest and equal capacity to reason	Determined • biological and social conditioning and individual differences
Response to crime	Punishment • proportional to the crime • fixed or determinate	Treatment • diagnosis on individual basis • indeterminate to fit offender
Crime prevention	Deterrence • pleasure–pain principle	Diagnosis and classification • early intervention
Operation of criminal justice system	Legal–philosophical approach • basic principles	'Scientific' approach • measurement and evaluation

The bottom line in each of these perspectives is that to deal with crime is a matter of dealing with individuals. The locus of change is the individual. However, other approaches within criminology, including the sociological positivist, place more stress on examining the social context of crime. As we shall see, specific types of criminal activity are analysed in terms of group processes, and as a result of broad societal changes. In other words, crime can be seen as fundamentally social in nature.

3 mainstream perspectives in juvenile justice

As we noted in the previous chapter, the traditional approaches to the study of crime and criminality tend to centre attention on the individual offender, and on the criminal act itself. The causes of crime are thus generally seen in terms of the offender's attributes (e.g., biological or psychological) or the offender's choices (e.g., rationality). In the specific case of juvenile justice, however, there emerged perspectives and theories which attempted to link the nature of a society, or of specific types of group interaction, with criminal or anti-social behaviour. In other words, a sociological approach was adopted in order to explain crime and the role of the criminal justice system as this pertains to young people.

The aim of this chapter is to provide a review of sociological approaches which have had a major influence on the character and institutions of juvenile justice today. The chapter beings by outlining the elements of a sociological form of analysis, and then explores various **strain theories** of crime. These theories essentially look at the structure of opportunities in society, and the ways in which behaviour is learned in groups, as a means to explain the origins and dynamics of crime. A second area of significant theoretical development from a broad sociological perspective is that of **labelling theories** or approaches. It will be shown how, in this instance, crime is seen as a social process involving varying forms of social reaction to particular behaviours and persons. The chapter will conclude with an introduction to the **republican theory** of criminal justice. Here the main focus will be on elaborating the normative and descriptive elements of a theory which is based upon reintegrating children and young people back into society in a particular way.

STRAIN THEORIES

Sociological approaches to the study of crime in many cases share a number of assumptions of the positivist approach as discussed in the previous chapter. That is, they attempt to apply natural science methods to the study of society. In particular, society is viewed as something external to the observer. The role of the social scientist is to quantify various 'social facts' through sophisticated empirical tools, such as surveys and questionnaires, and to intervene positively in providing appropriate technical answers to identified social problems. A consensus of values in society is sometimes, though not always, assumed. Rather than reduce deviant or criminal behaviour solely to the individual, however, a sociological perspective argues that in order to understand the nature and occurrence of crime we need to look at the structure of the society which moulds and shapes culture and behaviour. Individual action is thus attributable to social causes; crime can be seen as a matter of social pathology.

To illustrate the intellectual contribution of a sociological perspective, we consider some of the ideas of Emile Durkheim, and how these can be used to examine crime (Lukes 1973). Durkheim analysed society in terms of two basic concepts: the notions of a 'collective conscience' (or consciousness) and the 'division of labour'. The first idea refers to beliefs and sentiments common to a society which, while derived from individual beliefs, exist independent of us and which exert power over us in terms of influencing our behaviour. The second concept relates to how production is organised in a society, to the basic work tasks and roles available to a certain society. Combining these two ideas, Durkheim distinguished two kinds of society based upon the concept of 'solidarity'.

- *Mechanical solidarity:* pre-industrial society; individuals share same customs, culture, skills, beliefs, religion; little work specialisation; basically homogenous society.
- *Organic solidarity:* industrial society; wide variation in terms of wealth, ethnicity, religion, beliefs, culture; high degree of work specialisation; people linked together through law and interdependence.

Each form of solidarity is also linked to specific forms of punishment. According to Durkheim, the nature of the society in which one lives in fact determines the manner in which deviants are dealt with (Lukes 1973; Inverarity, Lauderdale & Feld 1983). Thus, he argued that the society of 'mechanical solidarity' generates **repressive** justice which reaffirms the common values and beliefs by distancing the deviant from the wider collectivity. The casting out of transgressors, either through exile or loss of life, serves to reaffirm the core values of the society. By way of contrast, the conditions of 'organic solidarity' are said to generate **restitutive** sanctions. Here the aim is to restore the disrupted values of the society by reintegrating the deviant back into the functioning of the organic whole.

For present purposes, the main point is that sociological perspectives argue that in order to understand behaviour it is necessary to acknowledge that different societies give rise to different social structures and different kinds of behaviour. The organisation of society—its division of labour, its collective conscience—determines the nature of crime and the regulation of behaviour. Durkheim argued that where you have an unhealthy division of labour (e.g., one based upon force rather than choice) or an unhealthy regulation of the collective conscience (e.g., norms not well established) then there is a greater likelihood of widespread crime (Taylor, Walton & Young 1973). In other words, the definition of, responses to, and causes of crime are inextricably linked to the nature of the society as a whole.

Durkheim believed that societies vary in their ability to impose social regulation, and that the values of a society vary in their ability to achieve a desired social integration. An important concept introduced by Durkheim is that of **anomie**. This is a condition of society (not of the individual) where the norms and values of a society are in flux or even partially destroyed. It describes a situation in which shared beliefs and values have broken down, and where moral guides to and constraints on behaviour have weakened (Brown 1979).

As applied to issues of crime, a distinction was drawn between 'anomie' and 'egoism', both of which revolved around social norms (see Taylor, Walton & Young 1973).

- *Anomie:* a lack of social regulation in which the unrestricted appetites of the individual conscience are no longer held in check (e.g., 'anything goes', 'just do it'). That is, a state of normlessness where appropriate norms are not in place to inhibit deviant behaviour.
- *Egoism:* a normative phenomenon in which a value has been placed on the unrestricted pursuit of individual desires (e.g., 'greed is good'). That is, norms are in place which actively encourage the development of unregulated aspirations, and which thus encourage and sustain deviant behaviour.

Using this kind of conceptual scheme, a social scientist could then examine the nature of a society in order to determine whether or not deviancy can be explained in terms of individual pathology in a healthy society, or whether it is linked to an inappropriately socialised individual in a pathological society.

Subsequent sociologists and criminologists shared this concern to connect wider situational factors (e.g., immediate opportunities, specific peer groups) and social structural factors (e.g., employment and educational patterns) with criminal activity. Crime was seen as essentially a **social phenomenon** which could not be reduced to personal psychology or individual biology. In one sense, then, the impulse to commit crime is 'normal' and is socially induced. The 'criminal' or 'delinquent' is a product of a specific kind of social order.

The underlying theme of the strain theories is that crime is due to social disjunctures or **social strains** within a society. The strains or sources of tension are generated by the society itself; they do not reside within the individual (as in the case, for example, of a person feeling strained or pressured by circumstance). The cause of crime is located in social structures and/or social values which in some way are unfair or socially pathological. To deal with crime, therefore, requires strategies and policies which are pitched at institutional reform, rather than solely changing or modifying the individual in some way.

By and large, strain theories see crime as something which is linked to strains between 'structural opportunities' and 'cultural processes'. Decisions are made by people in the context of whether or not they have the means or *opportunities* to achieve their goals relative to other people in society, and whether or not through social circumstance they associate with others who share their ideas and *cultural understandings* regarding acceptable and unacceptable behaviour. The key social conflict in this perspective is that arising from a disjuncture between social means and cultural ends. Deviant behaviour is viewed as a meaningful attempt to solve problems faced by groups of individuals who are located in particular disadvantaged positions within the social structure.

There are several different strands of thought within the broad strain theory. Some of these focus on opportunity structures relating to education and paid work; others concentrate on peer networks and the learning of particular norms and values.

Social Disorganisation

One of the earliest formulations of strain theory is that which examined crime in terms of social disorganisation. Also known as a 'social ecology' perspective, this kind of approach attempts to link the nature and extent of crime with specific social processes associated with urban life. The classic study in this area was provided by two Chicago-based researchers, Shaw and McKay, who were writing at a time of great social change, the late 1920s and the 1930s. The early decades of this century had been marked by events such as World War I (1914–18), the Russian Revolution of 1917, armed class struggles in Germany and other European countries in the early 1920s, the rise of Facism in Spain, Italy and Germany along with the entrenchment of Stalinism in the Soviet Union by the late 1920s, and the advent of the Great Depression in 1929. In this context of political turmoil and economic hardship, many people fled Europe to settle in other parts of the world.

Shaw and McKay (1942) sought to link these wider social processes to the incidence of crime in American cities. They examined the ways in which successive waves of immigrants moved into inner-city neighbourhoods of the urban spatial grid, and then gradually moved to the outer areas. This process of urban settlement and transition was seen to produce tensions and chaos; it was characterised by a high degree of social disorganisation. Against this backdrop, Shaw and

McKay examined the life histories of juvenile offenders, coming to the conclusion that juvenile offending is intimately linked to the transitional processes of social change. They argued that delinquency can be viewed as part of the natural social process of settling in experienced by new immigrants. Specifically, these communities were seen to exhibit a high degree of social disorganisation. Customary social norms which usually produce conforming behaviour were often inapplicable or in apparent conflict with the norms of the new society. The new immigrants were rarely integrated into the wider social, economic and political systems. Questions of language, education, work skills and social networks all came into play in shaping the life affairs of individuals and immigrant communities.

The hallmark of Shaw and McKay's version of strain theory is that behaviour is regulated via customary social norms and values (see Gibbons 1979). In the transient situation described above, it was claimed that:

- young people were not subject to the social controls that customarily produced conformist behaviour in their country of origin (this is similar to what Durkheim refers to as a state of normlessness or anomie)
- due to this state of social disorganisation, which cuts across material opportunities and cultural values, young people began to associate with like-minded individuals who shared the same transitory experiences. Since their neighbourhood was in a state of flux, the behaviour of such groups was often associated with various forms of delinquency.

While Shaw and McKay initially concentrated on the issue of social disorganisation and transient populations, changing social and economic circumstances in the 1930s prompted them to change their orientation somewhat. In particular, they began to speak not only of the link between crime, immigration and settlement patterns, but also of poverty and unemployment, and the social strains caused by economic deprivation. They stated that, while people had internalised the cultural goals of society, they were denied the opportunities to achieve these goals because of the stratified and depressed state of the economy.

Whether crime was viewed in terms of processes of rapid social change (e.g., waves of immigration) or in terms of relative deprivation (e.g., lack of opportunity), it was now seen to be more a matter of 'normal people in abnormal situations' than disturbed individuals acting out their pathology (Gibbons 1979). The themes of cultural clashes, cultural values, reduced opportunities and the impact of poverty were repeated in subsequent strain theories.

Opportunity Structures

The importance of analysing social values and social structures is a particularly strong feature of 'opportunity' theories. According to Merton (1957), for example, malintegration occurs where there is a disproportionate balance or disjuncture between the culturally defined goals of a society and the institutionalised means whereby these goals can be achieved. He argued that all individuals share the same cultural goal (in this case the 'American Dream' of financial success, fame and status) but they have different opportunities to achieve success through the established institutionalised means (such as education). That is, in a society where emphasis has been placed upon certain valued goals, but the universal provision of appropriate means to attain these goals has been neglected, malintegration is inevitable. In this sense, the society can be seen to be anomic.

An unstable social relationship between goals and means leads to a situation in which a fundamental factor in deviant behaviour is the thwarting of 'expressive anomie' at the level of individual experience. Depending upon one's location in the social structure, one chooses whether to accept or reject the culturally defined goals, and whether to accept or reject the institutional means to attain these goals. Accordingly, Merton developed a typology of individual adaptations to the goals and means of society. The typology was divided into the following categories:

- *Conformism:* This category comprises the majority of people, who are said to accept the culturally defined goals and the institutionally defined means of attaining them.
- *Innovation:* These individuals may subscribe to the culturally defined goals (of success), but they do not have the institutionalised means of achieving them (e.g., money to pay for education). The result is that they resort to 'innovative' means to achieve their goals, some of which include criminal activity (e.g., robbing a bank).
- *Ritualism:* Individuals acknowledge the culturally defined goals, but they also recognise that they cannot attain them. Nevertheless, they decide to pursue the institutionalised means anyway. To put it differently, these people simply go through the motions (e.g., attending school), even though they cannot achieve the goals set for them.
- *Retreatism:* Individuals choose to reject both the mainstream goals and the means of achieving them. Instead, they adopt a retreatist position, in which they opt out of the existing cultural and institutional framework (e.g., by taking drugs).
- *Rebellion:* The cultural goals are no longer seen as relevant, so they are replaced with something else. These individuals are not retreating into oblivion, but instead are creating their own goals and their own means of achieving these (e.g, counter-cultural activity).

Similar types of analysis are apparent today in Australia in the work of those criminologists who wish to examine the link between unemployment and youth crime. As with Merton, there is a tendency to see 'social class' in terms of degree of access to desired consumption goods (rather than as a relation to the means of production itself). Braithwaite (1991), for example, talks of the humiliation suffered by the poor and unemployed in society, and the need to address their economic needs. The importance of youth employment opportunities is stressed time and again as being a crucial variable in the conditions which give rise to varying forms of youth criminality (Wilson & Lincoln 1992; Braithwaite & Chappell 1994). The issue of individual opportunities and closed avenues for economic and social advancement is particularly pertinent in a period of generalised high unemployment. From the point of view of policy, great emphasis is placed upon enhancing and developing more opportunities for young people in the labour market so that the incentives to commit crime are reduced.

The key point of this perspective is that, ultimately, 'strain' or conflict is not seen to reside within the individual, but within society itself. It is the tensions existing between cultural goals and available means which provide the impetus for different types of individual adaptation. It is the structure of society and its institutions which thus shape the choices and opportunities available to young people, and which provide the impetus for different kinds of social behaviour.

Control Theory

The notion of opportunity also partially underlies control theory, which although not usually directly linked to strain theories per se, does share some elements with them. Here, however, the issue is not so much the presence or absence of opportunity, but the actual use of opportunity by young people. Control theory is premised upon the idea that it is an individual's bond to society which makes the difference in terms of whether or not they abide by society's general rules and values. From this perspective, all people are inherently anti-social, and thus all young people would commit crime if they dared. It is the nature of the bond that children have with their society which ultimately determines their behaviour (Empey 1982; Nettler 1984).

Hirschi (1969) theorised that the social bond is made up of four major elements.

- *Attachment:* the ties of affection and respect to significant others in one's life, and more generally a sensitivity to the opinion of others.
- *Commitment:* the investment of time and energy in activities such as school and various conventional and unconventional means and goals.
- *Involvement:* the patterns of living which shape immediate and long-term opportunities, for example, the idea that keeping busy doing conventional

things will reduce the exposure of young people to illegal opportunities.

• *Belief:* the degree to which young people agree with the rightness of legal rules, which are seen to reflect a general moral consensus in society.

It is the combination of attachment, commitment, involvement and belief which shapes the life world of the young person, and which essentially dictates whether or not they will take advantage of conventional means and goals of social advancement, or whether they will pursue illegal pathways to self-gratification.

In related work, Gottfredson and Hirschi (1990) argue that the central issue in explaining crime is that of self-control, that is, people differ in the extent to which they are restrained from criminal acts. This in turn is linked to the question of social bonding, and especially the problem of ineffective child-rearing. The theory incorporates elements of classical theory (in its acceptance of the idea that people are basically self-seeking), bio-social positivism (in its focus on the importance of proper 'conditioning' or training of the young) and sociological perspectives (which look to the nature of the family as a key variable in the development of self-control). The theory does not analyse specific social divisions (e.g., class, gender, ethnicity), but rests upon a conception of human nature which sees all people as essentially driven by the same 'universal tendency to enhance their own pleasure'. Given this, the crucial issue becomes how best to socialise all people to conform to society's values and to engage in conventional law-abiding behaviour. In policy terms, the answer to juvenile crime lies in redressing the defective social training which characterises offenders who have in some way 'lost control'. In other words, the emphasis from a practitioner's perspective is to reattach the young people to some kind of family, to recommit them to long-range conventional goals, to involve them in school and other constructive activities, and to have them acquire belief in the morality of law (Empey 1982: 269).

Importantly, the control perspective is premised upon the idea that 'deviancy' stems from lack of self-control, and that this is fundamentally a matter related to the processes of socialisation. Whereas Hirschi emphasised the significance of relationships within the family, by contrast most strain theorists have examined the impact of non-family members on the development and experiences of young people who offend.

Differential Association and Youth Subcultures

Writers have explored the impact of social strains as manifested in youth subcultures and individual learning processes. Sutherland and Cressy (1974), for example, argue that crime is essentially cultural in nature in the sense that it is learned behaviour. Crime is not simply determined by biological factors or youthful experiences of lack of opportunity. Over a period of years Sutherland

and Cressy developed a theory of **differential association** as a means to explain how criminal behaviour is learned in interactions between people. What is differentially associated is the behaviour, in that some individuals will associate with the holders of criminal norms, while others will not.

In summary form, the key elements of the theory of differential association include the following propositions (see Sutherland and Cressy, 1974).

- Criminal behaviour is learned.
- Criminal behaviour is learned in interaction with other persons in a process of communication.
- The principal part of the learning of criminal behaviour occurs within intimate personal groups.
- When criminal behaviour is learned, the learning includes techniques of committing the crime, which are sometimes very complicated, sometimes very simple; and the specific direction of motives, drives, rationalisations and attitudes.
- The specific direction of motives and drives is learned from definitions of the legal codes as favourable or unfavourable.
- A person becomes delinquent because of an excess of definitions favourable to violation of law over definitions unfavourable to violation of law.
- Differential associations vary in frequency, duration, priority and intensity.
- The process of learning criminal behaviour by association with criminal and anti-criminal patterns involves all the mechanisms that are involved in any other learning.
- While criminal behaviour is an expression of general needs and values, it is not explained by those general needs and values since non-criminal behaviour is an expression of the same needs and values.

The theory argues that a person learns to define a situation and to define their conduct in relation to the law and that this learning takes place within specific group contexts. One learns to associate certain classes of conduct, either legal or illegal, with the group's approval or disapproval. If we are to intervene in young people's lives to stop them from offending, then we must attempt to change the way in which certain groups define their immediate situations and their relationship to law-abiding or law-breaking behaviour.

The idea that decisions to engage in deviant or criminal behaviour are collective in nature has been the subject of those who look to **youth subcultures** as the source of the problem. Various writers, for instance, have argued that the strain between ends and means is reflected in specific class cultures. Cohen (1955) and Cloward and Ohlin (1960) point to the existence of working-class ways of doing things and concepts of the social world. Rather than focusing on the disappointed individual, who adapts in varying ways to the strain between opportunities and means to attain desired ends, these perspectives emphasise that crime is collective behaviour. Whether it be a conflict between middle-class values and working-class values, or the adoption of illegitimate opportunity structures specifically related to one's class background, delinquency and crime are seen to be collective phenomena.

The specific reasons for certain types of collective response to a general situation of blocked opportunity have been seen to include lack of self-esteem (Cohen 1955) and a sense of injustice (Cloward & Ohlin 1960). But others (Matza 1964; Downes 1966) have argued that working-class boys neither reject nor invert the dominant culturally prescribed values of society. Rather, youth subcultures often simply accentuate particular 'subterranean values' which are a part of normal society (e.g., risk, adventure, fun) but sometimes take them too far. In response to restricted access to opportunity, the response of young people is to resort to a form of 'manufactured excitement' of their own (Matza 1964).

Strain theorists have been criticised because they discuss young men more or less exclusively, and more generally because they have constructed theoretical explanations which simply do not explain the specific place and experiences of young women in similar class and social circumstances (see Naffine 1987; Campbell 1984). Women and girls were largely hidden from the analysis, or when they were included, tended to be analysed in stereotypical (i.e., sexist) terms. From a strain theory perspective, important questions remain regarding the specific sorts of strains impacting upon young women, and the variety of possible responses they have in relation to these strains.

The public concern about boys in groups doing the wrong things, and exhibiting the wrong ideas and appearance, has been reflected in various episodes in Australian history. These include the ways in which the pushes and larrikins of last century were policed (Finnane 1994), through to the moral panics associated with the bodgies and widgies youth subculture of the 1950s (Stratton 1992), to the manner in which 'riots' at the Bathurst motorcycle races have been socially constructed (Cunneen et al. 1989). The concern about young men (and young women) associating with the wrong crowd, and learning the wrong attitudes and behaviours, continues to permeate popular press reports on the activities of the young and on youth subcultures (see White 1993a).

From a strain theory perspective, the answer to the notion that crime is learned behaviour, which often takes place in a subcultural context, is to dismantle delinquent subcultures and replace them with something more positive. This can take the form of providing education and training programs which are of relevance and interest to the 'disadvantaged' so as to improve their legal opportunities for material success. It can also take the form of attempting to resocialise young offenders by separating them from each other, and by putting them into contact with individuals and groups which have a more positive, conventional outlook on society and criminal behaviour.

In summary, strain theories examine the nature of social constraints as they relate to behaviour; that is, the disjuncture between aspirations and opportunities, and between dominant values and subcultures. These kinds of disjunctures produce friction, frustration and strain, which result in criminal behaviour. The focus of such perspectives tends to be on working-class crime, particularly street crime, and various forms of anti-social behaviour.

Strain theory signalled a major shift away from the attempt to locate the causes of youth crime within the individual, toward an examination of the social structure. It is claimed that crime is not a matter of disturbed people acting out their personal pathologies; rather, crime is a case of normal people coping with abnormal or unequal situations. The policy options of the strain theories include such things as enhancing opportunities in order to overcome the disparity between ends and means, and encouraging the development of 'healthy' peer networks and relationships. On a personal level, this translates into the provision of training, educational, vocational and rehabilitation programs.

In some respects, strain theories can be seen as yet another variant of positivist criminology. They are often based upon the view that our behaviour and actions are to some degree determined by forces beyond our control. Furthermore, they often assume that society is or ought to be based upon a general consensus regarding the core values and norms which everyone is to share. The social world, including youth subcultures, is viewed as essentially 'out there', and the role of the social scientist is to record as accurately as possible the objective dimensions of this world. Crime is viewed as a 'given' (as recorded in laws or in social surveys of popular opinion) and the emphasis is on why people commit crime.

In their traditional form, strain theories have a number of problems or limitations (see Taylor, Walton & Young 1973). For a start, there is a general tendency to focus almost exclusively on working-class or street crime. As such, the approach accepts the conventional pyramid of crime, and sees the high incidence of working-class crime as a product of the strains experienced by this group. However, self-report studies of crime show that crime is committed by all sections of the class structure—the middle-class and the rich also engage in crime, and this too needs to be explained. A further problem is that the theory assumes a basic consensus on core social values (the American Dream) and crime (definitions of social harm). This denies the pluralism of values in society, and the wide range of aspirations, goals and means available to people, depending upon their particular individual and group ideologies, experiences and cultural background.

The approach tends to accept the general status quo, beyond the introduction of some reforms which are designed to enhance opportunities for the 'disadvantaged'. It is argued that the basic problem is a disjuncture between means and ends, which is also reflected culturally in various patterns of learned behaviour. The solutions offered point to improved educational or work opportunities and resocialisation efforts. However, strain theories fail to come to grips with the source of the disjuncture—the origins of the structural inequalities—in a society. The idea of reform therefore tends to aim at adapting the individual to the status quo, rather than removing the source of the inequitable distribution of opportunity. To put it differently, the theory does not deal with the reasons why there is poverty, unemployment or 'disadvantage' in the first place, nor does it identify the structural problems underpinning the lack of opportunities.

LABELLING THEORY

Labelling theories are closely associated with the 'interactionist' theories which argue that the social world is actively made by human beings in their everyday interactions (see Berger & Luckmann 1971). Such perspectives challenge the notion that the world and crime are objectively given. Instead, it is argued that crime should be viewed as a **social process**. That is, human beings do not simply respond passively to external stimulae; they possess choice, they are creative, and they bring to bear their own meanings upon situations. The meanings which people attach to situations and the manner in which they define situations has, in turn, an impact upon behaviour. Labelling perspectives therefore focus on subjectivity—our perceptions of ourselves are arrived at through a process of interactions with others and through negotiating the multiple possible definitions of a situation or event.

From this perspective, deviance or criminality is not something which is objectively given; it is subjectively problematic (Plummer 1979). The labelling perspective attempts therefore to provide a processural account of deviancy and criminality. The broad interactionist perspective focuses on how people typify one another (see each other as a particular type of person, such as 'mentally ill' or 'young offender'), how people relate to one another on the basis of these typifications, and what the consequences are of these social processes (Rubington & Weinberg 1978: 1). Essentially, it argues that deviancy itself can be the result of the interactive process between individual juveniles and the criminal justice system. Social control in the form of police intervention can thus actually produce deviancy.

In early versions of labelling theories, it was asserted that deviancy is not an inherent property of behaviour: it is something which is conferred upon the individual by society. In other words, deviance is created by **social reaction**. According to Becker (1963: 9), the impact of social reaction on certain types of behaviour or particular categories of people is crucial to explaining the criminalisation process:

social groups create deviance by making the rules whose infraction constitutes deviance, and by applying those rules to particular people and labeling them as outsiders. From this point of view, deviance is not a quality of the act the person commits, but rather a consequence of the application by others of rules and sanctions to an 'offender'. The deviant is one to whom the label has successfully been applied; deviant behavior is behavior that people so label.

The argument here is that we need to look at the impact of social reaction to behaviour, in terms of the application of certain labels (e.g., 'bad', 'criminal', 'delinquent'), in order to understand deviant behaviour. Public labelling, it is argued, may affect an individual's self-identity and transform them so that they see themselves in the light of the label. The process of labelling is tied up with the idea of the **self-fulfilling prophecy**. That is, if you tell someone sufficiently often that they are 'bad' or 'stupid' or 'crazy', that person may start to believe the label, and to act out the sterotypical behaviour associated with the label.

A further aspect of the public labelling process is that, in association with the labelling process, **stigmatisation** may occur. This involves the application of a negative label which becomes the 'master' definition of the person concerned. Regardless of current behaviour or past experiences, a person becomes known to the wider community mainly or solely in terms of the label which has been applied to them. A negative label, such as 'criminal' or 'delinquent' can colour the perceptions of people with whom the individual interacts and influence how the community in general treats the person. Where such stigma exists, it may lead to a situation where the 'deviant' begins to live up to the dictates of the label and change their identity and behaviour accordingly.

In order to describe the process of labelling, Lemert (1969) distinguished between primary deviation and secondary deviation. His concern was to explain how individuals come to be committed to the delinquent label, and to a delinquent career.

- *Primary deviation:* Most people at some stage in their development engage in activities regarded as deviant. They do so for a wide variety of social, cultural and psychological reasons. However, the important thing is that at this stage, when people engage in deviant activity they do not fundamentally change their self-concept. That is, the individual's psyche does not undergo a symbolic reorientation or transformation. There is no change in identity, and deviance is seen as nothing more than a passing event.
- *Secondary deviation:* The main focus of labelling theory is on secondary deviation. This occurs when the individual engages in primary deviation, and then there is some kind of official reaction to that behaviour. For example, an individual is apprehended by the police for truanting from school. The individual may begin to employ a deviant behaviour or role based upon this new status, which has been conferred upon them by state officials, as a

means of defence against or adjustment to the overt and covert problems created by the public social reaction to their original behaviour. Secondary deviation is said to occur when, because of the social reaction to the primary deviation, the person experiences a fundamental reorientation of their self-concept, and thus their behaviour.

Within the broad framework of the labelling perspective, a number of propositions and processes can be identified. Thus, for example, the labelling process can be described in terms of the following sequence of events.

- An individual commits an act which deviates from societal or legal norms.
- A public label is applied by police, courts, teachers, parents, counsellors, etc.
- Stigmatisation occurs: a blot on the record, a stain on the character.
- In response to this stigmatisation, a new identity is formulated as a means of defence to cope with negative public reaction.
- The new identity is constructed as the individual acts in accordance with the label and lines up to its content.
- The individual forms a commitment to the role of the label, learning the norms of behaviour identified by the label.
- Long-term pursuit of a deviant career follows, as dictated by the labelling process: the individual becomes a 'criminal' or 'delinquent'.

Labelling theories in criminology have had their greatest impact in the specific area of juvenile justice. This is not surprising, given the general view that young people and children are more impressionable than older people, and therefore more likely to respond to any labelling that might occur. It is argued that if a young person comes to court and is labelled as an offender, this process of public labelling and stigmatisation creates a new identity for the young person and as a consequence they will become committed to the roles and behaviour of the 'delinquent'. In terms of official processing of offenders, the impetus to further deviancy parallels the sequence outlined above:

- The deviant act is committed.
- Official detection occurs.
- The offender is taken to the police station and processed.
- The offender is brought before the Children's Court and branded a 'juvenile delinquent' or 'young offender'.
- This label 'sticks', even after the juvenile has been punished or dealt with by the criminal justice system.
- This long-term branding sets in train a whole process whereby the young person engages in further criminal acts.

At a theoretical level, much concern has been expressed over the issue of the social reaction to juvenile activity. Whether for good or bad, negative or positive, constructive or destructive, it is argued that labels do have effects on and consequences for subsequent behaviour.

Matza (1964), for example, investigated the question of 'delinquency' on the basis of the proposition that crime itself is ubiquitous—that is, most people at some stage engage in some form of criminal, deviant or anti-social behaviour. In studying youth subcultures and delinquents, a 'naturalistic' approach was adopted, one which was committed to providing an account that described youth experiences from the point of view of the young people. This not only enabled the researcher to reconsider the question of values and to challenge the idea that only working-class young people experience strain, but also to explore the motivational accounts provided by the actors themselves as to why they engage in certain types of activity. Sykes and Matza (1957) and Matza (1964) described the ways in which young people used certain **techniques of neutralisation** as a way of denying the moral bind of law (e.g., 'they started it', 'no one got hurt'). Furthermore, Matza argued that the actions of the juvenile justice system, and especially youth perceptions of the competence of officials and the application of sanctions, also affect the 'will to crime' of young people and form part of the ways in which they neutralise their moral restraint.

In studying young people, Matza found that juveniles eagerly explore all aspects of social life. In this process they tend to drift between the two poles of conventional and unconventional behaviour (including crime), without being fully committed to either. In the end, most juveniles drift towards conventional lifestyles and behaviours as their permanent pattern of experience. However, if during the teenage years of drift there is official intervention and social reaction to specific kinds of unconventional behaviour, it may precipitate the movement of the juvenile into a permanent state of delinquency.

Hence, the actions of juvenile justice institutions, and the impact of public labelling, are problematic in that they may propel some individuals into criminal activity who otherwise would have been law-abiding. The solution, according to Schur (1973), is to adopt a policy of 'radical non-intervention'. In other words, we should take a hands-off attitude to juvenile offending as far as possible, because any intervention may escalate criminal activity. As Schur (1973: 154–5) puts it:

> Basically, radical nonintervention implies policies that accommodate society to the widest possible diversity of behaviors and attitudes, rather than forcing as many individuals as possible to 'adjust' to supposedly common societal standards . . . the basic injunction for public policy becomes: leave kids alone wherever possible. This effort partly involves mechanisms to divert children away from the courts but it goes further to include opposing various kinds of intervention by diverse social control and socializing agencies.

The central policy concern of the labelling approach, therefore, is to find ways in which to prevent the young person from becoming a career criminal or long-term deviant. If we accept the proposition that contact with the criminal justice system, whether police, courts or detention centres, serves to sustain deviant careers, then the solution is posed in terms of **diversion**. The individual should be diverted away from the formal processes of the justice system, in order to escape any possible negative consequences arising from the formal public labelling process. In this way, future commitment to a deviant career can be averted.

Diversionary schemes and programs are an important feature of most juvenile justice systems today. They take a number of forms, from the introduction of informal cautions as an initial means of police intervention, through to the use of children's aid panels which attempt to divert young people from the official court system. The concern with labelling and the negative consequences of stigmatisation are also acknowledged. For example, the destruction of official records of juvenile offenders once they have reached a certain age, or completed a particular sentence, is one attempt to prevent them carrying a stigmatised reputation into their adult life. Tattoo removal schemes for young offenders have also periodically been used as a means to lessen negative perceptions of young people and to try to give them a conventional appearance in order that they may reintegrate back into society.

In summary, the labelling theory concentrates its attention on the social reaction to crime. It says that crime is maintained, perpetuated or amplified by the labelling process. Criminality is thus something which is conferred upon some individuals, and some types of behaviour, by those people who have the power to do so, who have the power to make a label stick. The implications of this perspective for juvenile justice are that we should do what we can to minimise the harmful effects of labelling and stigmatisation. This can be achieved through a wide variety of diversionary practices, methods of intervention which attempt to keep the young person from entering too far into the official criminal justice system.

Overall, labelling theory has been criticised for several reasons. For instance, the approach tends not to deal with the initial causes of deviance. It does not tell us why people have broken convention or engaged in illegal activity; its concern is mainly with the social reaction to the deviant behaviour. In a similar vein, it does not really explain how deviant behaviour can persist in cases where there has not been a negative social reaction. How do we explain continued deviancy in instances where individuals have not officially been labelled deviant, yet are still regularly and consistently engaging in socially deviant or unlawful acts? A further gap in some labelling theories is the failure adequately to theorise the nature of power in society. Why is it that some groups have a greater capacity to bestow a public label, and to engender social effects from this labelling, than others? The identity of the labeller makes a big difference in terms of the adoption or rejection of the label, and the social consequences of the labelling process for the person who has been labelled.

Difficulties also arise, at least in early versions of the theory, insofar as reaction to the labelling process is seen to be virtually the same in all cases. Contrary to this view, it is now recognised that people react in many different ways to a label (Plummer 1979). For example, once detected, those people who are officially processed and labelled may react in contrary ways. Some refrain from re-offending because they are ashamed about the whole process of being labelled 'bad'; in this instance the label has acted as a deterrent to future offending. Alternatively, some individuals see the label as a badge of prestige, reinforcing their self-image as someone who has a definite presence in the world. Others reject the negative label altogether, and persist in the activity for which they were apprehended since they do not view it as deviant. Some do not respond to the label one way or another. In short, for some individuals a label serves to amplify their deviance or criminality. Others view a label as undesirable, and are deterred from re-offending.

REPUBLICAN THEORY

The republican theory of criminal justice offers a perspective on juvenile justice which attempts to combine elements of strain theory and labelling (among other theoretical approaches) through a series of practical institutional measures. It is argued that the key to crime control is 'reintegrative shaming'. Before discussing what this means, it is useful to sketch some of the details of the normative basis of republican theory as a whole.

The core concept of this theory is the notion of 'republican liberty' or dominion. This refers to a form of 'negative liberty' where non-interference in our lives by other people (including state officials) is protected by law and general community norms. According to the authors of republican theory, Braithwaite and Pettit (1990), the prime goal of any society should be to maximise the enjoyment of dominion (personal liberty).

In this framework, crime is seen as the **denial of dominion**. This is so at three different levels.

- It is a negative challenge to the dominion status of the person who is the victim. That is, a threat to or disregard of the dominion of an individual attacks the status of that individual as someone who holds a protected dominion in society. If someone commits a crime against an individual, the criminal act asserts the vulnerability of the victim to the will of the criminal, nullifying the protected status of the victim.

- If successful, the criminal attempt not only disregards the victim's dominion status; it directly undermines, diminishes and perhaps even destroys the individual's dominion. For example, kidnapping or murdering someone destroys their dominion, while stealing a person's property diminishes their dominion by undermining certain exercises of choice they might have otherwise pursued.
- Every crime also represents communal evil. That is, not only does a crime affect the dominion status of the individual victim, but it endangers the community's dominion generally. This is because the fear of crime, or lack of action taken to assist the victim, can have the impact of reducing the liberty of those who fear possible victimisation of themselves.

If every act of crime represents damage of some kind to dominion, then the task of the criminal justice system is to promote dominion by rectifying or remedying the damage caused by the crime. What should the courts do in response to the convicted offender? Theoretically, in sentencing the convicted offender there are three considerations which need to be taken into account: recognition of the evil on the part of the offender; recompense to the victim for the harm suffered by them; and reassurance to the community as a means to restore confidence in collective dominion.

The focus of republican theory is on **restoring dominion**, for the victim, for the community and, importantly, for the offender as well. In other words, the theory is based upon an equilibrium model in which the needs of victim, offender and community are considered. Republican responses to crime, therefore, include the following three elements (see Braithwaite & Pettit 1990; Pettit & Braithwaite, 1993).

- *Recognition:* The offender must recognise the personal liberty of the victim in order to restore the dominion status of the victim. In order to do this, the offender must withdraw the implicit claim that the victim did not enjoy the dominion which was challenged by the crime. This can be achieved through some type of symbolic measure, for example, an apology on the part of the offender for their behaviour, a commitment not to re-offend, reconciliation with the victim.
- *Recompense:* In order to restore the victim's former dominion—which might not have been simply disregarded, but might have been destroyed or diminished—there must be some form of recompense for the damage done to the individual's personal dominion. This can be achieved through a range of substantive measures, such as restitution to the victim of whatever was lost in the commission of an offence, compensation where restitution is not possible, and reparation where restitution or compensation is not possible (e.g, compensation made to those close to and dependent upon a victim of murder).

- *Reassurance:* General reassurance must be given to the community at large of a kind that will undo the negative impact of the crime on their collective and personal enjoyment of dominion. This means that there has to be some guarantee that the community will be protected from future acts. For example, through a process of reprobation the criminal justice system should expose offenders in a constructive way to community disapproval, and reintegrate the victim and the offender back into community life.

In the specific area of juvenile justice, Braithwaite (1989) argues that the restoration of dominion can be achieved via a process of 'shame and reintegration'. It is argued that we need to distinguish between stigmatisation, which increases the risk of re-offending by the shamed actor, and reintegrative shaming, in which disapproval is extended but a relationship of respect is maintained with the offender. Stigmatisation is disrespectful of the offender. It is a humiliating form of shaming, where the offender is branded an evil person and cast out of the community in a permanent or open-ended fashion. **Reintegrative shaming**, by contrast, seeks to shame the evil deed, but sees the offender in a respectable light. The shaming is finite and the offender is given the opportunity to re-enter society by recognising their wrongdoing, apologising for their actions, and repenting. In this way, shame is seen as a useful means of combating crime as long as it is not applied in a stigmatising manner.

Braithwaite argues that we need in society a culture in which we promote a **self-sanctioning conscience**. That is, if certain norms and values are generally accepted and widely promoted, individuals will not engage in certain activities because their consciences will prevent them from doing so. Thus, the theory looks to both external processes of shaming (via the criminal justice system) and internal mechanisms of shaming (via socialisation through the family, media and schooling).

An important feature of the republican theory is the way in which it attempts to combine many elements of the different theories which we have considered to this point. Thus, for example, the theory tries to explain crime in terms of conditions affecting the individual and those occurring at a societal level. Crime is seen to stem from a combination of individual factors (e.g., unemployed, male, unmarried, young person), social processes (e.g., stigmatisation, criminal subcultural formation) and institutional structures (e.g., blocked legitimate opportunities, illegitimate opportunites).

A reintegrative shaming strategy works, or at least works effectively, only under certain conditions. These relate to the degree of **interdependency** (attachment to parents, school, neighbours, employer) experienced by the individual, and the degree of **communitarianism** (extent and depth of interdependent social networks) at the level of society as a whole. As Braithwaite explains it:

Interdependent persons are more susceptible to shaming. More importantly, societies in which individuals are subject to extensive interdependencies are more likely to be communitarian, and shaming is much more widespread and potent in communitarian societies. Urbanization and high residential mobility are societal characteristics which undermine communitarianism (1989: 101).

While the theory acknowledges the importance of economic variables (e.g., lack of opportunities for employment) and cultural variables (e.g., stigmatisation) in the construction of criminality, the main practical thrust of the theory is on the reintegrative shaming process.

In summary, republican theory as it relates to juvenile justice policy is framed in terms of responding to crime (rather than crime prevention *per se*), and doing so in a manner which distinguishes between 'reintegrative shaming' and 'stigmatisation'. The aim of any policy is to reintegrate the victim and offender into the society (and hence to restore dominion). The policy is thus aimed at reinforcing communal disapproval of the criminal act, while acknowledging and valuing the individual offender.

The republican theory has been criticised in terms of both its theoretical underpinnings and its practical applications (see Alder & Wundersitz 1994). For present purposes, it is enough simply to highlight a few areas of contention relating to its conceptual premises. The theory provides a list of variables (drawn from a wide range of traditional and mainstream theories in criminology) which indicate diverse causes of crime (see also Chapter 5); however, it fails to explain the basis for the existence of these variables. Unemployment, for example, is simply seen as a 'condition' affecting certain individuals. The causes and nature of structural unemployment are not explained in their own right. This must have some bearing upon the exercise of personal dominion in the first instance.

Another area of concern has to do with the concept of power. Here questions arise with respect to the notion of individuals exercising self-control and learning to act in accordance with a self-sanctioning conscience. Big issues surround the nature of social consensus (in relation to competing group experiences and ideologies), the distribution of community resources (the production and perpetuation of inequality), and the imposition of social control (those who actually exercise decision-making power). There is not a systematic theory of society or of the state, which means that the question of 'reintegration to what?' is not answered (White 1994c; Polk 1994). Without dealing with these kinds of issues in more considered and critical fashion, the republican theory may in fact find a number of difficulties in distinguishing between reintegrative shaming and stigmatisation when the theory is applied as a matter of practical policy.

CONCLUSION

The development of official responses to juvenile offending has been heavily influenced by the theories and perspectives outlined in this chapter. The 'special conditions' which have characterised the ways in which young people have been processed within the criminal justice system are in no small part due to the influence of ideas relating to the social structure and social processes as these impact upon youth behaviour. The responses of the system to young people are by no means uniform or consistent, and the multiplicity of programs and institutions in part reflects the many different ideas about the causes of juvenile offending.

The theories discussed in this chapter provide sociological explanations for youth behaviour and criminality (see Chart 3.1). Each attempts to make a link between particular kinds of activity and the nature of the society within which

Chart 3.1 Mainstream perspectives in juvenile justice

Issue	Strain Theory	Labelling Theory	Republican Theory
Definition of crime	• natural • violation of consensus	• conferred by those who have power to label	• denial of dominion
Focus of analysis	• structure of opportunities • nature of social learning • youth subcultures	• relationship between offender and those with power to label	• dominion of victim, community and offender
Cause of crime	• social strain, viz opportunity structure • learned behaviour	• stigmatisation and negative effects of labelling	• lack of self-sanctioning conscience and social connections
Nature of offender	• determined (by) social pathology	• determined (by) labelling process	• partly voluntary and partly determined, responsibility and opportunity combined
Response to crime	• provide opportunity to reduce strain, re-socialise offender	• diversion from formal system	• reintegrative shaming
Crime prevention	• expansion of opportunity and fostering of healthy peer group activity	• decriminalisation • radical non-intervention	• promotion of valued norms, fostering of communitarianism
Operation of criminal justice system	• individual rehabilitation and social programs	• greater tolerance and minimal intervention	• expansion of reintegrative shaming into social life of community

this takes place. Each tends to view crime as a social process which is not reducible simply to individual attributes of the offender, but which is closely connected to group interactions and social structural opportunities.

These theories have been described as mainstream insofar as many of the criticisms or perspectives offered by them have been incorporated into the practical workings and institutional practices of the contemporary juvenile justice system. The emphasis on groupwork and outreach work in some programs, for example, is related to the notion of peer-group influence and subcultural values, and how these shape a young person's attitude toward criminal or deviant behaviour. Provision of training and educational programs is clearly linked with concerns to enhance 'blocked opportunities' and encourage positive developmental outlets for young people. The decriminalisation of some juvenile offences, ongoing concerns to divert young people from the formal court system, and the development of alternatives to detention represent systemic responses to issues raised by the labelling theory (Coventry & Polk 1985). More recently, heightened interest in family group conferences, which bring together young offenders, victims and their families, and police cautioning programs, which do likewise, show the impact of republican theory on contemporary juvenile justice (Alder & Wundersitz 1994).

These theories can also be seen as mainstream in that they represent a liberal middle-ground in political terms. They tend, each in their own way, to provide a critique of the existing social order. But they do so in a manner which is geared to relatively minor institutional reform, rather than profound social transformation. The causes of delinquency are grounded in social structures and group interactions, but very often the policy prescription is simply to accept that 'the offender' (as legally defined) should be subjected to programs and forms of intervention (or non-intervention) which integrate them into the mainstream of society. The emphasis, therefore, is on conformity (in terms of a presumed social consensus) or tolerance (in regard to transient drifts from the socially acceptable norms).

These theories share another tendency: they often present a multi-factor explanation for youth crime, but fail to present a hierarchy of causes. The result of this is that immediate causes are cited (e.g., unemployment, racism, labelling, poor schooling), and a few minor reformist measures are advocated (e.g., training schemes, alternative schools), but little is done regarding substantial changes to the social structure as a whole. For those who wish to see major social change occurring, the questions of power and of social interests are of paramount importance. These are the concerns of the next chapter.

4 challenges to criminological orthodoxies

The theme of this chapter is radical challenges to orthodoxy in the area of criminological theory. These challenges have come from both the Right and the Left of the political spectrum. What unites these perspectives is a tendency to start from a vision of society as a whole, how it presently exists and how it ought to be structured, and then to work to specific propositions regarding the definition of crime and responses to it. The orthodoxy referred to can be seen as both the dominant ideas about crime and society within criminology, and the practical institutionalisation of crime control as this has developed over a long period of time. Thus, the challenge is often aimed both at the ideas behind the current system, and at the specific practices which have become the assumed common-sense way of doing things within this system.

The first two perspectives to be discussed—the Marxist and the feminist—are clearly tied to long-standing intellectual, social and political traditions. Their emergence in the field of criminology as significant, recognised perspectives in the 1970s coincided with major social changes occurring at all levels of society. The next perspectives—the New Right and the Left Realist—represent particular kinds of political interventions in the area of criminal justice. They tend to be rather eclectic in terms of theoretical elements and premises, but they do form specific viewpoints regarding the general direction and operation of the system. Both these perspectives really came to the fore in the 1980s, a time of substantial economic downturn and the rise of Right-wing parties and policies in many advanced capitalist countries. The chapter will conclude with a brief discussion of the possibilities and potentials of a new Critical Criminology, one which is relevant to the social conditions and criminalisation processes of the 1990s.

MARXIST CRIMINOLOGY

The 1960s saw sustained critique of many of our dominant social institutions. This was a time of general rebellion against the norms, values and activities of the mainstream society—as evidenced by resistance to the Vietnam War in Australia and elsewhere, by student militancy, the rise of feminism, demands for civil rights by Black and indigenous minorities, and so on. In the world of criminology, things also began to be perceived in a different light. In particular, whereas attention had traditionally focused on crimes committed by the less powerful in society (e.g., working-class young men, Aboriginal people), and the explanations for crime had tended to centre on individual attributes (e.g., choice, pathology, effects of societal strain on the individual), this was now called into question. Crime and the social response to crime began to be critically evaluated in terms of the concepts of power and social interests.

Previously, the dominant view within criminology was that society functioned relatively unproblematically to sustain everyone as a whole. It was thought that we shared the same values and the same interests. Thus, if an individual were to deviate from a social norm, the system acted to bring them back into line, to restore the social equilibrium. Individuals were socialised into a core set of values and norms. Even where conflict and competing interest groups were acknowledged to exist, the criminologist still often assumed that there was a basic consensus in society in relation to the appropriate means of conflict resolution (Pearce 1976). In other words, there may be inequality, there may be differences in the ability of people to conform to or gain advantages within the existing system, but overall there is also a capacity within the existing economic and political framework for individuals to move up (or down) the social ladder, and to challenge the status quo (via estabished parliamentary procedures) by introducing specific reform measures.

Marxist conceptions of society are based upon an analysis of structural power. A crucial aspect of the perspective is that power is increasingly concentrated into fewer and fewer hands; specifically, there is a ruling class. Those who wield decisive power in a society are those who own and control the means of production—the factory owners, the land owners, the media owners, the owners of information technology. In this view, an individual is defined, not so much by personal attributes or by reference to universalising statements regarding 'choice' and 'determinism', but by their position and opportunities as dictated by class forces. To understand crime, therefore, we need to examine the actions of the powerful in defining and enforcing a particular kind of social order, and the activities of the less powerful in the context of a social structure within which they have fewer resources and less decision-making power than the owners of the means of production. Criminality is intimately tied to class position, and is part of the logic of a system which is geared toward capital accumulation rather than the meeting of social needs (see Greenberg 1993).

A second key characteristic of Marxist conceptions of crime and criminality is their focus on the way in which institutionalised power is organised and exercised in society. Specifically, whereas 'liberal' analysis views the state as acting in the capacity of a neutral umpire or arbiter of conflict, as being independent of and not aligned to any particular class, Marxism sees the state as variously linked to the specific interests of the capitalist ruling class. Power is concentrated in a capitalist society, and the activities of the state reflect the interests of capital-in-general. These activities foster the accumulation of capital, maintain the legitimacy of unequal social relations, and control the actions of those who threaten private property relations and the public order. In other words, the state in a capitalist society is a capitalist state. As such, the general tendency of state institutions (such as the police, the judiciary, the prisons and community programs) is to concentrate on specific kinds of behaviour (usually associated with working-class crime) as being 'deviant' and 'harmful'. Other kinds of destructive or exploitive behaviour (usually associated with crimes of the powerful) are deemed to be less worthy of state intervention.

Within the Marxist framework it is argued that history can be seen in terms of a succession of different 'modes of production' (see, for example, Cornforth 1987). Each mode of production encompasses particular forces of production (tools, techniques), relations of production (lord–serf, capitalist–proletariat) and social institutions (monarchy, parliamentary democracy). Thus as we move from, for example, feudalism to capitalism, we see a shift in the mode of production across these areas: from agriculture to industrialisation; from power concentrat-ed in the hands of the aristocracy to power held by the bourgeoisie or capitalist class; from institutions based upon the notion of the divine right of kings and queens to those based upon the rule of law which binds the ruler as well as the ruled. The emergence of different modes of production has been associated with the rise of different kinds of class societies, where the central dynamic of each society is that of the expropriation of surplus from the direct producers and into the hands of those who own and control the overall means of production. For instance, in a slave-based economy (as in ancient Greece or Rome) the slave owner appropriates the surplus product of slave labour; in a feudal society the lord appropriates the surplus product of the serf; and in a capitalist society the factory owner appropriates the surplus labour of the worker. Hence, the concept of economic exploitation and class struggle are central to the Marxist perspective.

In terms of criminology, there are clear distinctions drawn between a con-servative (functionalist) and a radical (conflict) perspective on the nature of crime and law enforcement (see Chart 4.1). Where there are class divisions in a society, there are differing capacities to determine the content of the laws of that society. The powerful ruling class is able to shape the criminalisation process in such as way as to protect its own collective interests, and these interests reflect the interconnection between this class and a particular state form (see Chambliss 1975; Chambliss & Mankoff 1976; Quinney 1970, 1974). How issues are constructed, how crime is defined and how crime is responded to

Chart 4.1 Conservative and radical theories of crime

Issue	Conservative (functionalist)	Radical (conflict)
Definition of crime	Offends the morality of the people.	Reflects ruling class interests, especially property rights.
Use of law	To control those who offend against moral consensus.	To repress class struggle and threats to capitalist social order.
Causes of crime	Inadequate socialisation of members of working class via families, school, adults.	Class division as manifest in economic, social and political inequalities.
Extent of crime	Constant in all societies as each society needs crime to mark boundary of agreed-upon rules, norms and values.	Varies from society to society, depending upon the political and economic structure.
Consequences of crime	Makes people aware of the interests and bonds they have in common.	Diverts attention from exploitation and repressive nature of the system as a whole.
Responses to crime	Focus on working class due to lower level of internalisation of societal consensus.	Focus on working class because ruling class has power to label certain groups as criminal and controls the state law-making and enforcement processes.

Source: Adapted from Chambliss (1975), and Chambliss and Mankoff (1976).

relates directly to one's position in the class structure. If social power is concentrated in the hands of those who own the means of production, they will influence and generally dictate what behaviour is defined as criminal and which is not. For example, shop stealing may be considered theft, but false advertising may be viewed as only a trade practices violation. Similarly, those with power are capable of influencing the nature of societal reaction to behaviours deemed to be socially harmful. For example, industrial homicide may be prosecuted as murder or simply seen as accidental or a result of negligence.

A major contribtution of Marxist criminology is that it directs attention away from an exclusive focus on street crimes or working-class crime, toward the social harms perpetrated by the powerful within society. It attempts to demonstrate how class situation is linked to specific types of criminality. Thus, where you are located in the class structure will influence the kinds of criminal activity you engage in, the propensity for you to engage in such activity, and the intensity of that involvement.

According to the Marxist view, a broad distinction can be made between the **crimes of the powerful** and the **crimes of the less powerful** (see Chart 4.2). The initial difficulty in determining the 'crimes' of the powerful is that, if the laws reflect the interests of the ruling class, many types of social harm may not be

Chart 4.2 A Marxist perspective on types of crime

Crimes of the Powerful	
Typical crimes	**Examples**
Economic	Breaches of corporate law, environmental degradation, inadequate industrial health and safety provisions, pollution, violation of labour laws, fraud.
State	Police brutality, government corruption, bribery, violation of civil rights, misuse of public funds.
Motivations	**Examples**
Maximisation of profit	Structural imperative to minimise costs and maximise economic returns in a competitive capitalist market environment.
Augmentation of wealth	Attempts to bolster one's own personal position in the economic and social hierarchy.

Crimes of the Less Powerful	
Typical crimes	**Examples**
Economic	Street crime, workplace theft, low-level fraud, breach of welfare regulations, prostitution.
Socio-cultural	Vandalism, assault, rape, murder, resistance via strikes and demonstrations, public order offences, workplace sabotage.
Motivations	**Examples**
Subsistence	Gaining illegal income to meet basic income needs, attempting to supplement low wages and income relative to subsistence levels.
Alienation	Separation of people from mainstream social institutions such as education and work, and a structural and emotional sense of powerlessness.

incorporated into the criminal law if to do so would go against capitalist interests. In such circumstances, there is a need to establish wider criteria relating to the nature of offences. Thus, for example, crime has been redefined in a broader sense to encompass any activity which interferes with basic human rights and causes social injury (Schwendinger & Schwendinger 1975). Crime in the case of the powerful is seen to be linked to both a personal desire to augment one's wealth, and a structural imperative to get an edge in the overall capitalist economic competition.

The impact of the crimes of the powerful is often diffuse, yet the crimes affect a large number of people directly or indirectly simply because of the capacity of the capitalist to do harm on a large scale. For example, tax avoidance and environmental destruction can have a considerable social cost, but they are not visible in the public domain in the same way as street crime. In defending themselves against prosecution, the powerful have greater social resources at their disposal with which to protect their interests. Furthermore, the sheer cost associated with investigation and prosecution of white-collar and corporate crime often makes it prohibitive for the state to proceed, or to cast a net widely enough to catch violations beyond the exceptional few that are prosecuted. Crimes of the powerful can have significant structural effects in terms of deaths and financial losses. Because such crimes are usually directed in the first instance against other capitalists or against the rules governing the market-place, they are rarely perceived by the general public as being of special interest to them personally (except in the case of events such as industrial homicide).

By way of contrast, the crimes of the less powerful tend to be highly visible and to be subjected to wide-scale state intervention, involving police, welfare workers, social security officials, tax department officials, the courts, prisons, and so on. Such crimes stem from a combination of economic and social motivations. In the first instance, they are related to efforts to bolster or supplement one's income relative to subsistence levels; in the second, they may represent anti-social behaviour linked to varying types of socio-cultural alienation. People who are separated from mainstream social institutions and feel powerless can make efforts to supplement their income through illegal means (e.g., theft, fraud) or commit street crimes which express deep alienation, such as assault and vandalism.

A feature of relative powerlessness is that the crimes committed tend to be individualised and thus to have a discrete impact. There are usually only a few victims, whether personal or business or household, and the impact of the offence is limited to the actual household or person violated. The major institutions in society are largely oriented toward stopping these kinds of crimes, regardless of the comparatively greater amount of damage caused by crimes of the powerful. The lack of access to resources, such as control of the media and legal experts, means that working-class people are more vulnerable to apprehension, prosecution and punishment at the hands of the capitalist state. They are exposed to societal control mechanisms in such a way that they feel the full force of the state for any transgression they might commit.

For example, arising from concerns with class and class analysis of society, attention was drawn to the specific ways in which the activities of working-class juveniles have been subject to particular processes of criminalisation. The Birmingham Centre for Contemporary Cultural Studies in England, for instance, re-examined the issue of youth subcultures from the point of view of the unequal material circumstances of working-class boys and girls (Hall & Jefferson 1976). It was argued that class was central to any explanation of the experience of growing up, and that the relationship between young people and social institutions—such as the school, employment, and the legal system—is characterised by different forms of class-based resistances to the dominant relations of power. Certain youth subcultural forms were seen to 'solve', in an imaginary way, problems experienced by working-class young people (e.g., unemployment, educational disadvantage) which at the material level remained unresolved (Clarke et al. 1976; Brake 1985).

From the point of view of social control and policing, various studies pointed to the ways in which the media portrayed certain types of youth subcultures, which in turn led to a form of 'deviancy amplification' (Cohen 1973; Young 1971). That is, the sort of public labelling which pertained to some groups of young people actually generated further 'deviant' behaviour in the group so labelled. More generally, the link was made between the actual cultural, social and economic experiences of working-class young people, and the manner in which the state, particularly the police, intervened in their lives both coercively (e.g., arrest rates) and ideologically (e.g., through the promulgation of 'moral panics' over their behaviour and attitudes).

In this type of criminological approach, the concern is to highlight the inequalities of a class society (e.g., wealth versus poverty; business profits versus low wages), and how these impact upon the criminalisation process (Spitzer 1975). The powerful are seen as designing the laws in their own collective interests, while having greater capactity to defend themselves individually if they do break and bend the existing rules and regulations. The less powerful in society are propelled to commit crime by economic need and social alienation. They are also the main targets of law enforcement and wider criminal justice agencies. This is reflected in statistics which show an over-representation of the unemployed and poor in our prisons, our police lock-ups and our courts. By providing a structural perspective on social institutions, social processes and social outcomes, Marxist approaches argue that revolutionary or profound social transformation is needed if 'crime' is to be addressed in a socially just manner.

Aspects of Marxist writing in criminology have been criticised for the romantic image some writers have of the criminal as 'primitive class rebel', and for the rather conspiratorial overtones of some analyses regarding, for example, the direct involvement of members of the ruling class in dictating the operational activities of the police (Hall & Scraton 1981). Similarly, it has been acknowledged that not all laws are, strictly speaking, 'class' laws, in that some deal with class-neutral questions such as rape. This also raises the issue that power and powerlessness exist in a sense outside the class structure, as in the power of men over women. In addition, laws are enacted to fetter the activities of specific capitalists (e.g., insider trading), although it must be recognised that such laws ensure the smooth operation of the market-place, which is in the interests of capital-in-general. A further point of critique is that one cannot reduce crime to a simple equation with poverty or alienation. If this were so, then we would need to explain why it is that many people living in poverty do not commit crime, and why some well-off people engage in crimes ranging from vandalism to homicide.

There are many diverse interpretations and explanations for crime from within the broadly Marxist framework. Some of them offer rather simplistic formulations (e.g., the ruling class directly defines what is criminal or not) and some of them provide detailed, sophisticated accounts of how class power is exercised via the state to enforce basic class rule (e.g., through analysis of personnel, decision-making processes, limits to reform). Overall, however, it can be said that the strength of such approaches is that they attempt to locate social action within the wider structural context of a class-divided society. In doing so, they elevate the issue of power and control to the foreground of criminological analysis. They stress the ways in which social background and social processes give rise to certain propensities (on the part of the powerful and on the part of the less powerful) to engage in criminal activity.

FEMINIST CRIMINOLOGY

Feminist criminology developed in the early 1970s and reflected the resurgence of feminist political intervention in all spheres of social life. The Women's Liberation Movement represented a second wave of feminism, following the first wave of struggles by the so-called suffragettes at the turn of the century to gain the vote. This time the agenda was very wide. There were concerted efforts to make women the subject of history, of politics, of economics, of social life, rather than to present the social world in male-only terms, or in ways that did not recognise the existence, contribution and active part played by women in that social world.

Feminism proceeds from the point of view that a fundamental division in society is that between men and women. The differences between men and women are both biological in nature, and socially and historically constructed. A major emphasis in contemporary social analysis is to explain the different experiences and social realities of men and women in society, and to understand why it is that women and men have different positions, roles and status in society. To appreciate the complexities and debates over questions of such differences it is essential to distinguish between 'sex' and 'gender'.

- *Sex:* a biological classification, indicated primarily by (genital) sexual characteristics. Thus, we would speak here of someone being 'male' or 'female'.
- *Gender:* the learned culture of the individual, such as their dress, use of gestures, occupation, social networks, and aspects of personality. Thus, we would speak here of someone as being 'masculine' or 'feminine' in presentation, activity and outlook.

In the late 1960s and into the 1970s the Women's Liberation Movement put the issue of women's place in society on the political agenda. The political activity of women focused on questions such as the need for greater autonomy for women, the need for equal rights and a fundamental alteration of women's role in society, and the necessity for wider social and political responses to the oppression of women in society.

The different political strands of the Women's Liberation Movement, involving many different tactics and strategies for social change, were and are reflected at the levels of theory and practice. There are in fact many different interpretations and explanations for the subordinate position generally of women in Australian society. These are roughly set out in the following list, which provides some idea of the central concerns of various approaches within feminism (see Eisenstein 1984; Tong 1989; Segal 1987).

- *Liberal feminism:* questions of rights and equal opportunity legislation, and women's freedom in the public sphere to compete equally in economic and political life without sex-based discrimination.
- *Marxist feminism:* how the work of women in the paid labour force and domestic sphere serves the interests of capitalism, and how women's oppression can only end with the abolition of classes and private property.
- *Radical feminism:* the common experiences of all women, how they are all subject to male domination, and how oppression occurs at economic, political, psychological and social levels in both the public and private spheres.
- *Socialist feminism:* the interrelationship between capitalism and patriarchy (male domination), the unequal distribution of oppression among women, and the need to gain power and liberation in areas such as production, reproduction, the socialisation of children, and sexuality.
- *Cultural feminism:* the 'discourses' of everyday life and the ways in which institutions, language and interactions are structured to include and exclude female experiences in certain ways, and the need for women to separate themselves from dominant culture via a women-centred analysis and way of life.

There are a number of complex, sophisticated and diverse perspectives dealing with the origins, causes and nature of women's oppression and exploitation. It is useful to recognise that, while feminists are united in wanting to change aspects of women's lives in terms of equality, justice and self-determination, there is no single theory or perspective of feminism *per se*.

Feminism challenged criminology in at least two ways. First, there was the relative neglect within criminology itself of issues relating to female crime and women as victims of crime. Secondly, the theories and studies that did exist tended to reinforce certain stereotypes and conservative portrayals of the 'proper' place of women in society. There were problems with each of these, and feminist writers sought to rectify them by critique of both the criminal justice system, and the dominant sexist assumptions underpinning mainstream criminological theories of crime (Smart 1976; Naffine 1987).

It was pointed out, for example, that the neglect of women in criminological inquiry was due, in part, to the overwhelming dominance of males in both the criminology discipline and the criminal justice system. In terms of research and theory, and at the level of the practitioner, the system was composed mainly of men. Judges, barristers, solicitors, prison officers and police were predominantly male. Even where some men challenged the overt sexist practices of the law and law enforcement, this did not change the overall orientation of the system toward women. Similarly, it was recognised that women were well represented in social control agencies such as welfare, social work, and the medical professions. Nevertheless, the criminal justice and welfare systems together tended to police the behaviour of women in ways which reinforced the notion of women as wives, mothers, sexual partners, nurturers and domestic workers, rather than as complete persons in their own right.

The neglect of women generally within criminology is attributable to the subordinate position and limited participation of women within the criminal justice system. It is also related to the fact that women appear to be less statistically significant as a problem than men. That is, they generally commit fewer crimes, and the crimes they do commit are less serious and less violent than those committed by men. Furthermore, while women are overrepresented in some categories of victimisation (e.g., rape, domestic violence), in general they did not appear to be victims of crime to the same extent as men. As a consequence, investigators within criminology did not regard the female offender or the female victim as worthy of much research attention.

One of the problems with this overall attitude and perspective on women and crime was that when criminologists did look at female crime they did so within a male framework. Since mainstream criminological theories tended to concentrate on male experience (e.g., strain theory and male subcultures), there was a problem in trying to extrapolate these experiences into analysis of women's place in crime (Naffine 1987). For example, what does strain theory tell us about the opportunity structures and cultural goals of women? Similarly, labelling theory argues that it is particularly the less powerful in society who suffer most from the detrimental effects of labelling. How then do we account for the fact that powerless women are not involved in crime to the same extent as powerless men? What is it about the sex variable which influences the specific conditions under which male and female offending (and victimisation) occurs? The vast majority of traditional and mainstream criminological theories have ignored these questions altogether.

When such theories attempted to explain female crime as a distinct and specific social phenomenon, they accepted a narrow, conservative view regarding the place and position of women in society, and more often than not did so on the basis of a form of **biological reductionism**. This refers to instances where female experiences and behaviour are reduced to the imperatives of biology—the biological sex of a person is seen to dictate or determine appropriate social roles and practices (social constructions of femininity).

A key contribution of feminist criminology has been to critique one-sided, distorted views of women in the traditional literature that did exist on female offending. The basis of the critique had to do with the conflation of sex and gender (failure to distinguish the biological and the social) in much of the analysis on offer, and the misogynist (women-hating) character of some of the writing. Here we can point to several different theories which have ultimately based their conclusions upon the idea of innate female social characteristics linked to female biology.

Biological Explanations

These explanations view female crime as stemming from biological causes (see, especially, Smart 1976; Naffine 1987). Most focus on sex-specific biological differences as the standards by which to compare men and women, and as explanations for particular kinds of activity. They vary in substantive emphasis, but the overall message of biological determinism remains the same.

- In early theories it was argued that the true, biologically determined nature of women was antithetical to crime. Such views were based upon stereotypical notions of women as being passive, non-aggressive creatures. Criminality was linked to 'maleness' and 'masculine' traits such as aggression and physicality. Therefore the female offender, who was seen as exhibiting male traits, was considered doubly deviant, both socially and biologically: she was an exception to the usual sex of the offender and, as a woman, she went against her biological nature and thus was not fully female.
- Some theories discussed female criminality in terms of the physiological differences between the sexes. In this view, women conceal their offending behaviour (and thus have lower report and detection rates than males) and use their sexuality to attain (presumed) greater leniency by the police and the courts. This behaviour proceeds from their inherent deceitful and manipulative nature. This is turn is linked to their physiological make-up, in that women are capable of concealing their sexual arousal (unlike men) and thus in the most intimate human acts they have the opportunity and ability to manipulate those around them.
- In some recent theories, research on hormonal disturbances and social behaviour has tried to establish a link between menstrual cycles and the propensity of women to engage in criminal activity. In a similar vein, it is sometimes argued that post-natal depression is responsible in some instances for infanticide. In other words, as the female body fluctuates in terms of hormonal activity, the woman may engage in a wide variety of anti-social and criminal activity.

Socialisation Theories

A common way in which to explain female crime is to point to differences in the ways in which men and women are, or should be, socialised (Smart 1976). These types of explanations are generally closely tied to specific notions of appropriate sex roles. The problem is usually seen as inadequate socialisation, leading to a violation of the behaviour appropriate for members of the female sex. Again, very often the approaches reduce crime causation to essentially biological factors.

- Some theories see deviancy or delinquency as a form of 'acting out' on the part of young women. It is stated that women have traditionally been socialised to be passive and need affection, and that this explains their lower crime rates. However, if they have been abnormally or poorly socialised, then they may be susceptible to manipulation by men, and this manipulation can result in sex-related deviancy such as prostitution.
- A variation of this theory is that which argues that the key issue is the under-socialisation of individual female offenders. The maladjustment of the offender to mainstream social norms manifests itself in the form of sexually inappropriate conduct, such as promiscuous sexual relations. The desire of girls and women for acceptance and approval may result in gratuitous sexual relationships because this is seen as the only way in which the young women can assert themselves—through their sexuality.
- Some theories begin by arguing that crime is due to the disconnection felt by some women. The psychological absence of love produces instability in these females and this in turn leads to various 'acting out' of an anti-social or deviant nature. The argument assumes that emotionality is an inherent biological feature of the female sex. Women are said to have a need for dependencies because they are primarily emotional creatures—again, a biological reductionist argument.

The Feminist Response

The response of feminist writers to these kinds of biological explanations and socialisation arguments is that they represent a double standard in terms of morality and power. Underpinning this double standard is a blurring of the distinction between 'sex' and 'gender'. Females are presumed to have a fixed biological nature which is indistinguishable from their fixed social role. Any maladjustment to this stereotypical femininity is said to be the consequence of biological defect or inherent biological weaknesses of the female sex. Woman's social nature is thus thought to be given naturally by her biological being.

The crucial issue from a feminist perspective is that of relative social power and access to community resources. The criminalisation process itself is heavily laden with sexist assumptions which reinforce and reproduce structural inequalities of gender in society (Gelsthorpe & Morris 1990). This occurs both with respect to the construction of offending behaviour, and with respect to the portrayal of victims (see Chart 4.3). The central proposition of much feminist analysis is that women are treated differently in and by the criminal justice system because of the persistence of traditional gender-role expectations regarding 'appropriate' and 'feminine' behaviour for women (and men).

Underpinning this gendered division of the sexes is the question of power. That is, society is male dominated, and this is reflected in a myriad of social institutions, including the law and the criminal justice system. Thus, feminist jurispruedence has been concerned to demonstrate the gender biases built into

Chart 4.3 Women and crime

	Women as offenders	Women as victims
Nature of crimes	• Sex-specific offences, e.g., prostitution, infanticide. • Sex-related offences, e.g., shopstealing, fraud.	• Sex-specific offences, e.g., rape, sexual assault. • Sex-related offences, e.g., consumer rip-offs.
Mainstream explanations	• Related to issues of female sexuality, e.g., biological drives and hormonal activity. • Related to notions of gender, e.g., constructions of 'feminine' behaviour, and socialisation into these. • Categories of 'mad' and 'bad' based upon essentially passive and/or deceitful nature of women.	• Categories of 'deserving' and 'undeserving' victims based upon sexuality and relationship to men, e.g., married. • Related to notion of 'weaker' sex and dominant sex roles and social functions, e.g., housewife. • Sex-specific victimisation explained in terms of male biological drives, e.g., rape and 'provocation'.
Feminist explanations	• Double standards of morality, e.g., sexualisation of offences for women but not men. • Prior status of women as victims, e.g., persistent abuse, economic dependency. • Attempts to control and regulate female behaviour by criminalising certain offences as sex-specific. • Different social opportunities linked to male-dominated institutions and cultures.	• Emphasis on women as victims of male violence generally. • Sex-specific victimisation linked to patriarchial cultures and institutions. • Relative powerlessness of some women to protect themselves from personal and property crime. • Traditional gender-role expectations shape victimisation process.

Source: White and Haines (forthcoming).

the very processes of the law (for example, the 'reasonable man' argument in legal reasoning), as well as specific overt instances of gender inequality (for example, laws which allowed rape in marriage). The status of women as 'property' and as 'rights holders' has been examined historically and as part of an ongoing struggle to assert women's place and position in a patriarchial system and society (Scutt 1990; Graycar & Morgan 1990; Naffine 1990).

The nature of female offending is placed into a wider social, economic and political context, rather than one which reduces female experience to biological or psychological determinants. Women who commit homicide, for instance, have in many cases been victims of violence themselves. Similarly, women who commit social security fraud or other minor forms of fraud and theft usually do so, not for themselves, but to support children and dependants. Hence, the generalised violence against women as a social category, and the relative disadvantages they suffer economically, are explored as vital preconditions to any individual offending behaviour.

In the case of victimisation, much attention is paid to the ways in which crimes against women have historically not been considered as such (e.g., domestic violence) or are subject to trivialisation and sexual bias (e.g., rape trials involving sex workers). It has been argued in some cases that a woman who has been victimised is herself judged in relation to a man, rather than a specific offensive action. For example, an injury to a married women may be seen as a 'serious crime' insofar as it affects her status as her spouse's 'sexual property' or 'domestic homemaker'. An unmarried woman who has a sexual history of multiple partners may be treated by the courts as having actually provoked a criminal assault. Questions of what is an 'offence' and who is a 'victim' are thus often intertwined with gender stereotypes and biases which reflect a general inequality between the sexes in society.

In summary, the feminist perspectives within criminology challenge the male biases and neglects of mainstream criminology. Criticism is levelled at historical and contemporary examples of the double standards applied to women and men in the criminal justice system. As well, active intervention has been called for in areas such as inappropriate responses to female offenders (e.g., imprisonment), law reform which prevents discrimination against women (e.g., equal employment opportunity), the legal recognition of certain crimes against women (e.g., sexual harassment), and active enforcement of laws to protect women from male violence (e.g., domestic violence, incest, rape).

The feminist perspectives have been criticised on two main grounds. The first is that they do not deal adequately with questions relating to class, ethnicity and 'race' in discussions of the female offender and the female victim. Yet as various recent studies show (e.g., Carrington 1993), the 'race' of the person is a crucial factor in terms of overall representation of some groups within the criminal justice system. Likewise, the class background of the offender or victim has significant consequences with regard to the actual nature of the criminalisation and the victimisation process. A second area which is generating more attention is the notion that, instead of providing a women-centred analysis, feminist criminology needs to foster a non-sexist criminology which focuses more broadly on gender relations in their entirety. Specifically, it has been suggested that issues of female and male criminality need to be examined in terms of the social constructions of both 'femininity' and 'masculinity', and with regard to the relationship between each of these social constructions. We explore these issues in greater detail in Chapter 8.

More generally, the issue of power, and how it is manifested institutionally, remains an area where more research and discussion are required. This is particularly so with respect to feminist conceptualisations of the state. Meanwhile, an immediate problem confronting feminist writers and activists is that of the conservative backlash against many of the concepts and issues raised by feminists generally. The profile of female victims and the dilemmas and inequities surrounding the processing of female offenders have been actively raised by feminist criminologists. But in the light of contemporary calls for greater law and order, there is a fear that such work will be subverted and/or swamped by the simplistic moralising, and simplistic answers, of the New Right.

NEW RIGHT CRIMINOLOGY

The term New Right refers to a particular political orientation, rather than to a systematic, coherent theory in its own right. The discussion of radical feminist concerns with victimisation (of women) provides an ironic backdrop to the conservative or New Right criminology which emerged in the 1970s and 1980s. This particular strand of thought wanted to direct attention to victims, and to the need for of the state to 'get tough' on offenders.

The rise of a more conservative perspective in criminology, one which was directly opposed to the liberalism of strain theory and labelling theory in particular, occurred at a time when the long boom of economic properity in the advanced capitalist countries was coming to an end. The mid-1970s saw a world economic recession, which was followed over the next two decades by periodic and, in some instances, devastating economic slumps. In this context there was bound to be an increase in property and personal crime, and the alienation and marginalisation of a significant layer of the population, many of them young people, was associated with a range of anti-social and deviant behaviours.

Politically, by the 1980s there had been a swing to the Right at the level of policy formulation and development, regardless of the political party in power. The economic ideas of Margaret Thatcher in Britain and Ronald Reagan in the United States, the advent of 'Rogernomics' (named after the Treasurer) in New

Zealand, and the approach adopted by Hawke and Keating in Australia all signalled an **economic rationalist** platform for dealing with contemporary issues. This emphasised the notion of economic efficiency above all else in policy development. In each country it led to tax cuts for the rich, and the curtailment of universal provision in the allocation of the services and benefits of the welfare state. The catch-cry was 'wealth creation', which it was assumed would be to the benefit of all; yet the effect was to exacerbate the growing distance between the rich and the poor in society.

In this context of increasing economic hardship and an ideological swing to the Right, supported largely by an economic rationalist mentality, there was a rise in law-and-order politics, both domestically and internationally. For example, internationally, the former concern with the preservation of human rights propounded by world leaders was quickly transformed into an emphasis on terrorism and the drug trade, and the necessity to combat these 'by any means necessary'. Domestically, the law-and-order push assumed the tone of a 'war on crime' and an attack on the disorder of society. This translated into a cry during the 1980s for increased police personnel, powers and resources, for longer gaol sentences, the provision of more prisons, stronger discipline within families and schools, and a return to more traditional values generally. For young people there was the demand for 'greater responsibility', which translated into more punitive attitudes in the area of juvenile justice.

The main elements of New Right criminology include a combination of conservative moralising and free-market competitive ethos. These sometimes contradict each other at the level of specific policies. However, the overriding message is that there is a need to 'get tough on criminals', to hold them responsible for their actions, and to punish wrongdoers in a consistent manner and such that they get their 'just deserts'. New Right criminology challenges directly the orthodox criminologies as described in the previous chapter. That is, it is opposed to perspectives that emphasise treatment and reform rather than punishment. And it opposes the views of orthodox positivist criminology which have a deterministic model of the causes of crime; rather, it asserts that people do make choices, and that they therefore must pay for these choices. In a nutshell, the argument is that if you 'do the crime', then you must 'do the time'.

There are several different strands to the broad New Right criminological perspective (see Tame 1991; Young 1981). These include: philosophical views regarding the nature of human activity; specific areas of interest such as retributivist concerns with sentencing; and economic analyses of the causes of crime and the social responses to it. For present purposes, however, we will illustrate the broad orientation of these perspectives by examining two general views on the nature of crime and crime control. Each is concerned with the punishment and disciplining of offenders, but their overall analysis of crime in society nevertheless differs.

Right-wing Libertarian

This perspective harks back to the days of classical liberalism, characterised by competitive free-market capitalism and minimalist state intervention, including welfare provision. In this approach, human beings are conceived of as rational entities with free will. It is based upon a moral philosophy of egoism (selfishness), in which the only constraint on behaviour is the duty not to initiate force over others. In many ways, this perspective reflects many of the elements of classical criminological theory, with its stress on the individual and the social contract.

The notion of a competitive ethos pervades this perspective. This is usually tied to the idea of rights to private property as being the first virtue of the legal and criminal justice system. Accordingly, crime is defined in terms of the infringement of private property, including infringements of one's physical self. Since human nature is conceived of as being possessive and individualistic, and since crime is conceived of mainly in terms of private property, then the role of the state should be restricted to those instances where other people actually come to harm by one's social actions (see Tame 1991). So called 'victimless crimes' therefore should be decriminalised insofar as they do not directly affect those beyond oneself. In other words, 'anything goes'—people should have complete liberty to do as they will, as long as they do not infringe upon the property of others in an illegal way.

In reinforcing notions of individual selfishness, rights and individuality, this perspective simultaneously asserts that criminological theorising of the recent past has made excuses for individuals, by taking away people's responsibilities for their actions. Its proponents argue, for example, that to speak of biological drives or social determinants such as poverty is to take away any notion of choice in the selection of behaviour and activity. In fact, from the point of view of **rational choice theory** we need to assume that most 'criminals' are rational agents who can be deterred from committing additional crimes by an increase in the punishment they might expect to receive (Buchanan & Hartley 1992). According to the advocates of this approach, the most economically efficient way to manage the crime problem is to privatise institutions such as prisons, and to increase the probability of detection and conviction of offenders. The broad philosophical orientation of rational choice theory is also closely related to the adoption of prevention techniques directed primarily at reducing opportunities for crime (see Felson 1994), rather than at the structural reasons for offending behaviour or the criminalisation process itself.

In response to perspectives which see behaviour mainly in terms of psychological or social influences, this approach calls for a 'moralising' of society. Morality is seen to be rooted in the individualistic ethos of personal responsibility and self-control. Where this is breached, as in the case of the commission of an offence, the offender should be punished. The perspective generally promotes retribution, deterrence, incapacitation and punishment as its responses to crime. Furthermore, it favours the enforcement of restitutive measures with respect to the victims of crime. That is, compensation should be paid by the offender to the victim for any harm caused in the commission of the offence.

Traditional Conservative

This perspective takes a broader view than the Right-wing libertarian of what constitutes a crime. The conservative view of crime includes not only that activity which endangers property or the person, but morality as well. Hence, attacks on certain traditional values and people's respect for authority generally may be viewed as criminal.

From this point of view, crime is not only a matter of free choice: it is linked to certain intrinsic aspects of humanity. In particular, people are seen as possessing certain 'natural urges' which go against the more civilised or divine purposes of society. In order to constrain these urges, it is necessary to establish a strong order based upon personal sacrifice, self-discipline, and submission to authority (Tame 1991). Order must take precedence over all else, including justice. Crime is said to be caused by the unwillingness of people to accept discipline, the undermining of traditional loyalties—such as to the (patriarchial) family—and the pursuit of immediate individual gratification without appropriate hard work.

According to this approach, punishment is an essential part of deterrence. This is so not only because it establishes personal responsibility for one's actions, but also because it has an important symbolic impact on society as a whole. That is, punishment has to be seen in terms of its effect on the establishment of moral solidarity through stigmatisation. Strong emphasis is placed upon the importance of morality in the maintenance of social authority. Thus, someone who does something deemed to be wrong or harmful must be punished swiftly and appropriately in order to set the moral standard.

There are conflicts between libertarians and traditionalist conservatives. The latter, for instance, generally possess anti-libertarian views with respect to pornography, sexual behaviour, drug use and abortion; that is, they favour intervention in areas regarded as victimless crimes. Indeed, the conservative point of view often favours increased state intervention in everyday social life because it is felt that only strong coercive measures will ultimately keep people in line and teach them the discipline they require to live as members of a civilised community.

Authoritarian Populism

Whether it be linked to a libertarian project centring on unbridled human freedoms, or a conservative project oriented to upholding traditional values, New Right criminology tends to revolve around the individual in society, and to provide a moralistic and punitive approach to issues of crime and criminality. While recent academic work has provided sophisticated defences of these ideas (Tame 1991; Buchanan & Hartley 1992), in the public domain the 'get tough' approach has generally been associated with populist appeals to the public at large. This has proved to be electorally expedient and attractive, even if the consequences of the adoption of such measures leave something to be desired.

Populism is not a political ideology as such, but is a loosely defined mood. It is an appeal to people on the basis of 'us versus them'. The 'us' is always viewed as virtuous. The 'them', whoever they are, are viewed as parasites destroying the social body. In terms of crime, the essence of populism exaggerates the dangerousness of crime, and the foreign or alien nature of the criminal. The criminal is seen to be outside the society—its networks, institutions, communities, mores, values, methods of income, ways of life. Insofar as criminals are seen not to be bound by normal social rules of conduct, it is argued that normal rules of order should not necessarily be adhered to if criminals are to be brought to book for their offensive activities.

The rhetoric of populism reduces all crime problems to very simple solutions. Offenders are made entirely responsible for their actions, particularly since they exist outside the mainstream institutions of society. They are not seen as members of the community, and indeed are sometimes presented as not being members of the human race (described as 'animals' or 'savages'). Insofar as this social distancing occurs at the level of rhetoric and policy development, it is a short step to encourage ever more draconian solutions to the crime problem. If the problem is constructed as being one of 'us' against 'them', as a 'war' which implies violence and destruction, then redemption of the situation is seen to lie in enhanced state power.

Authoritarian populism refers to a process in which crime is ideologically conveyed in a series of moral panics about law-and-order issues (Taylor 1981; Hall 1980; Hall et al. 1978). The extent and seriousness of crime is highlighted (but not necessarily backed up by statistical and other research findings), and this in turn is used to justify harsher penalties, and the assertion of state authority in more and more spheres of everyday life. As part of this process, specific groups or categories of people are singled out for special attention: young people, Aborigines, welfare recipients, striking workers, sole parents. In this way, 'we' are protected by ever-greater state intervention into the affairs of 'them', the most likely candidates for membership of the criminal class. Again, the rationale behind such intrusion is usually a combination of protection of private property, and the differential treatment that should be meted out to the moral and immoral in society.

The broad appeal of authoritarian populism is due in part to the pervasive influence of the print and electronic media in conveying particular types of images regarding crime in society (see Grabosky & Wilson 1989). The flooding of the media with stories of street crime has the real and pertinent effects of heightening the fear of crime, feeding the stereotypes regarding the 'typical offender', over-emphasising the extent of extremely violent and serious crimes, and fostering acceptance for policies which promise to 'get something done' about the crime problem. The politically important role of New Right criminology is thus related to the basic electoral appeal of 'authoritarian populist' rhetoric. One consequence of the popularity of such perspectives was the emergence of a response from the Left, a response which promised likewise to 'take crime seriously'.

LEFT REALISM

The origins of this perspective lay in Thatcher's Britain, where the idea of a 'short, sharp shock' as a way to deal with young offenders, and greater use of prisons for adult offenders went hand in hand with authoritarian populist rhetoric. Law and order became a major election issue, and the Conservative Party was able to keep the media spotlight on the 'crime waves' besetting the nation. A persistent campaign based upon skewed statistics, superficial analysis and simplistic solutions was used to fuel existing fears of crime and to garner support for the political party which promised to do something dramatic and concrete about the problem. The electoral success of the conservatives and the adoption of hardline criminal justice policies indicated that a response to New Right theories was needed within criminology, particularly if public debate was to be guided by other than 'get tough' rhetoric.

The whole focus of the debate within criminology shifted from 'what causes crime?' to 'what can we do to control crime?' Previous theories had tried to provide holistic and processual accounts of the causes of crime and to link these to particular juvenile justice strategies (e.g., strain theory and retraining, labelling theory and diversion), or had provided critiques of basic definitions of 'victims' and 'offenders' from the point of view of differential social power in society (e.g., Marxist theory and feminist theory); now the focus narrowed to the specific issue of crime control. This orientation in criminological circles was especially apparent among the New Right. But it also became the central guiding principle of various liberal analyses, including the republican theory (discussed in the previous chapter) and Left Realism.

At an analytical level, Left Realist writers wished to distinguish their type of research and analysis from Marxist criminology by describing the latter as simply a type of 'Left Idealism' that had little practical application to the real world of crime (Young 1986). Specifically, it was argued that Marxist criminology had tended to ignore actual working-class crime because of its concern with crimes of the powerful; that it had tended to romanticise working-class criminals (the so-called Robin Hood syndrome); and that it had failed to acknowledge that working-class people want protection, now, from crime and that something had to be done, now, to stop their victimisation. Politically, the Left Realist concern was to provide an avenue for parties such as the British Labour Party to intervene in the law-and-order debate with something meaningful in electoral terms. In short, the Left Realists argued for a pragmatic position on crime issues, one that 'takes crime seriously' in such a way that concrete reforms can be proposed (Lea & Young 1984).

Both the republican and Left Realist perspectives were sparked, in part, by liberal concerns to provide some kind of constructive response to the conservative, punitive direction of New Right criminology. Interestingly, both republican and Left Realist views are also similar in that they acknowledge the multifaceted nature of crime causation, and are reticent in reducing crime causation to any one 'structure' or 'social factor'. Indeed, the issue of what causes crime tends to be glossed over, and discussion concentrates on issues relating to crime control.

The Left Realist position is based upon a series of interrelated propositions which indicate that its main focus is on crime in working-class neighbourhoods and on developing strategies to deal with this (see Hogg 1988: 28–9, White & Haines forthcoming).

- Crime is a major problem and needs to be taken seriously by the Left.
- Street crime is a growing problem and requires some sort of active response by the state and community.
- Most personal crime such as robbery and assault is intraclass. That is, it involves sections of the working class preying upon other sections of the working-class.
- The most vulnerable sections of the working class—the poor, the aged and the unemployed—are disproportionately affected by crime.
- The police are inefficient in dealing with crime in working-class neighbourhoods and in protecting the interests of working-class victims of crime.
- The police are hostile and discriminatory in their activities, especially in regard to young people and particular ethnic minorities.
- Mutual antagonism between the police and particular communities at a local level sets in train a cycle of non-cooperation, in which there is a reduced flow of information about crime from the community to the police, and the police respond with heavy-handed tactics in dealing with community members.
- Inner-city working-class communities are concerned about local crime; they want effective policies to control it, and they see the police as playing a central role in crime control.

- Effective policing involves the police and community working together in dealing with crime at the local level.
- Greater community control over policing policies, and a shift away from intrusive and heavy-handed policing, will allow for more effective intervention, particularly with respect to those crimes deemed to be most serious by the community.

The object or target of Left Realist analysis is **street crime**, which includes violence against the person, and property crimes such as 'break and enter' forms of theft (what republican theory would refer to as 'predatory crime'). The focus on street crime directs attention particularly to young people, given their involvement in these types of crimes (like break and enter, car theft, minor assaults, etc.) and given the ways in which young people use public space in our society (see Chapter 6). In examining this type of crime, the Left Realist approach concentrates on two areas: the extent and nature of victimisation, and the role of crime-control agencies such as the police in dealing with this victimisation.

The main tool of research favoured by the Left Realist is the victim survey. From the results of their own 'unofficial' victim surveys in working-class neighbourhoods, the Left Realists argued that official crime statistics considerably underestimate the problem of crime. In part this is because many crimes are not reported, which in turn is related to public alienation from and mistrust of the police. The various surveys undertaken not only highlighted the deficiencies in existing police practices, but, also uncovered the extent and distribution of certain kinds of crimes, such as domestic violence, which hitherto had not been taken seriously by the state agencies.

The 'practical' solution to the problem of street crime proposed by Left Realists is to make policing more effective. This, they argue, requires efforts to democratise policing, to forge a new and active co-operation between members of the community and the police. To put it differently, the approach called for demands a transformation of the police force into a police service. Hence there is a tendency in Left Realist writing to emphasise the importance of policing and police styles as a crucial variable in the prevention of crime.

The Left Realist position has been criticised for a number of general and specific reasons (Hogg 1988). For example, its conception of the state ignores the structural basis of social power in society, and the role of agencies such as the police in sustaining and legitimating social inequality and division. Likewise, its conception of crime as 'street crime' has been characterised as too narrow, and as simply adding legitimacy to the idea that it is such 'conventional crimes' which cost the community the most. Victim surveys, for example, fail to deal with issues of corporate crime, nor do they generally tap into other types of crimes such as environmental degradation, industrial homicide, state crime, and so on.

The primary focus on street crime serves to fuel media-driven notions as to what actually constitutes serious crime, and what the appropriate strategies should be to combat it. Ironically, the victim survey may well spread the fear of crime amongst members of the community (as in the case of 'discovering' higher rates of domestic violence), and reinforce the logic of crime control (e.g., greater use of state officials to fight the crime menace). It is a strategy which tends to privilege increased state intervention, albeit under greater community control, rather than a transformation of basic economic and social relationships across the society as a whole.

While professing to be socialistic in orientation, there is little in the Left Realist perspective which speaks to the causes of crime beyond that of poor policing. A concentration on the police has tended to preclude discussion and debate on alternative measures to reduce crime, such as wealth redistribution, employment creation, participatory activities and so on, at the local community level. This is significant: if policing were to be 'more effective' and offenders apprehended, then we can ask what the effects of the criminalisation process would be on those people who come from communities where there are obvious structural factors (e.g., poverty, unemployment, racism) propelling them into various criminal and anti-social activities.

Even where the structural effects of racism, class division and sex discrimination are recognised, there is very little analysis of the generative structural causes for these social phenomena. This is partly because of the way in which the 'working class' (or sections thereof) are presented as 'victims' in general (of capitalist economic restructuring), whereas victims of crime are presented in a much more immediate and less abstract manner. One consequence of this is to highlight the extent of victimisation, rather than the social relationships which underpin the criminalisation process. Another is to obliquely reinforce the notion that, while victimisation in general is unevenly distributed in relation to class background, it appears to affect individuals in a random fashion beyond their immediate control. Conversely, by emphasising responsive policing as a means to deal with street crime there is an implication that the offender is consciously choosing crime, that criminality is indeed voluntary (as argued by the New Right). This raises major issues regarding the limits to choice, and the parameters of meaningful decision-making as these are determined by wider structural factors and social forces.

CONCLUSION

The challenge for criminology in the 1990s is twofold: first, to provide a critical analysis of the relationship between social structure, criminality and the criminalisation process; second, to develop strategies and policies which address issues relating to inequalities and abuses within the existing criminal justice system and in society generally.

The theoretical perspectives outlined in the last three chapters have provided competing, and at times complementary, explanations regarding the causes of crime and the appropriate responses to it. While some theories concentrate on determining individual differences in the commission of offences, some focus on the role of state agencies such as the police in creating further crime, while others explore the way in which changing social circumstances and the nature of society itself impinge upon particular groups and classes in society. The specific level of analysis and the particular political orientation of the writer in essence dictate the definitions, explanations and control strategies that ought to be adopted. In a similar vein, the notion of 'scientific truth' in terms of theoretical understanding and 'effectiveness' with regard to actual criminal justice practices will vary according to the paradigm within which one is working.

In our view, a critical criminology is one which is based on a particular political project—social equality and political emancipation (in its many dimensions). The goal is one of human liberation, and analysis is prompted by acknowledgement of the substantive inequalities and oppressive structures which shape everyday life in Australian society. Issues of class division, racism, sexism and homophobia are central to this analysis, as are issues relating to the marginalisation of specific groups and classes in society and their criminalisation by the mainstream criminal justice system.

The development of a critical criminology is premised upon the idea that, while variation in perspective may exist and hence no researcher or scholar is impartial in the criminological enterprise, nevertheless 'taking a position' does not necessarily imply unscientific or subjective analysis. It demands objective analysis of values, structures and processes, while still maintaining a vision of a society in which human dignity is cherished and preserved.

A critical criminology for the 1990s is one which can build upon the knowledge and innovative conceptual contributions of radical challenges to orthodoxy, and so provide a clear, unambiguous picture of the existing field while retaining a critical edge. Its task is to delineate the really important issues of the day and to define and redefine matters which are or should be of legal and criminological concern. One purpose of our review of criminological perspectives is to familiarise the reader with where, broadly speaking, the discipline has been theoretically and politically. This provides a basis on which to compare basic concepts and strategic intervention options, and to understand the strengths and weaknesses of the perspectives we have covered. If we are to comprehend the situation of young people today, and to interpret their location within the field of criminal justice, then such analysis must be theoretically informed as well as empirically validated.

part two

the dynamics of
juvenile justice

5 the nature of contemporary juvenile crime

Our discussion in earlier chapters on the history and theories of juvenile offending and juvenile justice should have alerted us to the definitional problems which arise when we come to discuss the nature of juvenile crime. It is important to recognise at the outset that a complete picture of juvenile crime cannot be obtained. Our sources of information limit the picture of juvenile offending for a variety of reasons. Each source of information at the most provides only a selective glimpse—and, like any partial view, may actually disguise as much as illuminate. Sources of information about juvenile offending include official statistics and self-report studies. We should also not underestimate the role of popular culture through film, video, music and literature, as well as the ubiquitous role of the media as definers of law-and-order news, in structuring our knowledge and understanding of both juvenile offending and the range of possible responses.

EXTENT

Official sources of information deal with the end process of intervention by police, courts and juvenile justice authorities. These sources may be useful in terms of understanding some juvenile offending patterns, and also for telling us about the priorities, practices and nature of intervention by state agencies: for instance how many young people receive a police caution instead of being arrested and charged, or how many matters are processed by way of a panel or conference rather than through the Children's Courts.

However, we need to be aware of the limitations of the official statistics which are, in the end, a product or outcome of a social and political process. Cicourel (1976), in an important study of juvenile justice in the 1960s, analysed the social processes which create knowledge about an 'offender'. In particular, he was concerned with the way police and probation officers construct documents and textual accounts which develop 'evidence' about an individual. In this sense the routine bureaucratic processes incorporate and transform the young person into a 'juvenile delinquent'. We will return to this point later in the book, but for now it is necessary to note that official statistics concerning young offenders derive from these processes. Equally important is the fact that our knowledge of the occurrence of 'crime' is also dependent on a range of factors. In summary, for an event to become classified as a crime, a number of things must occur. Some act or situation must be perceived by someone and then defined as being illegal. The person then must decide to report the incident to police. The police must then decide that what is being reported to them constitutes an offence, and record it as such.

We know that a great deal of crime is not reported to the police in the first instance. Crime victim surveys in Australia and overseas repeatedly show that between 60 per cent and 70 per cent of offences of violence and theft are never reported to authorities (Mukherjee and Dagger 1990: 53). Other British studies have shown that between one in four and one in five crimes which are reported by the public to the police are subsequently not accepted by police as being crimes and are therefore not recorded (Bottomley & Coleman 1981; Sparkes, Genn & Dodd 1977). What emerges in the crime statistics as the official level of crime is clearly a partial picture.

There are also factors specific to juvenile crime which further limit the utility of official figures. These are:

• the level of unreported juvenile crime, particularly where young people are also the victims
• changes in enforcement practices with a specific focus on young people
• distortions caused by the nature of juvenile offending itself.

Young people may be reluctant to report crime to police for a variety of reasons. It has been noted that young women who are the victims of violence, either at home or in public, report few of these incidents to the police (Alder 1994: 170–1). Homeless young people are also vulnerable to violence, and their already strained relationship with authorities makes reporting of incidents unlikely. Specific groups of young people from non-English-speaking backgrounds and indigenous young people, who are either suspicious of police or have a history of poor relations with police, are unlikely to report offences when they have been victims. Interviews with people working in youth services have noted that a sense of resignation and powerlessness often prevents young people from reporting offences (Underwood, White & Omelczuk 1993: 14).

Changes in juvenile justice enforcement practices and law can have dramatic effects on official figures, particularly in amplifying the incidence or participation of specific groups of offences or offenders. For instance, a police crackdown on graffiti groups can immediately boost arrests and court appearances for offences related to property damage. Yet this does not mean there has necessarily been any increase in the level of offending. Similarly, changes in legislation can 'cause' an apparent increase in court appearances. A recent example of legislative change leading to more arrests and court appearances of young people was the introduction of the New South Wales *Summary Offences Act 1988*, which redefined the elements of offensive behaviour and increased the penalties for the offence. The number of Children's Court appearances for offensive behaviour rose from 336 matters in 1985–86 (prior to the legislative change) to 1192 matters in 1989–90 (Cunneen 1993: 186). The 255 per cent increase in the number of matters heard by the court was primarily the result of changes in legislation and police arrests.

There are also a number of specific features of juvenile offending which increase young people's representation in crime statistics. Young people are more likely to get caught by police than adult offenders, for the following reasons.

• Young people are less likely to be experienced and accomplished criminals.
• Young people tend to commit offences in groups, which leads to greater visibility and risk of detection.
• The social dynamics of the offence may lead to easier detection if it is public, gregarious and attention-seeking.
• Juvenile crime is often episodic, unplanned, opportunistic, and related to the use of public space in areas like public transport and shopping centres where there is more visibility and surveillance.
• Young people tend to commit offences close to where they live. As a result, they are more likely to be identified by the victim and reported.

These issues have been discussed more fully in a number of reports (Mukherjee 1983; Mukherjee 1985; Freiberg, Fox & Hogan 1988). There are also a number of other factors which lead to distortions in the figures on juvenile offending. These include the following.

• Because young people commit offences in groups, several young people are often arrested for a single offence, which distorts the statistics on the relationship between offenders and offences.
• The offences for which juveniles are most over-represented compared to adults are also offences which have high reporting rates because of insurance requirements (motor vehicle theft, burglary).
• Motor vehicle theft and burglary are also offences where police clear-up rates are very low. The apparent high level of young people's participation in these offences may in part reflect their inexperience and greater likelihood of being apprehended.

An example will clarify some of the points noted above. Young people are likely to steal cars for different reasons to professional thieves. They are more likely to get caught joy-riding because of the nature of their public behaviour and their youth. If they have committed the theft in a group, the theft of a single car produces multiple offenders in police and court statistics. The vast majority of car thefts are not solved. In fact, about 86 per cent of reported motor vehicle thefts are not cleared by police (Mukherjee & Dagger 1990: 47). Thus, while we know juvenile offenders comprise some 47 per cent of those who are caught by police for motor vehicle theft in Australia (see Table 5.1), this figure is itself based on a low percentage (14 per cent) of cleared crimes. In addition, the 47 per cent proportion of juvenile offenders is not equivalent to saying that juveniles accounted for 47 per cent of car theft where offenders are known, because of the likelihood that there were several young people involved in each incident. A similar scenario is applicable to burglary (break and enter), where inexperience and the propensity to commit offences in groups lead to a greater chance of apprehension and a distorted presence in the offender statistics. For example Mukherjee (1985: 36) found that nearly 80 per cent of adults arrested for breaking and entering were apprehended acting alone. Conversely, the majority of young people arrested for breaking and entering were apprehended in groups of two or more.

The Proportion of Offences Committed by Young People

The official police figures can be used to give some indication of the participation of young people in reported crime. One set of data which is available relates to offences cleared by police. Table 5.1 shows the percentage of juveniles as offenders in offences cleared by police throughout Australia. Generally, the offences for which the highest proportion of young people are apprehended are related to property theft or damage. There are difficulties in drawing too many conclusions from police clear-up figures because of the assumptions underlying them and their mode of collection (Tait 1994), but they do tell us something about who gets arrested for particular offences. Some 50 per cent of break-and-enter offences cleared by police involved young people, and a similar proportion of young people accounted for those arrested for motor vehicle theft. Well over one-third of those arrested for shoplifting, theft and arson were also young people.

The Youth Justice Coalition (1990: 21) has concluded that juvenile offenders tend to be under-represented in the more serious offence categories. Such an argument is consistent with earlier findings by Mukherjee (1983) that juveniles were not over-represented proportionate to their population for violent offences. A similar finding was made by Freiberg, Fox and Hogan (1988: 40–1) when comparing arrest rates between juveniles and adults. Arrest rates for

Table 5.1 Percentage of juveniles as offenders in offences cleared by police, Australia, 1989

Offence	Juveniles (%)
Offences against person	12
Sexual assault	14
Robbery and extortion	22
Fraud	11
Breaking/entering/burglary	50
Motor vehicle theft	47
Shop theft	38
Other theft	38
Arson	38
Property damage	28
Public order	15
Drug offences	8
Total offences	26

Source: Adapted from Potas, Vining and Wilson (1990: 21).

juveniles showed that they were under-represented for homicide and serious assault. Juvenile arrest rates were the same as adults for robbery, and higher than adults for burglary and motor vehicle theft. The higher juvenile arrest rates for burglary and motor vehicle theft are open to influence by the factors we have discussed above: the commission of the offence in company, lack of criminal experience and greater likelihood of detection (Freiberg, Fox & Hogan 1988: 41).

Not only are young people not over-represented in the most serious offence categories: the offences they do commit are less serious than adult crimes for the following reasons.

- There is a greater likelihood that the attempted property crime or robbery will be unsuccessful.
- There is less frequent use of weapons when committing an offence.
- When injuries to victims occur, they are less serious than those caused by an adult offender.
- The financial loss suffered in theft offences is less than that caused by adult offenders.

While the overall picture shows that about one in four offenders in offences cleared by police is a juvenile, young people are overwhelmingly concentrated in less serious property offences.

Apprehensions by Police

Another way of considering the information available on young people who come into conflict with juvenile justice agencies is to look at the apprehension of young people by police. A young person who is apprehended is not necessarily arrested and charged, and does not necessarily appear before the Children's Court. As will be discussed later in the book, in most States a range of options is available to police which might divert the young person from the court system. In short, the information on apprehensions shows the nature of the offences for which young people are likely to come into contact with police.

Table 5.2 is based on South Australian police data and shows the top ten offences for which young people are apprehended by police. It shows that offences relating to theft are the major reasons for contact with police. Shoplifting, in particular, far outnumbers any other reason for apprehension. In relation to drug offences, the overwhelming majority of apprehensions (87 per cent) were for the possession or use of cannabis or for possession of drug implements.

Table 5.2 Top ten offences for juveniles apprehended by police, South Australia, 1991–92

Offence	Juveniles (n)
Stop theft	3358
Drug offences	2007
Breaking/entering/burglary	1890
Property damage	1512
Other theft	1492
Motor vehicle theft	1057
Under-age drinking offences	746
Minor assaults	670
Disorderly behaviour	494
Weapon offences	473

Source: South Australian Government (1993).

Court Appearances by Young People

Another source of information on young people's contact with juvenile justice agencies is available through the Children's Courts. As we noted above, not all young people who come into contact with police end up before the Children's Court. However the court data does provide important information on who is selected for prosecution. Young people appear in the Children's Courts for a variety of offences, from the very serious such as homicide to minor forms of youthful misbehaviour. Table 5.3 relates to 12,537 criminal matters determined in the New South Wales Children's Court in 1992–93, and shows the different offences for which young people come before the courts. The major offence categories relate to property theft. The break-and-enter category of offences comprised the largest single proportion of all offences (17 per cent), followed by other stealing and theft offences (11.2 per cent) and motor vehicle theft (9.9 per cent). Offences against good order comprised 9.1 per cent of offences. Assault (7.8 per cent), shoplifting (7.8 per cent) and property damage (7.6 per cent) were the next major categories of offences.

Table 5.3 Criminal matters in the Children's Court, New South Wales, 1992–93

Offence	Male		Female		Total	
	n	%	n	%	n	%
Homicide	20	0.2	2	0.1	22	0.2
Serious assault	608	5.7	127	6.9	735	5.9
Assault	786	7.3	197	10.7	983	7.8
Sexual offences	99	0.9	3	0.2	102	0.8
Other offences against the person	44	0.4	6	0.3	50	0.4
Robbery and extortion	268	2.5	25	1.4	293	2.3
Fraud	240	2.2	138	7.5	378	3.0
Break and enter	1 982	18.5	150	8.2	2 132	17.0
Motor vehicle theft	1 049	9.8	115	6.3	1 164	9.9
Shoplifting	664	6.2	321	17.5	985	7.8
Other stealing/theft	1 254	11.7	146	8.0	1 400	11.2
Possession stolen goods	522	5.2	98	5.3	620	4.9
Property damage	867	8.1	92	5.0	959	7.6
Justice offences	445	4.2	91	5.0	536	4.3
Against good order	946	8.8	193	10.5	1 139	9.1
Serious driving	235	2.2	24	1.3	259	2.1
Drug offences	652	6.1	101	5.5	753	6.0
Other	24	0.2	3	0.2	27	0.2
Total	10 705	100	1 832	100	12 537	100

Source: Adapted from New South Wales Department of Juvenile Justice (1993: 7–25).

Overall, the majority of matters determined in the Children's Court relate to some form of property theft or stealing. If we combine the offence categories relating to these types of matters (robbery, fraud, break and enter, motor vehicle theft, shoplifting, other stealing and possession of stolen goods) they account for well over half of the appearances (56.1 per cent) of young people.

Offences against the person (homicide, serious assault, assault and other offences against the person) account for 15.1 per cent of offences. Some of the offences within the robbery category (assault and rob, armed robbery) could be classified as either property crime or offences against the person. However, the percentage is small and does not alter the overall picture.

Broadly speaking, the data from the New South Wales Children's Court is comparable with other jurisdictions in Australia. Wundersitz (1993: 30) has analysed various jurisdictions and concluded that 'property theft dominates the charge profile of young offenders processed by the system'. She reported the following findings.

- In South Australia, Victoria and New South Wales, over 50 per cent of charges dealt with were property offences.
- In Tasmania and Western Australia, around 45 per cent were property offences.
- It was generally the less serious categories of 'other theft' and 'shoplifting' which predominated, although Table 5.3 shows a variation to this in New South Wales.

• Offences against the person were relatively infrequent in most States, constituting 2 per cent in Victoria, 3.3 per cent in Western Australia, 4.5 per cent in Tasmania, and 7.9 per cent in South Australia. At the time of the Wundersitz comparisons, the highest recorded figure was in New South Wales. The more recent data in Table 5.3 confirms this, with 15 per cent of matters classified as crimes against the person.

American juvenile arrest data suggests almost identical patterns, particularly if compared to the New South Wales data. In United States during 1990, crimes against the person accounted for 14 per cent of arrests, compared to 57 per cent of arrests for larceny-theft (Lundman 1994: 7).

Returning to the New South Wales data in Table 5.3, some further comments can be made on a number of offence categories which give a greater indication of the actual nature of the offending behaviour. In the homicide category, 16 of the 22 offences related to driving in a manner which caused death. In the offences against good order category, half the offences related to offensive behaviour or offensive language. Finally, in the drug offences category, more than 50 per cent of the 753 cases related to possession of cannabis and a further 19 per cent of cases related to the possession of drug utensils.

Changes in the Rate of Juvenile Offending

There has been a great deal of public discussion about whether cime rates are rising and whether young people are committing a greater number of offences now than in the past.

One way of finding out whether there has been an increase in juvenile offending is to look at trend data in terms of the number of interventions by the juvenile justice system ('interventions' refers to all court appearances and other formal diversionary processes, such as cautioning and/or appearances before panels). Over the last fifteen or so years there has been a relatively stable proportion of young people facing some form of intervention by juvenile justice authorities in Australia. Wundersitz has analysed the rate per thousand of youth population for matters processed by juvenile justice systems in each State for the period 1979–80 to 1990–91. She found that, with the exception of Western Australia, the rates remained stable across jurisdictions with only small variations (Wundersitz 1993: 22–3). In other words, at the beginning of the 1990s the rate of intervention in Australia was much the same as it had been more than a decade previously. Even in Western Australia, where the data showed a major increase in the rate of intervention during the 1980s, this trend was reversed at the end of the decade. By 1991 Western Australia was processing juvenile offenders at about the same rate as it had been in 1981.

Despite perceptions of rising juvenile crime rates, the figures for the decade of the 1980s show remarkable stability. However, consideration of arrest rates of juveniles during an earlier period, from the 1960s up to the end of the 1970s, shows a slightly different pattern. The data for this period is available only for a limited number of offences, including homicide, serious assault, robbery, burglary, fraud, and motor vehicle theft. The arrest rates increased for all these categories for both boys and girls (Mukherjee 1985: 30–1). Although the arrest rate for girls remained much smaller than that for boys, there were some important changes during this period, with the arrest rate increasing more rapidly for girls compared to boys, and girls compared to women. For instance, in 1964 the ratio of arrest rates for serious assaults for women and girls was 3:1 (three women arrested for assault for every one girl per 100,000 of population) and boys and girls 25:1 (twenty-five boys arrested for every one girl per 100,000 of population). By 1981 this pattern was reversed between women and girls, with girls having a higher arrest rate than women, while the ratio for boys to girls had dropped to 6:1 (Mukherjee 1985: 28).

The figures for the period 1964–81 which Mukherjee (1985) has compiled are not completely compatible with the Wundersitz (1993) collection for 1979–91, because one is based on arrest data for a limited number offences while the other looks at total interventions for all offences. However, they imply that the apparent increase in juvenile arrests experienced during the period of the 1960s and 1970s has levelled off during the last decade or so. Such a finding is compatible with overseas data. American data shows an increase in juvenile arrest rates from 1960 to 1980, with an uneven decline since then (Lundman 1994: 8).

Another factor which needs to be taken into account is the extent to which increased levels of policing produce increases in arrest figures. It has been noted that an increase in the number of police per head of population as well as greater expenditure on policing, as has occurred in Australia, 'may increase crime figures without there having been any change in the underlying rate of crime' (Freiberg, Fox & Hogan 1988: 35). Similarly, total intervention rates are susceptible to fluctuations because of changes in juvenile justice policy. In particular, changes in approach to formal diversionary mechanisms may lead to the processing of more young people (net-widening) (Freiberg, Fox & Hogan 1988: 43–8).

There is also some evidence to suggest there has been an increase in the seriousness of offences for which juveniles have been apprehended (Youth Justice Coalition 1990: 21). In New South Wales, both the number and proportion of charges for offences against the person determined by the Children's Court doubled between 1985–86 and 1989–90. However, this pattern does not seem to have occurred in other States, and offences against the person still constitute a relatively small proportion of offences even in New South Wales (See Table 5.3).

Self-report studies provide an alternative method to official statistics for gaining a picture of the extent and nature of offending by young people. Such studies rely on young people themselves to provide information on their involvement in behaviour that could constitute a criminal offence.

Early studies in the 1950s compared self-reports on delinquency between male high-school students and males in a juvenile detention centre. While both groups admitted committing offences, those who were incarcerated admitted more frequent and serious offences (Lundman 1994: 12). However, self-report studies do suggest that juvenile offending occurs more uniformly among young people than suggested by arrest data. Two points are of particular relevance to issues discussed further below. Firstly, self-report studies indicate that both boys and girls engage in a range of activities definable as delinquent (Alder 1985: 54–5). Secondly, groups of both black and white youth have reported similar levels of offending or delinquent behaviour (Gale et al. 1990: 17).

Generally there has been more attention to self-report studies in Britain and particularly the United States than in Australia. However, some studies have been conducted locally (Kraus & Bowmaker 1982; Warner 1982).

Contact with the Juvenile Justice System

There are a number of ways we can consider the question of how many young people come into contact with the juvenile justice system in Australia. Firstly, there are figures on arrest rates of juveniles from various States which indicate formal police contact. These figures are available only for the more serious offences of homicide, serious assault, robbery, break and enter, motor vehicle theft and fraud. They do indicate, however, quite substantial differences between jurisdictions, with the highest arrest rate in Northern Territory at 72.1 per 1000 of the juvenile population compared to 15.8 per 1000 in New South Wales (Freiberg, Fox & Hogan 1988: 39).

Secondly, there are the formal intervention rates which combine court appearances with data from formal diversionary appearances (police cautions and panel or conference appearances in jurisdictions where these diversionary alternatives exist). Wundersitz (1993) has recently compiled data from these sources and estimated that the intervention rate is 40.8 per 1000 young people. She concludes that about 4.1 per cent of juveniles come into formal contact with juvenile justice agencies in any one year. These figures range from around 3 per cent in Victoria and New South Wales to 6.4 per cent in Western Australia. The Northern Territory and the ACT were omitted from the analysis because of the problem of obtaining accurate data (Wundersitz 1993).

Another of way of considering how many young people come into contact with the system is through the use of cohort studies. In South Australia, Morgan (1993) is conducting research on two groups of young people (or cohorts) who were born in 1962 and 1972. The research indicates that about one in five young people appeared before either the South Australian Children's Court or Aid Panel during their adolescence. The analysis has shown that approximately one in four of boys, compared to one in ten girls, had contact with either the court or panel. Over half of the Aboriginal youth in the 1972 cohort had contact with these agencies.

Thus, the intervention rates indicate that in any one year only a very small proportion of young people come into contact with the juvenile justice system. But a different picture emerges from studies that consider the likelihood of contact over the entire period of adolescence. In general terms, the majority of young people have no contact with juvenile justice agencies; however, some 20 per cent of young people (based on the South Australian study) do find themselves at some stage before the authorities. There are also important differences between male and female, Aboriginal and non-Aboriginal.

SOCIAL DIMENSIONS

The are a number of key social dimensions which must be considered when looking at offences by young people. Many of these factors will be considered in more detail throughout the book; for the present it is important to put juvenile offending within the context of social relations. The key social dimensions are:

- age
- gender
- ethnicity
- indigenous status
- social class
- family.

An understanding of these social dimensions allows us to contextualise and understand both the nature of offending by young people and the response to offending by state agencies.

Age

Age is an important characteristic in understanding juvenile offending and its classifications. Firstly, not all jurisdictions legally define 'child', 'juvenile' or 'young person' in the same way. Most Australian jurisdictions have now legislated for criminal responsibility to begin from the age of ten years. However, in Tasmania it is set at the old common-law age of seven years. Similarly, the age at which a young person is treated as an adult by the criminal justice system varies from seventeen to eighteen years, according to the State of residence.

We often see references to 'juvenile crime' as if all young people were equally likely to be offenders. However, the level of offending is also related to age. This is demonstrated in a number of ways.

- Offending rates for particular offences peak during the teenage and early adult years, depending on the type of offence, and then decline dramatically. According to Mukherjee (1983: 36), the peak age for theft is sixteen; for robbery seventeen; for homicide nineteen; and aggravated assault twenty-one years of age.
- A large proportion of juvenile offenders stop offending as they get older—they 'grow out of crime'.
- A small proportion of juvenile offenders go on to commit a large number of offences.

Two recent studies in New South Wales and South Australia have confirmed the phenomenon that most juveniles brought before the courts do not reappear on further offences (Coumarelos 1994; Morgan 1993). The New South Wales study involved a sample of 33,900 young offenders brought before the Children's Court between 1982 and 1986. It was found that 70 per cent of the young people did not reappear in the Children's Court. A further 15 per cent had two appearances. The average age of the first appearance was sixteen years.

The study also confirmed that a relatively small group of re-offenders accounted for a large number of court appearances. The 15 per cent of young people who had more than two court appearances accounted for 45 per cent of all Children's Court appearances, and the 3.4 per cent of young people who had more than six court appearances accounted for 20 per cent of all Children's Court appearances during the period under examination (Coumarelos 1994: 7). In line with these results, it was found that the probability of returning to the Children's Court increased as the number of appearances increased. There was a low probability that a young person appearing for the first time would return to the Children's Court. About half the young people who had two appearances returned for a third appearance. However, about three-quarters of those who had six appearances returned for further appearances (Coumarelos 1994: 19–20).

The South Australian study had similar findings. The majority of children had only one appearance before either the Children's Court or the Aid Panel (69.3 per cent of the 1962 cohort and 64.6 per cent of the 1972 cohort) (Morgan 1993: 176). However, a small number of young people accounted for a large number of offences dealt with by either the court or panel: 5 per cent of young people accounted for one-third of offences (Morgan 1993: 180).

This research, identifying peak ages for various offences and showing that most young people appear before the Children's Court only once, has given weight to the notion that young people grow out of crime. The maturation process is as important as any rehabilitative or reformative measure (Mukherjee 1985: 33). There is considerable research from various countries which lends weight to these ideas. A famous study of juvenile males in Philadelphia by

Wolfgang, Figlio and Sellin (1972) confirmed that about half those with a police record were only apprehended a single time, while a small group committed a large number of offences. Hirschi and Gottfredson (1983) have also found consistency in the age distribution of crime across countries and various time periods. The British study by West (1982) found that with increasing age there was increasing conformity among those previously designated as delinquent. In terms of policy, such approaches have led to an emphasis on developmental strategies which reinforce the role of the home and the school and argue against the use of incarceration (Rutherford 1986).

Gender

There are enormous differences in the numbers of young men and young women arrested and brought before the Children's Courts. While levels of unreported crime and differential treatment by state agencies may obscure some criminal behaviour by young women, the overwhelming feature of the data is that boys are about five to six times more likely to be charged with a criminal offence and appear in court. Table 5.3 shows the magnitude of difference in court appearances in New South Wales. Such a difference is typical of all Australian jurisdictions (Wundersitz 1993: 27).

Another feature of intervention specific to girls is that proportionately they are more likely to receive a diversionary outcome (caution, panel, etc.) than boys. Such a finding is typical across Australian jurisdictions where information is available (Western Australia, Victoria, New South Wales and South Australia) (Wundersitz 1993: 28).

The data from New South Wales shows that, once before the court, the offence categories for males and females tend to be similar (see Table 5.3). There are some exceptions. The major offence categories for girls are shoplifting (17.5 per cent), assault (10.7 per cent), offences against good order (10.5 per cent), and break and enter (8.2 per cent). The major offence categories for boys were break and enter (18.5 per cent), other stealing (11.7 per cent), motor vehicle theft (9.8 per cent) and offences against good order (8.8 per cent).

However, there were no offence categories where the number of offences by girls comes near that of boys. Table 5.3 shows that the closest parity is for fraud, where 36 per cent of court appearances were by girls. The next closest was assault (20 per cent of appearances by girls), followed by offences against good order (17 per cent), justice offences (17 per cent) and serious assault (17 per cent).

As we noted previously, offence categories are groupings of distinct criminal offences. The one specific offence where the number of court appearances by young women exceeds that of young men is prostitution (which is classified as an offence against good order). In New South Wales just on 90 per cent of prostitution offences were by young women (New South Wales Department of Juvenile Justice 1993: 8).

A further feature of the difference between males and females brought into the juvenile justice system is their relative likelihood of re-offending. The South Australian cohort study showed that females were significantly less likely to appear more than once before the Children's Court or Aid Panel than were boys. Some 37 per cent of boys went on to reappear, compared to 13 per cent of girls of the 1962 cohort (Morgan 1993: 176).

Ethnicity

During the period since World War II, Australia's population has become increasingly culturally diverse as a result of immigration. By the mid-1980s it had been estimated that between one in five and one in six young people between fifteen and twenty-four years old were either born in non-English-speaking countries, or had one or both parents born in non-English-speaking countries (Federation of Ethnic Communities' Council of Australia 1991: 3). The cultural diversity of Australia's young people has posed a number of issues relating to juvenile crime and the administration of juvenile justice.

Some of those issues have concerned the over-representation of specific groups of young people (Indo-Chinese, Lebanese and Pacific Islanders) in court appearances, and whether discrimination is a matter of concern (Human Rights and Equal Opportunities Commission [HREOC] 1993: 251). In New South Wales there was an increase of over 200 per cent in the number of Indo-Chinese juvenile detainees between 1991 and 1993. Indo-Chinese detainees were also spending three times longer (16.3 months) in juvenile justice centres than the average custody (Cain 1994a: 5).

In addition some socio-demographic indicators such as unemployment, poverty, refugee status and lack of family support in Australia place at least some young people from non-English-speaking backgrounds (NESB) in high-risk categories for contact with juvenile justice agencies.

There has also been concern over insensitivity and police harassment of NESB young people (New South Wales Office of the Ombudsman 1994; Youth Justice Coalition 1994). A recent report from the Youth Justice Coalition found that the rates at which young people from Asian, Aboriginal and Pacific Islander backgrounds were contacted, searched, questioned, fingerprinted and detained by police indicated unacceptably high levels of racism. 'Our survey shows that young people from Asian backgrounds are nearly twice as likely to be searched, four times more likely to be arrested and three times more likely to be injured during their contact with police than young people describing themselves as from as Australian background' (Youth Justice Coalition 1994: 1).

Ethnicity has in the main been ignored as a factor in juvenile justice policy. Yet clearly, specific groups of young people come into contact with agencies in a way that calls into question whether their ethnicity is a factor in intervention.

Indigenous Status

A key social factor of young people who are processed by the juvenile justice system is the over-representation of indigenous youth. We will discuss the evidence of over-representation at greater length in Chapter 7. For now it is important to note that a key characteristic of the juvenile justice system is the extent to which Aboriginal and Torres Strait Islander young people, more than other identifiable groups, dominate arrest, court and detention figures.

The over-representation has been persistent and severe and needs to be understood within the context of colonial and neo-colonial politics. In other words, there has been a distinct and special relationship between indigenous young people and non-indigenous authorities since the time of colonisation. Aboriginal and Torres Strait Islander young people have historically been treated differently and it is by no means self-evident that the current over-representation of Aboriginal young people is simply the result of greater levels of offending.

Many of the factors commonly associated with young people who are arrested and brought before the courts simply do not hold true for indigenous young people. For example, the South Australian cohort study showed that the observation that the majority of young people only appear once before courts or panels was reversed for Aboriginal young people. Some 60 per cent of Aboriginal young people were brought into the juvenile justice system on two or more occasions (Morgan 1993: 177). Aboriginal young people who come into contact with juvenile justice authorities are also more likely to come from rural backgrounds, to be female, to be younger, and to be incarcerated.

Social Class

A determinant in relation to social class and the likelihood of contact with the juvenile justice system is unemployment.

Unemployment is characteristic of young people brought before the Children's Courts. One study indicated that 67 per cent of young people over the age of fifteen years who appeared in the Children's Court were unemployed (cited in Freiberg, Fox & Hogan 1988: 50). Similar findings were made in a South Australian study where over 60 per cent of school-leavers who appeared were unemployed (Gale et al. 1990: 56).

We will deal more fully with the issue of unemployment in the next chapter. For now it is simply important to note a number of essential features.

Unemployment is not equally distributed across the population in terms of age, gender, ethnicity or geographic location. Unemployment rates among 15–19-year-olds are regularly two to three times higher than the general unemployment rate. There are gender differences in that employment opportunities for young women in the 15–19-year age bracket have contracted, compared to those for young men and to older women.

Unemployment is also differentiated by area. Many of the working-class suburbs of Australian cities have significantly higher rates of unemployment than affluent areas. It has been noted that the suburbs with the highest number of young people appearing in court are also the ones with high levels of unemployment and disadvantage on other social indicators including welfare dependency, etc. (Freiberg, Fox & Hogan 1988: 49–50; Gale et al. 1990: 59; Carrington 1993: 15). Unemployment is also concentrated in particular groups and this factor tends to be registered in Children's Court appearances. The unemployment rate for NESB young people (aged 15–19) is higher by over three percentage points than the general rate of youth unemployment. Among specific groups, such as Vietnamese male youth, it is double the general youth rate (HREOC 1993: 223; Blacktown Youth Services 1992: 16). Similarly, among Aboriginal young people the unemployment rate is considerably higher than the general youth rate. In some communities the level of unemployment amongst indigenous young people is almost total (Cunneen and Robb 1987: 27). In South Australia it was found that the unemployment rate among Aboriginal school-leavers who appeared in court or before an aid panel was 91 per cent (Gale et al. 1990: 56).

Unemployment is not equally distributed across the general population or across the youth population. Particular groups of young people are susceptible to a greater likelihood of being without work. Unemployment is also a factor strongly associated with those young people who appear in the juvenile justice system.

Family

It is apparent that many young people who appear before the Children's Courts do not live in nuclear families. These include young people who live with one parent, with relatives, with other young people, or in a de facto relationship, or who are homeless.

There are a number of complex issues here relating to culture, economics and politics. Some young people live in extended families because it is part of their culture of child-rearing and familial relations. For instance, in South Australia, three-quarters of Aboriginal young people brought before the courts or panels lived outside a nuclear family (Gale et al. 1990: 57). Young women who are homeless and brought before the courts may well be there as a result of escaping from an abusive home situation (see Chapter 8).

Another way of considering the issue of family is that juvenile justice agencies may seek to supervise what are defined as abnormal families through the Children's Court. There are two aspects to be considered here. Firstly, there is the question of the perceived abnormality of the sole-parent family. In a South Australian study about one in four appearances were of young people from sole-parent families (Gale et al. 1990: 57) and in a New South Wales study specifically of girls, about one-third were from sole-parent families (Carrington 1993: 73). The prevalence of sole-parent families among these young people was about three to four times the national average. Secondly, there is the issue of the extent to which all family members, including all the siblings, come under surveillance. In one study of fifty-nine girls who were institutionalised, over half of the siblings appeared in the Children's Court at some time (Carrington 1993: 73).

Family background is an important social characteristic of those young people brought into the juvenile justice system. It is those young people without family, those living in what is defined as an abnormal family relationship, and those in the most economically marginalised families who are the most susceptible to intervention. As we will discuss further in later chapters, young people who live outside 'normal' family arrangements are subject to different responses once inside the system.

The social dimensions which surround those young people who are apprehended and brought before the courts is clearly an important issue. Not all young people are equally likely to find themselves in this position. Questions of sex, age, ethnicity and cultural background, employment, family and social status, all operate to select certain young people.

EXPLANATIONS

Many of the attempts to identify the predictors for juvenile offending have been tautological, highly generalised and often profoundly ideological in nature. For instance, it has been argued that the background characteristics of delinquents are: below-average intelligence, parental criminality, sibling criminality, low income, and discordant family environment. Others cited are poor academic performance, anti-social behaviour, and inadequate parental supervision and discipline (see Potas, Vining & Wilson 1990: 52–4).

Braithwaite (1989: 44–9) has outlined the strongest known variables which relate to crime. With the exception of white-collar crime, crime is disproportionately committed by males aged 15–25 years, by unmarried people, by people in cities, and by people who have experienced high residential mobility. People who are disadvantaged by socio-economic status, who are unemployed, and who belong to an oppressed racial minority group have higher offending rates.

In addition, young people strongly attached to school are less likely to commit offences; young people who do poorly at school are more likely to engage in crime. Young people with high educational and occupational aspirations are less likely to commit offences. Young people who are strongly attached to their parents are less likely to engage in crime. Young people who have friendships with criminals are more likely to engage in crime themselves.

The list which Braithwaite has developed shows the danger of making sweeping generalisations concerning young people and juvenile justice. In the end, all that can be said is that these factors are *associated* with young people brought into the juvenile justice system. This is a very different proposition from stating that these factors are the *cause* of juvenile crime. The most fundamental difficulty with predictors or factors associated with juvenile offending is whether they can be divorced from the operation of the system itself. Are young people who have trouble at school more likely to commit offences, or are they more likely to be reported to authorities and become the subject of surveillance and intervention? Are the young of minority groups more likely to appear in arrest rates because they commit more offences, or because they are members of minority groups and subject to differential treatment and sometimes racism?

In other words, the factors that are often presented as predictors of delinquency may in fact be the predictors of intervention. Rather than present arguments about the causality of juvenile crime, we have preferred to provide an analysis of the key social characteristics of young people who end up in the juvenile justice system. We have sketched such a profile in terms of age, sex, ethnicity, indigenous status, social class and family.

REPRESENTATIONS

For many years there has been concern about the way the media present images of youth, particularly in relation to crime and social disorder. For most people, their knowledge concerning crime does not come from the direct experience of victimisation, offending or detection by authorities, nor does it come from academic studies or policy documents. Rather, knowledge about juvenile offending and juvenile offenders is partly mediated and partly constructed through the stories circulated in the news broadcasts and cop shows, the daily tabloids and talk-back commentaries. What we have are constructed simulations dealing in images of youth.

These images cover a limited terrain of possibilities. We have identified four broad categories in the contemporary representations of young people: the 'ideal' young person; the young person as 'threat'; the young person as 'victim'; and the young person as 'parasite' (White 1990: 107). Evidence presented below indicates that the dominant representation of young people is as a threat. The media are big business, and their representations need to be understood within the context both of profitability (what sells) and of discourses about social normality.

There is a tradition in criminological writings that has looked at the relationship between young people and the media. Stan Cohen's classic work on the clashes between the mods and the rockers in England during the 1960s showed the power of negative representation in amplifying disorder and bringing about a political crackdown on youth (Cohen 1973). Similarly, Hall and others analysed the creation of a phenomenon of 'mugging' and its association with young people, in particular black British youth (Hall et al. 1978). In Australia, researchers have looked at the role of the media in riots at the Bathurst motorcycle races through their amplification of anti-police sentiment and limited portrayal of events (Cunneen et al. 1989). Others have noted the media representations of bodgies and widgies (Stratton 1992) and contemporary youth subcultures (Walton 1993). An underlying theme in this work is the way young people and their subcultures are portrayed as deviant and criminal.

Many empirical studies have confirmed the media's preoccupation with crime (see Cunneen et al. 1989). In addition, recent empirical work has looked at the media association of youth and crime. In an examination of newspaper reporting about youth in Western Australia between 1990 and 1992, Sercombe (1993) found that the major issue reported in relation to young people was crime. As Table 5.4 shows, crime stories easily dominated the reporting agenda. The study also found that two sources of information (police and courts) dominated the news in relation to youth. Sercombe suggests that the reason for this lies in the economics of news production and in the news values of the media. In terms of production, statements from the courts and police are routine, cheap, and easy to collect. The close connection between the police and journalists has been commented upon in a number of Australian studies (Grabosky & Wilson 1989; Cunneen et al. 1989). The propriety or otherwise of these connections has been questioned in judicial inquiries such as the Fitzgerald inquiry in Queensland and the New South Wales Royal Commission into the arrest of former police officer Harry Blackburn.

Table 5.4 Newspaper reporting on youth, *West Australian* 1990–92

Issue	n	%
Crime	1644	63
Health	242	9
Education	215	8
Misadventure	156	6
Economic issues	145	6
Place in society	118	5
High achievement	57	2
Homelessness	36	1
Total	2613	100

Source: Sercombe (1993: 16).

Official views, whether through press releases, spokespersons or government statistics, dominate what is said about young people. Young people themselves are in a particularly disadvantaged position in terms of having their own opinions or views on matters heard in the media. They have neither official legitimacy, nor the institutional means of making their views known.

The representation of particular groups of young people is also an important issue. Sercombe found in Western Australia that 87 per cent of newspaper articles that identified young people as Aboriginal were primarily about crime (Sercombe 1993: 4). One of our own studies found that Aboriginal people were the only group who had their ethnicity or racial background mentioned in newspaper reports if they were arrested or convicted of an offence (Cunneen 1987).

Similarly, there has been concern about the reporting of young people from non-English-speaking backgrounds. The New South Wales Ethnic Affairs Commission, in a report on fights between young people in Marrickville and Bankstown, was highly critical of what it saw as superficial and selective reporting by the media which presented the conflict in racial terms. It described some of the headlines as sensational, misleading and hysterical (Ethnic Affairs Commission 1986: 3). There have been similar concerns with the reporting of Indo-Chinese young people and crime. One article described Vietnamese young people who had arrived in Australia as unattached minors as follows. 'They live in transient, shared households, stay up late, smoke, drink and watch hours of cheap "chop socky" videos. They roam in packs, drifting from pool halls to petty crime to drug-taking' ('Suburbanasia!', *Time Magazine*, 8 April 1991, p. 23). The single empirical study on Vietnamese young people and juvenile crime showed quite different results. According to Easteal, unaccompanied Vietnamese minors in fact had a significantly lower rate of offending than other Vietnamese young people, and Vietnamese young people in general had lower offending rates than the wider population (Easteal 1989).

Finally, we need to consider how the representations of young people coincide with their positioning as a law-and-order problem within electoral politics. Virtually all State and Territory elections in Australia now have law-and-order issues as a central component of the campaign. In most elections, the extent of juvenile offending and the appropriate responses to it have been used as an electoral issue. Often Labor and conservative parties have attempted to outdo one another to be seen as the more punitive.

In the post-election period, punitive policies are often put in place as a result of earlier promises. Examples are boot camps in Western Australia, and changes to juvenile cautioning procedures and the introduction of the *Summary Offences Act 1988* in New South Wales. Electoral politics and the role of media reporting on young people and crime go hand in hand, and neither is fettered by appeals to rational discourse about the nature of juvenile offending. Empirical evidence and calls for reasoned debate on juvenile justice policy are lost when populist politics are in command. The potential appeal of the politics of law and order, 'getting tough' on juveniles and the collapsing of media into government is shown by the Western Australian 'Rally for Justice'. The rally was organised by Perth Radio station 6PR and a local talk-back radio commentator. One result was the introduction of the *Crime (Serious and Repeat Offenders) Act 1992* (WA) (see White 1992).

The role of the media in representing young people as delinquents can have tangible results—from changes in legislation to variations in policing practices. More broadly, a certain reality is constructed which inhibits our understanding of the nature of juvenile offending and limits the way we conceive of the possible responses.

YOUNG PEOPLE AS VICTIMS OF CRIME

Ironically, an important and neglected aspect of the relationship between young people and the law is that they are often the victims of offences. Usually the images and public knowledge about young people and crime paint a picture of youth as perpetrators of offences. However, a number of writers have identified the extent to which young people are also the victims of crime. This recognition is in line with the current focus on victims' rights and the move towards 'restorative justice' which emphasises the participation of victims in dealing with young offenders. Unfortunately, despite all the emphasis on the role of the victim in the new methods of dealing with young people, there is no recognition in the official literature that young people are as likely to be victims as perpetrators (or some cases more likely). For all that has been written about victims' rights, one is hard-pressed to find official literature that deals with the simple empirical observation that young people are indeed victims themselves.

Using South Australian police data, Tait (1994: 70) makes the point that young people between the ages of fifteen and twenty were the most likely group to be the victims of robbery, and that more young people reported being victims of robbery than were apprehended by authorities as perpetrators of the offence. Alder (1991) has identified the high levels of victimisation of young people who are homeless. Underwood, White and Omelczuk (1993) surveyed youth workers in a number of different youth services, such as refuges and drop-in centres, throughout Western Australia. The survey ascertained that young people were exposed to incidences of violence both in the private sphere of the home as well as in the public sphere (Underwood, White & Omelczuk 1993: 15–17). Similarly Mukherjee (1983: 71) has noted that children (under sixteen years) are about four times more likely to be victims than suspects in homicide cases.

There is also a large body of research which identifies young people as being susceptible to violence on the part of the authorities, particularly police. We will return to this issue in Chapter 10.

CONCLUSION

The nature of juvenile offending is not as straightforward as it might seem at first glance. The official figures are limited for a range of reasons: some general to all recorded offending rates as well as those which are specific to juvenile offending. Arrest rates and court appearances show that property crimes predominate amongst young people. The available data also shows that juvenile offending is less serious than adult offending because of a number of factors.

We know that most young people who are apprehended for an offence come into contact with the juvenile justice system only once during their adolescent years. We also know that in any one year a very small proportion of young people will be brought before the police, courts or diversionary mechanism. Over the length of a person's adolescence the likelihood of contact is much greater, but still the majority of young people have no contact. We also know that there is a range of social factors which increase the likelihood of a young person's contact.

Finally, we need to acknowledge that the dominant images of young people and crime which circulate in the social world are not real reflections of youthful offending. These images magnify the social threat of young people and particularly isolate groups of young people such as indigenous youth and youth from non-English-speaking backgrounds. Politicians grab eagerly at these simulated images of youth and develop public policy that has more to do with the image of threat than the reality of the world in which young people live.

6 class and community

The actual processing of young offenders is heavily oriented toward working-class young people, in particular the most marginalised sectors of the youth population. In the previous chapter we analysed in general terms the extent and nature of juvenile crime. The aim of this chapter is to explore the economic reasons why certain categories of young people engage in specific types of crimes, and how the state attempts to enforce a particular kind of order with regard to the public presence of working-class and minority young people on the streets. It will be argued that the impetus or motivation for offending by young working-class people lies in the limited availability of adequate means of subsistence, and in the denial of the opportunity to participate in a meaningful way in consumption and social activities. In particular, we will explain the high incidence of property crime among juveniles (see Chapter 5) through the application of the concepts of class and marginalisation.

Australian society is a capitalist society, which is divided into a number of identifiable classes (e.g., capitalist class, small business class, working class). As a structural relation, class reflects the different positions and capacity of people to marshal economic and political resources as dictated by their relationship to the means of production. The ownership of the means of production (e.g., factories, banks, telecommunications, mining companies, farms) is central to the distribution of wealth and power in society, and to the overall allocation of community resources. The working class is comprised of those people who live by the sale of their labour power on the labour market in return for a wage or salary. Indeed, the wage is a crucial determinant in the well-being and social status of working-class people. Unemployment, and the threat of unemployment, is therefore one of the conditions of the working class, given the importance of the wage for economic survival and a general dependency on business to provide work in return for a wage or salary.

Youth unemployment and youth poverty, in particular, are and will continue to be among the most disturbing and profound issues of the 1990s and into the twenty-first century. Specific studies and overviews of the youth studies literature indicate that young people are seriously 'at risk' across a range of broad social indicators—whether suicide, health, employment patterns, or other facets of youth lifestyle, all of which have been affected by wider economic conditions (White 1994ab). One consequence of the vulnerability of many young people to economic and social hardship is the creation of a marginalised 'underclass' stratum of the working class. Members of this social stratum are part of a wider 'surplus population' which has been progressively swelled by the advent of structural, long-term unemployment.

From the point of view of juvenile justice, it is essential to understand the broad processes of **marginalisation** which economically, socially and culturally separate certain young people from mainstream institutions, and which provide fertile ground for various kinds of low-level property and interpersonal crime. Such processes are also associated with varying degrees of alienation, anti-social behaviour, riots and violence, which in turn are symptomatic of a system which privileges the economic over the social, and which relegates the needs of the majority behind the dictates of the market.

In a similar vein, it is likewise important to consider the manner in which marginalisation is related to particular processes of **criminalisation**, whereby certain groups of young people are targeted above others for state intervention. In essence, it will be demonstrated that the criminalisation process is by and large directed at the comparatively powerless and most marginalised sectors of society. Thus, the young people who are most vulnerable to being discarded by the formal labour market and to experiencing difficulties within institutions such as schools and the welfare system are also the most vulnerable when it comes to the activities of coercive state institutions such as the police, courts and gaols.

The chapter provides an examination of the relationship between young people, crime and community resources. In so doing, it poses the question of how we address issues relating to the definitions and causes of particular types of youth crime, and official state responses to youth offending, in a period of gross economic and social inequality. Our approach to youth crime is in terms of political economy: this approach offers the prospect of an integrated analysis which incorporates structural, situational and personal factors in explaining youth behaviour. It also exposes some of the limitations of existing state responses to this behaviour.

A POLITICAL ECONOMY OF CRIME

The basis for a political economy of crime is an appreciation of the profound changes occurring in the spheres of production and consumption as these have affected young people in recent years. The marginalisation of young people in the sphere of production, specifically in relation to paid work, has had a profound impact upon their well-being and life opportunities. Indeed, there can be little doubt that many young people are experiencing life in this sphere as victims and are bearing the brunt of the economic recession.

The Sphere of Production

Under capitalism, the key mechanism for the distribution of economic resources is the market. The sale of one's labour in return for wages is the basis for economic well-being. For those who, for whatever reason, are excluded from participation in the labour market or who simply cannot earn enough to make ends meet, there is the welfare state. In essence, the welfare state plays a residual role in Australian society, compensating for the shortfalls in resource distribution in the market sphere (see Watts 1987). A third area in which economic and other resources are transferred is that of informal community structures and networks (Jamrozik 1984). This area includes both informal economic activities of an illegal nature (see below) and the sharing of resources within a particular family, household or community.

Changes in resource allocation in the dominant sphere of the market affect each of the other spheres as well. Certainly the phenomenon of widespread unemployment constitutes the biggest single factor, but by no means the only factor, in the transformation of the relationship between the market, the state and informal community sectors. For example, in 1992 there were over 300,000 children living in families dependent on unemployment benefits, and an even greater number living below the after-housing poverty line (Australian Council of Social Services 1992; see also Carter 1991). While structurally playing a residual role *vis-à-vis* overall resource distribution, the state has come to be a primary or major source of economic resources in the lives of a large proportion of Australian residents. This in turn has placed considerable pressures on the state to balance the demands of the economy through fiscal, monetary and labour market polices, with the demands of social policy. The latter stem from the general decline in living standards accompanying the movement of people out of paid work and into the welfare queue.

The result of the state's balancing act has been manifest: the tightening of regulations covering benefit provision; moves toward the privatisation of public services (through the sale of assets, the introduction of user-pays principles into areas such as education, and the farming out of government functions to private contractors); more selective allocation of state resources via tests on means and assets; and redefinitions of areas of state responsibility and private responsibility. Simultaneously, the ways in which the Australian state has intervened in the market sector, particularly in the areas of taxation and wages policies, have served to erode the living standards of the majority of those in the paid workforce. All of this adds up to enormous hardships for people as a result of the substantial rise in unemployment over the last decade.

For young people in particular, the impact of the changing nature of work has been especially profound and, in some instances, devastating. For example, teenage full-time employment has plummeted in the last twenty-five years. It has been pointed out that the 'proportion of all 15–19-year-olds in full-time employment fell from 58 per cent in August 1966 to 20 per cent in August 1991' (McDonald 1992: 18). Many young people today in this age group are in fact in some kind of training or education program. Even so, youth unemployment generally has continued to rise dramatically in recent years. Thus, in late 1992 the official national unemployment rate of young people not in training was approximately 38 per cent.

By way of contrast, part-time employment for 15–19-year-olds has increased from 3.5 per cent in 1966 to around 23 per cent in May 1992 (McDonald 1992: 18). The majority of young people in part-time work are also students; employers appear to have a preference for these workers over the full-time unemployed (Sweet 1987; White 1989).

For those who are out of work and out of school, the chances of gaining employment are diminished considerably. Indeed, the 'average length of time a young person is unemployed has increased from 2.9 weeks in 1966 to 25.1 weeks in 1991' (Australian Youth Action and Policy Association 1992: 15; see also Larwill 1992). In terms of actual numbers, it has been noted that:

> There are currently around 230,000 young people—17 per cent of all 15–19-year-olds—who can be categorised as being 'at risk'. This includes those not in full-time education and either unemployed, employed only part-time or not in the labour force (i.e., discouraged young people who have given up looking for work or training) (McDonald 1992: 19).

Hence, a considerable proportion of young people are currently in a vulnerable situation in terms of employment, and are therefore unable to secure community resources for themselves.

As the nature of the labour market changes, so too does the position of young people in the overall economy. Here we can point to five interrelated spheres of activity which are crucial to an understanding of the economic position of young people: the formal waged economy, the informal waged economy, the informal non-waged economy, the education and training sector of the economy, and the criminal economy. Pressures in one sphere have direct and indirect consequences for activity in the other spheres.

In terms of unemployment, a significant proportion of working-class young people have effectively been squeezed out of the full-time formal **waged economy** (Senate Standing Committee on Employment, Education and Training,

Chart 6.1 Spheres of economic activity

Sphere	Issues
Formal waged economy	• low wages • poor working conditions • insecure tenure • underemployment • health and safety • harassment
Informal waged economy	• low pay • loss of award benefits • insecure • illegal • open to exploitation and harassment without legal remedy
Informal non-waged economy	• difficult to assign a value to one's labour • abusive • over-work • social isolation • infantilisation
Education and training sector	• cost of study • poverty • level of government assistance • stringent requirements for claiming assistance • pressures to work in informal waged economy
Criminal economy	• irregular income • illegal activity • possibly dangerous • open to exploitation

1992). They have been obliged to rely on state benefits and/or to find income from other sources. For those young people in the paid workforce, there are strong pressures to accept low wages and poor conditions under the threat of dismissal. Here we have to recognise that youth wages in the 1980s in fact declined: the ratio of junior male to adult male wages was the lowest since 1964, and for females it was the lowest since figures were first recorded in 1962 (Australian Council of Trade Unions 1989; see also McDonald 1991; and Australian Youth Action and Policy Coalition 1993).

For many young working people, the lack of paid work in the formal economic sector leads them to pursue alternative work arrangements in the **informal waged economy**. This includes, for example, the so-called cash-in-hand phenomenon where workers are paid 'under the table' for their efforts. However, here also many young people find themselves competing on unfavourable terms with others for the work at hand. The oversupply of workers in the formal economy ultimately spills over into the cash economy (see White 1989).

If paid work is not available in these two sectors, young working-class people, especially young women, are in many cases forced to be active in the

informal non-waged economy. Thus, in return for lodgings and board, young women are placed in the position of domestic servants due to their dependent and vulnerable economic status. This may also entail a process of infantilisation, whereby young women in particular are treated like children, whose duty it is to obey the whim of the providing parent. It can also mean that these young people are restricted by financial means and household chores to spend most of their time in the home, rather than outside with friends, engaged in activities of a recreational and creative nature. Thus, the question of social isolation looms large in this kind of situation. So too, do the issues of sexual abuse, incest, and exploitation of child labour.

Many young people have been forced to undertake some kind of **training or education.** For instance, it has been pointed out that 'whereas in 1966, 63 per cent of 16–19-year-olds were employed and 30 per cent were in education, by 1989 only 37 per cent were employed and 58 per cent were studying' (Maas 1990). This shift is partly a reflection of young people trying to improve their own individual employment chances. But it is also linked to the imposition of more stringent requirements related to the receiving of state benefits such as the Newstart Allowance. One of the problems here, of course, is that the level of payment and/or financial resources tends to be very low, especially in the light of the costs of books, transport and the like which are part of the price to be paid for further education or training. While not directly a part of the sphere of production, this sector is nevertheless vital because it prepares people for the world of paid work. It also exists, in part, as a 'holding tank' for those unable to find jobs in present economic circumstances. Even so, education and job-search allowances for young people have consistently been well below the poverty line (Sheen & Trethewey 1991). Students are often forced by immediate economic pressures to participate simultaneously in other economic sectors, whether waged or unwaged, legal or illegal.

Thus poverty-stricken young people may be forced to be active in the **criminal economy.** Activities in the criminal economy differ from those in the informal economy in that the latter are not themselves different from 'legitimate' economic transactions in the formal waged economy. Income in the criminal economy, however, is generated through irregular commission of offences, ranging from shoplifting to burglary. It may involve individual, one-off offences and spontaneous spur-of-the-moment activity, or be linked to group activities including, at the extreme, organised crime. For most young people such activity is sporadic and contingent upon their immediate situation. Few young people end up having a 'career' in the criminal economy.

The well-being of working-class young people is intimately linked to the stresses and strains associated with movements into and out of each of these sectors of economic activity, and the pressures of securing an income in each particular case. There are shifts between these sectors (e.g., from employment to unemployment), and changes within each sector (e.g., from receiving a youth wage to receiving a training allowance), and young people may find themselves periodically drifting into and out of different spheres.

The transformations in the material resources available to young people have had a profound impact on their lifestyle and life opportunities. The issue of economic provision is not, however, simply quantity but quality as well. For example, an important distinction can be made between physical survival and social functioning. The first refers to basic human needs, such as nutrition, necessary for the sustenance of life itself. The second is more closely related to the question of life chances. Social functioning, as Jamrozik (1987: 48) explains, 'depends on the provision of, and access to, an adequate quantity and quality of material resources sufficient for the achievement of a certain minimum standard of living and a certain quality of life'. The cash resources available to young people, whether through the labour market or as a result of state transfers, therefore mean different things in real terms, depending upon the overall economic situation of particular young people, their position in the class structure, family and community resources that can be drawn upon, and their immediate work, study or lifestyle requirements.

Social problems such as unemployment, poverty and declining opportunities directly affect the physical and psychological well-being of young people (White 1994b). The marginalisation of young people economically, socially and politically undermines their own self-conceptions of 'worth'. It also is linked to feelings of resentment at promises unfulfilled, boredom and frustration in their present social state, and a search for meaning and satisfaction in an era of no jobs. As Pixley (1993) demonstrates, people who are excluded from mainstream work become powerless, and experience significant problems in coping with their lack of status in society.

The Sphere of Consumption

The exclusion of young people from the traditional means of income and social status in the sphere of production has also altered their position in the sphere of consumption. It is in this sphere of activity that young people are most prevalent as **offenders**, and are most likely to be identified as threats to existing consumer practices and institutions. To understand this, we have to consider the nature of juvenile crime, and the ways in which non-offenders have been implicated in the commission of such crimes.

The sphere of consumption concerns the position of young people as consumers in society. That is, examination of their activity in this instance focuses on their ability to purchase and their patterns of behaviour in relation to goods and services sold as commodities on the market. One of the significant features of the post-war period has been the important position of young people as consumers. The rise of the 'youth consumer' in the 1950s and the ability of business to incorporate previously 'rebellious' fashions and fads into the commercial orbit were important elements in the changing pattern of relationships involving young people in the sphere of consumption. Working-class young people, in particular, broke the ground at a time when paid work was readily available and a disposable income there to be spent.

One consequence of the shifts in spending ability and market weight was the construction of leisure activity, time and space. As Stratton (1992: 163) points out: 'With the advent of an increasingly consumption-oriented society independence came to be measured more and more as a function of possible expenditure. This relates directly to the rise of institutionalised and commercialised leisure activities'. The position of young people as consumers also carried with it the tacit acceptance by shopkeepers, businesspeople and state officials of a new status for the teenager in society.

Today, however, the importance and composition of the youth market has diminished in relative terms, due to the deepening recession of the 1990s. The decline in the ability of young people to be consumers in recent years has cast a shadow over previous portrayals of 'the young'. The effects of sustained periods of high unemployment, economic polarisation, and visible evidence of poverty and homelessness have rendered the notion of 'young consumer' less powerful as a defining characteristic of the ideal or typical young person. Instead, the image is one of greater dependence upon others (family, the state, friends) and fewer options in terms of work and spare-time pursuits (as influenced by availability and cost).

There was and still is considerable variation in community response to youth subcultures, depending upon class, gender and ethnic differences (Brake 1985; McRobbie & Nava 1984; White 1993a). Nevertheless, media-generated moral panics regarding youth 'crime waves' and the stereotyping of certain young people as being particularly 'troublesome' or 'dangerous' can stimulate general fear and anxiety at a popular level (see Cohen 1973; Pearson 1983; White 1990). Coupled with the concerns of businesspeople and market traders regarding actual losses suffered due to offending behaviour, such images affect large numbers of young people, offenders and non-offenders alike.

The suspicion which (some) shopkeepers and traders have of (some) young people is grounded to a certain extent in experience. However, the overall statistical picture on youth offending certainly does not warrant the treatment usually meted out by the mainstream media. As we saw in the previous chapter, most youth crime is of a trivial nature. Indeed, crimes of violence by young people constitute a particularly low percentage of all offences cleared by the police (see Table 5.1). As we demonstrated, a small proportion of young people are responsible for a large fraction of reported offences (Morgan 1993); the rate of official intervention has remained constant over the last five years or increased only slightly (except in the case of Western Australia); and the vast majority of youth crime consists of property offences (Wundersitz 1993). Significantly, however, shop stealing constitutes the largest category of offences for which juveniles are actually apprehended by police (as shown in Table 5.2), and it has been estimated that shoplifting constitutes half of the total direct costs of juvenile offending (Potas, Vining & Wilson 1990). The main victim of youth offending, therefore, is not the individual citizen *per se*, but business enterprises of varying kinds.

Given the prevalence of shoplifting as an offence, it is useful to explore more fully the meaning of such offences in the lives of different groups of young people. More research is needed, for example, to examine the dynamics of shoplifting as activity which plays different possible roles in relation to personal situation and household economic relations. Do young people steal items for their immediate use value, or for their exchange value, that is, as something to be exchanged in the criminal economy for cash? In what ways can shoplifted items, or cash from their sale, be linked to immediate physical needs (e.g., fast food, drugs), youth culture (e.g., items related to dress and appearance), psychological needs (e.g., self-esteem, status, peer-group pressure), or to purchases of other goods and services on the market (e.g., commercial entertainment)? As well, it would be of interest to investigate class, gender and ethnic differences in the patterns and content of shoplifting. Clearly there are bound to be differences in perceived causes of such behaviour, which will range from issues of powerlessness stemming from general social restrictions placed upon all young people, through to immediate economic needs relating to physical survival. In other words, if we are to understand the nature of juvenile offending of this kind, we need to have insight into the significance and meaning of such activities in the lives of the young people involved.

Nevertheless, it is logical to suggest that, given the poverty, unemployment and homelessness affecting large numbers of young people in Australia in the present day, shoplifing represents one means to 'consume' when one does not have the resources to pay. And in a consumption-oriented society, there are considerable pressures on young people to participate in consumption activities regardless of their financial ability to do so.

One of the consequences of both the prominence of shoplifting as a youth crime, and the visibility of the social impact of the recession, is what can be called the 'criminalisation of the non-consumer'. For many young people, the central logic of the shopping centre or mall—to consume—is either not realisable or is not the primary reason for their use of this space. Other motivations for young people to congregate in such centres include social activity and escape from close parental or adult control. But the social response to young people will be shaped by their position as consumers (and producers) in the context of general street life. For example, young people who do purchase goods and services, or who exhibit a level of affluence which makes them appear as potential consumers, are rarely seen as problematic by businesspeople or the police.

On the other hand, the social position of the dispossessed, the obviously poor and the visible minority group member is usually mirrored in the suspicion and confrontational attitudes of those around them. From the point of view of consumption, these young people are virtually and literally worthless. They are unable or unwilling to purchase the goods and services so tantalisingly displayed. Meanwhile they are using the consumer space as public space for uses of their own. The shopkeeper can see this as unacceptable on at least two grounds. First, such young people are often implicated in or suspected of shoplifting, which directly affects profit levels in a period when many small businesses in particular are finding it difficult to keep afloat. Secondly, even if no offence has been committed, the very presence of these young people may put off other consumers. That is, 'riff-raff' hanging around one's shop can dissuade potential customers from entering into the shop and thus are bad for business.

Production and consumption are inextricably linked in the formation of personal identity, self-esteem and social value. The marginalisation of young people in the first sphere invariably shapes their position in the second sphere. In addition to questions of income, however, there is also a need to consider space itself as a community resource. Increasingly, it seems to be the case that public space is being redefined as and constricted to 'consumption' space. As such, it is also subject to intensive and extensive forms of social control (White 1993b; White & Alder 1994). The private ownership and/or state regulation of public space—based primarily on the construction of this space in commercial terms—thus forms part of the context within which other kinds of 'offensive' behaviour on the part of the young is occurring.

SOCIAL INSTITUTIONS AND YOUTH ALIENATION

The conventional approaches to 'delinquency' and youth crime often begin by asking what it is that makes young people become delinquent. The answer, for many, lies in the relationship young people have with the dominant institutions of society and, especially, the school. In a period of high youth unemployment, the school has become ever more important as an indicator of future life chances, and as a necessary (although not sufficient) requirement for the attainment of paid work. The school plays a major part in establishing the position of young people in society as producers and as consumers.

The school also reproduces many of the contradictory aspects of what it is to be young in Australian society. As Corrigan (1979) points out, young people occupy a position as 'actual and potential labour': schools need to teach flexibility to suit the labour market, but in fact, constrained by resource and discipline concerns, they teach inflexibility. Young people also occupy a position as 'actual and potential consumers': they are meant to be treated as adult consumers with individual rights based on money, but they are treated as children who lack adult rights. Indeed, it has been argued that schooling embodies a number of structural alienations (see Polk 1988). While schools are meant to prepare students for later work and social life, they do so in ways which segregate them from other segments of the population, prolong their economic dependence, build in passivity, routinely deny natural justice, and perpetuate unequal competition between pupils and between schools (Polk 1988).

The necessity of schooling as a means to get ahead is reflected in increased retention rates in post-compulsory schooling over the last decade. Between 1981 and 1991 there was a general increase in retention rates across the educational sectors. For example, apparent retention rates for state schools went from 29 per cent in 1981 to 67 per cent in 1991 (National Youth Affairs Research Scheme/Australian Bureau of Statistics 1993). By way of contrast, it is also notable that in New South Wales the high schools which consistently show the lowest retention rates across the State are precisely in the areas with the highest Aboriginal population (e.g., Bourke, Brewarrina and Walgett). Going to school is seen as an opportunity for the enhancement of one's job prospects, especially given the rise of credentialism (employer demands for certificates). It is presently an employer's market, where those who have the highest qualifications are more likely to be hired than others, even though the qualification may have no direct relevance to the area of employment. There is also often a financial incentive to stay on at school, because government assistance rewards school attendance more generously than unemployment or job-seeking.

For many young people, schooling is a terribly alienating experience, which appears to rob them of their autonomy, creativity, and efforts at self-development and expression. Furthermore, there is no guarantee that upon leaving school that they will get paid work. The high retention rates indicate that there are many young people at school who do not really want to be there. Economic incentives and the ideology of enhanced job opportunities have generally reinforced the 'value' of schooling. The sheer number of students remaining in, or returning to, high school, coupled with resource pressures on public education, has generated a range of difficulties which impact upon the school experience and the out-of-school activities of young people. Compounding these difficulties has been the traumatic effect of school closures, which in Victoria have caused large numbers of students to discontinue their formal schooling (Charikar & Seiffert 1994).

A big issue today in Australian schools is discipline. This refers both to unruly or challenging behaviour in the school, and to truancy. The latter is particularly significant in the light of the earlier discussions of use of public space by young people. In explaining disciplinary problems, it is useful to refer to varying forms of and reasons for **resistance** in the school setting (see Polk 1988; Walker, 1993).

In addition to in-school factors which help to explain the different forms and types of resistance, it needs to be acknowledged that much resentment of schooling and education generally arises from the sense of a promise unfulfilled. That is, education is sold as a means of enhancing job opportunities. It is furthermore sold as a key component of self-development. Yet the high rates of youth unemployment belie its presumed economic role (for large numbers of young people). Simultaneously, the selection and labelling processes associated with competitive schooling can entrench notions of 'failure' and the status of 'no-hoper'. Far from preparing young people for roles as producers and consumers, the school may reinforce their marginal status in society.

Chart 6.2 Sources of resistance to school

Source	Comments
The content of schooling	Often students do not see the relevance of the academic content of schooling; they just want to get a piece of paper which will help them win a job, or they want training in some sort of 'practical' skills; alternatively, some young people, for example Aborigines, may resent the fact that their views of history, culture and science are not represented in the mainstream curriculum at their schools.
The structures of authority	Authorities seek to promote expressions of autonomy and responsibility, but as soon as students exhibit these qualities they are cut down because they are seen contradicting authority.
Teachers	Although working-class young people are seen as 'anti-school', it is often the case that they do want a 'proper' education; however, teachers spend more time with students from high-income backgrounds, and many refuse to take working-class students seriously.
The process of education	Education is supposed to promote knowledge, and the sharing of knowledge; yet the system is geared to privatised notions of knowledge acquisition via the stress on competition and stringent rules about cheating (i.e., sharing information).
Racism and violence	Students may be thrown into a situation where bullies and racist violence are not confronted by teachers or the school. One consequence of school closures has been to shift certain school populations (e.g., migrant children) from familiar environments and put them into uncertain new environments, thereby increasing the potential for violence.

Social alienation is a condition where people are separated from developmental institutions (Polk 1994) such as the educational system. For many young people, the dynamics of these institutions translate into loss of rights, inadequate provision of facilities and services, forms of hostile control, and unaccountable decision-making. The general result is to reproduce class divisions—working-class kids end up in working-class jobs or no jobs, and kids in underclass environments remain in those environments. In behavioural terms, the consequence is activity which is anti-social or rebellious. It is activity which disconnects one, in some fashion, from the dominant institutions, while bearing a relationship to those selfsame institutions. A sense of powerlessness and vulnerability can manifest itself in varying kinds of self-destructive and anti-social behaviour. Suicide represents one such response. But so too do racist violence, gay bashing, sexual assault and thuggery, all of which target the personal integrity of individuals. The devaluation of young people in and through our major institutions, including work and school, has a real and lasting impact on the society as a whole.

MANAGING A YOUTH 'UNDERCLASS'

Perhaps the main irony and tragedy of contemporary reactions to youth crime is that young people themselves are seen as the **focus for action**. The reasons for this relate directly to perceptions regarding the position of young people as part of a new underclass in society, and an emphasis in official policy on policing this section of the marginalised population.

In the last hundred years, young people in general have been socially positioned as a vulnerable category. The weight of social institutions such as schools, social welfare and the police; the enforced economic dependency of young people on their families via state policies; and the ideological constructions of 'youth' as a period of less responsibility and less autonomy based upon the criterion of age: all these have contributed to the marginalisation of young people, as young people, from mainstream social life. Regarding legal and civil rights, all young people are subject to varying degrees of freedom and constraint; the same, however, cannot be said of social resources (Edgar, Kean & McDonald 1989; Burdekin 1989). It is working-class young people, for example, who are bearing much of the burden of the economic recession. It is young women who are suffering the discriminations of male-dominated heterosexist society in areas of work, welfare and personal relationships. It is Aboriginal young people who are so often the targets of law-and-order campaigns and media-generated moral panics (see Australian Youth Policy and Action Coalition 1992; White 1989; Cunneen 1990a; Polk and Tait, 1990).

The marginalisation of young people economically, socially and politically is therefore uneven, and it is based upon wider social divisions in Australian society linked to class position, ethnicity, indigenous background, and gender relationships. Whether it be unemployed school-leavers or old-age pensioners, young sole parents or factory workers, an impoverished social condition is ultimately dictated by lack of ownership and control of the means of production, and by distance from the meaningful exercise of state power. The result is that it is working-class people, broadly defined and including many people from middle-income households, who are experiencing the so called 'broken transitions' of youth, and it is the affairs and activities of these people which the state is most anxious to manage and keep under close control.

The extent of youth marginalisation has been indicated in previous figures relating to unemployment levels and duration, and those pertaining to poverty levels. Because of the sheer extent and scope of such marginalisation, much concern has been directed in recent years to the concept of 'underclass'. Such a notion carries with it various connotations, including the distance of certain groups from the mainstream institutions and processes of society. For example, it has been used to distinguish different categories of unemployed people on the basis of their relationship to the labour market (Morris & Irwin 1992). Thus, the unemployed can be divided into two main groups.

• *Outside the labour market:* These people by virtue of their age or disability are ineffective in competing for jobs; they are outside the labour market because they lack 'marketability'. These people suffer systematic disadvantage in the market. At an experiential level, they still maintain an interest in entering the labour market, and state policies relating to education and training—i.e., labour market re-entry—are central to their lifestyle and efforts to become employed.

• *Excluded from labour market:* These people are non-participants in the labour market, and have no stable relationship to employment. They are in essence excluded from the job market through a combination of long-term unemployment, inadequate work histories, and declining motivation to compete in apparently hopeless circumstances.

Each category of the unemployed constitutes a sizeable proportion of those people living in poverty (which also includes aged pensioners, sole-parent families, etc.) and as such includes people who would under normal circumstances rely upon state welfare provisions of some kind. The important distinguishing factor is whether individuals are defined as 'deserving' or 'undeserving' with regard to the claiming of these state benefits or services. It is crucial to acknowledge here the ways in which social policy encapsulates and structures the social division of welfare (Rodger 1992; White 1995). In the Australian context, it is clear that more stringent conditions for the claiming of state support simultaneously constitute rules of inclusion and exclusion in relation to state welfare provision. (For example, to receive the Newstart Allowance one must be engaged in training or job-seeking.) For those who play by the established rules of the game, the reward is a meagre sum with which to achieve some modicum of physical survival. However, there are many who persistently find it difficult to succeed within the terms of the policy agenda (because more training does not necessarily guarantee greater employability); who refuse to accept the notion that welfare resources exist principally as a privilege (rather than a right); or who exhibit high degrees of alienation, resentment and loss of faith in themselves or the system (through accummulated 'failures'). Such people may find themselves subject to the label of 'underclass'.

The concept of **underclass** can therefore refer to an objective position of exclusion (from the labour market and/or state welfare provision), and a subjective dimension of experience (general social attitudes, values and behaviour). It is the 'habitual' and long-term unemployed who are seen as a threat to the economic fibre of the nation; it is the 'culturally impoverished' and 'socially deviant' unemployed who are seen to threaten the standards of decency and respectability in society. As a substratum of the working class, the so-called underclass can thus appear as a highly visible blight on the social landscape and an 'unnecessary' drain on public and private resources.

Discussion of the underclass could be used to heighten awareness of social polarisation and human deprivation, and as a means to focus attention on the structural conditions which exclude some categories of people from community resources. However, in popular discourse the concept has largely been appropriated by those who use it as a stigmatising label, referring in the main to forms of (undesirable) behaviour. It is the perceived behavioural threat from an emerging underclass which has informed various law-and-order policies and which partly shapes the way in which law-enforcement agencies operate in relation to the unemployed. As has been pointed out, this approach to dealing with members of the underclass focuses on kinds of people rather than on social conditions (Rodger 1992).

The high rates of youth unemployment (which are incredibly high in the case of Aboriginal people) clearly shape perceptions of young people who are visible in the public domain. Periodic media coverage of apparent 'crime waves' involving young people creates a particular kind of social awareness, not only of the alleged offences, but of the kinds of young people most likely to commit these offences. Invariably, the focus of such media stories is on street crime, and the main message conveyed is of danger and the vulnerability of ordinary citizens to this kind of crime. The images presented have no small effect on political decision-makers and on the police officer patrolling at street level.

One consequence of the perceived threat posed by unemployed young people who hang around shopping centres and streets is increased state intervention in the affairs of these young people as a matter of course. The impact of pervasive and strong official intervention into their lives in this manner combines with the prior difficulties of economic hardship, low self-esteem, few social resources and general boredom associated with exclusion from the spheres of production and consumption to make an explosive mix of desperation and anger. Young people caught up in the web of no money, no job and no future nevertheless often have very creative survival skills and a rebelliousness sparked by knowledge that they are most disfavoured and disowned by society. The existential dilemmas of many of those on the margins of society reduces the probability that they will care either for the legitimate institutions of society (e.g., private property) or for those who wield the sanctions designed to protect the interests of the propertied and the respectable (e.g., the police, private security firms).

The social costs of marginality are inevitably translated into the economic costs of crime (White 1989; Potas, Vining & Wilson 1990; Box 1987). But the social costs of marginality are also transformed into behaviour which is officially recognised as 'anti-social' and 'dangerous'. As much as anything, this reflects the ways in which the state attempts to manage the underclass at the ground level. In other words, official social reaction to the marginalised in turn exacerbates the tensions and conflicts involving young people who are visible in the streets. This is partly reflected in the fact that most police report they have been assaulted or harassed by young people in the course of their work. While most of this consists of verbal taunts, and the like, Alder et al. (1992) also found that a majority of police officers have at some time been punched by a young person, and many have been kicked or had an object thrown at them. In institutional terms, offence charges such as 'resisting arrest' and 'assault' have to be seen as, in part, a reflection of the aggressive physicality of policing itself and the consequences of persistent harassment of the least powerful groups in society by the forces of law and order.

All of this is bound to have an impact on the self-image of marginalised young people and their efforts at self-defence in a hostile environment. The pooling of social resources and the construction of identities which are valued by others (if only one's peers) finds expression in a range of cultural forms, including various youth subcultures. Masculinity and femininity, Aboriginality and ethnic identity all find new expressions according to the dictates of economic circumstances, state policies, historical legacies, and different intrusions into the life of the young. But too often the cultural expression of social difference is itself taken as a cause for alarm, and efforts are made to force the young to conform to unrealistic social norms or to render their activities invisible from the mainstream society.

CRIME AND COMMUNITY

The actual behaviour and activity of young people is thus shaped by their position as producers and consumers in society, their relationship to the major social institutions, and by the ways in which they are subject to various social control measures by the state and private policing agencies. Structural dislocations are being experienced by a large and growing number of young people, giving rise to a range of experiences. These experiences are shaped by situational factors, such as the nature and extent of policing in particular social locations, and young people respond with diverse personal coping strategies, from substance abuse and suicide through to petty crime. Any strategy designed to address youth crime must therefore seek to transform the reality of young people at the structural, situational and personal levels.

While acknowledging the constraints and limitations imposed on the Australian economy from outside the country, it is still important to recognise the ways in which the state has been implicated in creating the conditions for the emergence of a marginalised underclass stratum of the working class. Regardless of a rhetorical commitment to social justice, the federal Labor government has ushered in an era of redistribution of income from labour to capital, thus deepening inequalities in income and wealth generally (Eaton & Stilwell 1993). The consequences of economic rationalism at a policy level (Pusey 1991), and adoption of corporate management models at an administrative level (Considine 1988), have been disastrous in terms of social policy funding and service provision. The result of this has been a steady emphasis on making the welfare system leaner and meaner, oriented toward excluding people from its benefit and service allocations as a cost-control measure.

While the state is implicated in the making of the youth underclass, through a combination of ill-judged economic policy and grossly inadequate social policy provision, it is also directly involved in the control of those in need. Thus, the fall of the 'social state' is intertwined with the rise of the 'repressive state' (White 1995). That is, the creation of the underclass has been accompanied by measures designed to 'get tough' and regulate the activities of the marginalised in Australian society. Portrayals of the underclass as threatening, dangerous, irresponsible and immoral serve to justify the introduction of more hurdles for claimants of state benefits, and the enactment of law-and-order policies which target particular groups of young people, and penalise certain types of behaviour. This represents a movement from concerns about welfare to the **criminalisation of the poor**.

If we are to respond adequately to the issue of youth crime, then it is essential that we come to grips with changes occurring in the spheres of production and consumption, and how these are radically transforming the life experiences of young people in Australia today. Indeed, it could well be argued, especially in the light of the United Nations *Convention on the Rights of the Child*, that the biggest crime of all is that the economic and political order has denied young people basic human rights across a range of institutional areas. It is common to relegate unemployment, poverty and inequality to the too-hard basket. This postpones vitally needed societal reform and reconsideration of political priorities. It also tends to push people in the direction of short-term and medium-term 'solutions' which, ultimately, do not address the real determinant factors behind youth offending or the substantive role of official social reaction in shaping the criminalisation process. It also raises the question of whether policies to prevent juvenile crime are genuinely seeking to change the existing situation or merely seeking to control it via new methods of widening the net (see Cohen 1985).

A realistic, meaningful and humane response to the issues surrounding young people, crime and community would have to be built upon interrelated policies which acknowledge and attempt to transcend the unequal distribution of power and resources in current socio-structrual arrangements. Briefly, these might include the following.

- *More action to redistribute community resources:* The right to the means of life should not be contingent upon activity but should be based on need. For both the working poor and the unemployed, there is a great need to increase social resources such that physical survival and enhanced social functioning are guaranteed institutionally.

- *Concerted action on employment and job creation:* The right to work could be concretely grounded in policies which recognise the transformation of paid work in the late twentieth century, the essential creativity and necessity of labour in the self-worth of human beings, and the necessity to involve all members of society in the carrying out of tasks essential to preserving and improving the social and natural environment.

- *Acknowledgement of the importance of community space in the construction of social life:* The right to space of one's own means that there needs to be greater community control over privately owned areas which have a high public usage, such as shopping centres, and the managers of such space should be encouraged to provide greater control and usage of such space by young people.

- *Greater community involvement in local decision-making, particularly public service provision:* The right to accountability is crucial in the case of institutions and agencies such as the police. As the wielders of legitimate violence in society and the holders of considerable social power, the police must be fully accountable for their actions, and the orientation of policing must be toward peace-keeping rather than policing the community.

Such measures are central to a reform program which sees young people first and foremost as active, valued members of their communities. When society disenfranchises the young and the communities of which they are a part, youth crime and greater state intervention in the lives of the young necessarily follow. Expanding the range of real and significant personal choices for young people is still the best way to guarantee that they will become responsible and full participants of society.

CONCLUSION

The distribution and allocation of community resources is ultimately a question of politics, one which goes to the heart of power by asking who controls and manages the means of production in Australian society. Criminality associated with economic marginalisation and social alienation stems from the subordinate position of the working class in society. Unemployment and the threat of unemployment constitute central factors of the capitalist organisation of paid work. This means that social vulnerability via the growth in surplus populations, and social polarisation via unequal distributions of community wealth, will be endemic in our society. In such circumstances, working-class crime will flourish even as the state redoubles its efforts to contain it.

7 indigenous young people

In this chapter we consider why Aboriginal and Torres Strait Islander young people have high levels of contact with juvenile justice agencies. To answer this question involves analysing many interlocking issues, including the history of colonisation, the links between welfare intervention and criminalisation, the effects of social and economic marginalisation, and the extent to which racism and discrimination are part of the regulatory practices of juvenile justice agencies.

We also consider some indigenous responses to the current situation, including demands that Australia respect its international obligations in relation to its treatment of indigenous young people. Finally, there is discussion of the methods by which Aboriginal and Torres Strait Islander people deal with youth who engage in offences within their communities.

To gain an appreciation of the extent to which Aboriginal people are caught up in the juvenile justice system, it is worth noting the level of over-representation in juvenile institutions. The figures in Table 7.1 show that the majority of detainees in Queensland, Western Australia and Northern Territory are Aboriginal and Torres Strait Islander (51, 62 and 82 per cent respectively). The highest rate of indigenous incarceration is in Western Australia, at 849 per 100,000 of the Aboriginal juvenile population. We can also ascertain the level of over-representation of Aboriginal young people from Table 7.1 by comparing Aboriginal and non-Aboriginal rates. Again looking at the Western Australian figures, Aboriginal young people are forty times more likely to be incarcerated than non-Aboriginal young people (849 per 100,000 compared to 21 per 100,000).

Another way of understanding the extent of intervention into the lives of Aboriginal young people is to look at the number of juveniles who, at some time in their life, come into contact with juvenile justice agencies. The only Australian research (Morgan 1993) which has been able to consider this question is the study of cohorts in South Australia to which we referred in Chapter

5. The research found that 55 per cent of Aboriginal youth born in 1972 appeared either in the Children's Court or before a panel during their juvenile years. When categorised by sex, nearly seven out of ten Aboriginal boys and four out of ten Aboriginal girls had formal contact. These figures can be compared to the general figures in South Australia of nearly three out of every ten boys and one out of every ten girls (Morgan 1993: 173–4). The figures give some idea of the extensive formal contact of Aboriginal young people with Children's Courts and panels.

Table 7.1 Rates of detention and incarceration for young Aboriginal and Torres Strait Islander people, compared to non-indigenous young people[a]

State	% detained		Rate of incarceration [b]	
	ATSI	Non-ATSI	ATSI	Non-ATSI
New South Wales	22	78	541	35
Victoria[c]	15	85	248	8
Queensland	51	49	364	13
Western Australia	62	38	849	21
Southern Australia	37	63	648	19
Tasmania	0	100	0	20
Northern Territory	82	18	219	23
ACT	0	100	0	30

a   During late 1992 and early 1993
b   Rate per 100,000 of the respective juvenile populations
c   Junior Youth Training Centre figures

Source: Adapted from Atkinson (1994: 26).

The two sets of data presented above show the formidable nature of the dilemma. It is impossible to consider the operation of juvenile justice agencies without looking at their impact on Aboriginal and Torres Strait Islander young people. And it is impossible to understand the position of indigenous young people in Australia without considering the extraordinary level of criminalisation.

We now turn to look at explanations for this relationship.

HISTORY AND CULTURE

Indigenous societies in Australia differed and continue to differ from the mainstream in their cultural notions in relation to childhood and young people. Generally, there is not the same separation or exclusion of children from the adult world. Responsibility for children and young people is allocated through the kinship system and the wider community (Watson 1988; Sansom & Baines 1988). Colonisation has wrought changes in these social patterns to varying degrees, either through disruption of whole communities and nations by expropriation of land or through specific policies aimed at the removal of Aboriginal children and young people. However, it is also important to recognise that distinct cultural patterns relating to child-rearing have remained intact.

There have been at least three modes of intervention into the lives of Aboriginal and Torres Strait Islander young people during the last two centuries. These forms of intervention have included the period of open warfare and resistance; the period of 'protective' legislation; and the contemporary period of criminalisation. The different phases of colonial expansion over the last two centuries have caused overlapping of these modes of intervention. For instance, in the mid-nineteenth century, when the Native Mounted Police were engaged in open violence on the frontier in Queensland, the Victorian government was introducing protective legislation.

During the period of open colonial warfare, Aboriginal young people were treated the same as Aboriginal adults. The massacre of Aboriginal tribal and kinship groups meant young people were killed along with other members of the group. Age was irrelevant at this level of state intervention: an over-riding concern was Aboriginality. Aboriginal people were murdered *because they were Aboriginal*, because they were the indigenous people in possession of the land and because they resisted colonial expansion. The accounts of various massacres by mounted and other police suggest that the killing was indiscriminate. Elder (1988) has described massacres by state forces in Tasmania, New South Wales, Victoria, Queensland and the Northern Territory. It is also important to remember that the killing of Aboriginal adults and children by punitive parties went on at least until the late 1920s in the Northern Territory and Western Australia (Cunneen 1994: 129).

Both missionaries and colonial administrators saw children and young people as targets of interventionist policies. Their policies removed Aboriginal children from their families and kinship groups (Attwood 1989; Markus 1990). From the beginning of colonisation, 'those seeking to absorb Aborigines into European culture have looked to children as their best hope' (Markus 1990: 22). Some of the earliest institutions established by whites to deal with the 'natives', such as the Parramatta Native Institution established in 1814, were designed to remove Aboriginal children (Brook & Kohen 1991). Indigenous young people were captured to be sent to the institution, and those who were there often absconded. The plan by Governor Macquarie to use the institution to 'rescue' these children needs to be seen alongside the simultaneous use of punitive expeditions against the indigenous peoples around the Sydney settlement (Brook & Kohen 1991).

By the mid-1800s, Victorian missionaries were concentrating on the removal of Aboriginal children from their families to dormitories. The policy was designed to prevent the continuation of Aboriginal culture (Attwood 1989: 18). By 1850 all the missions which had come and gone in eastern Australia had tried to raise Aboriginal children separate from their parents (Edwards & Read

1988: xi). The removal of children was often vigorously contested. In 1838 at Wellington, in midwestern New South Wales, an entire Aboriginal camp left the missionaries after a baby was removed from its mother to a dormitory (Edwards & Read 1988).

PROTECTION LEGISLATION

The removal of Aboriginal children from their families and communities started at the beginning of the colonial period. However, the scale of removal by the missionaries was relatively modest compared to what was achieved under the so-called protection legislation introduced in the late nineteenth and early twentieth centuries. The legislation legitimated intervention into Aboriginal life by police and the Aboriginal Protection Board in an unprecedented manner. The removal policy was large-scale; it was designed to prevent Aboriginal children growing up to identify as Aboriginal adults (Edwards & Read 1988: xiii). Read (1982) has estimated that more than 5600 Aboriginal children were removed in New South Wales alone between 1909 and 1969 when the legislation was repealed.

In the following discussion we use New South Wales as an example of the policies which were introduced. The aims of the New South Wales Aborigines Protection Board have been identified as: reducing the Aboriginal birth-rate by the removal of adolescents, particularly girls; preventing Aboriginal children from identifying with the Aboriginal community by isolating them from families; and preventing of the return of those removed to their families or the Aboriginal community at the end of their term of 'apprenticeship' (Wootten 1989: 18–19). In the board's own words, the purpose of child removal was to counter the 'positive menace to the State' which the ever-increasing and non-assimilated Aboriginal population was supposed to represent (Read 1982: 5).

A feature of the legislation was the absence of procedural justice (Chisholm 1988: 321). The New South Wales protection legislation of 1909 was found inhibiting by the board because it had to be demonstrated before a magistrate that the child or young person was neglected before they could be removed. The children whom the board wanted to remove were not neglected, and the board failed in a series of court cases because it was unable to demonstrate neglect (Goodall 1990a). The legislation was amended in 1915 to allow removal of Aboriginal children without a court hearing if the Aborigines Protection Board considered removal to be in the interest of the child.

The change in the New South Wales legislation was achieved after a public campaign aimed at convincing parliament and the public that generally Aboriginal parenting was negligent. The board gained greater powers and, in the process, reinforced racist assumptions about Aboriginal parenting. These assumptions about the incompetence of Aboriginal parenting and child-nurturing permeated the views of police and others when carrying out Protection Board policies (Goodall 1990a). It is also important to understand how this process of intervention and removal was gendered. Between 1900 and 1940 Aboriginal girls bore the heaviest impact of removal policies. The policy was targeted at pubertal girls; in its early years, some 80 per cent of the children removed were female, the majority of whom were twelve years and older (Goodall 1990a).

The human devastation wrought by the regime has been told in Aboriginal autobiographies (Tucker 1977), by historians (Read 1982), and in the inquiries of the Royal Commission into Aboriginal Deaths in Custody (Wootten 1989). Life for Aboriginal children in homes such Kinchela and Cootamundra was appalling. For instance, the manager at Kinchela Boys' Home had to be warned against being drunk on duty, using a stockwhip on boys, tying them up, and denying them food as punishment (Read 1982: 11). The links between early removal on welfare grounds and later juvenile and adult criminalisation are clearly articulated in the Royal Commission's inquiry into the death of Malcolm Smith (Wootten 1989). At the age of eleven, Malcolm Smith was removed from a caring family in rural New South Wales by the Aborigines Welfare Board on the complaint of being neglected. He was placed at Kinchela and denied access to his family. He was later released as a teenager, still without access to his family, into inner Sydney, without support and functionally innumerate and illiterate. He was charged with stealing, and institutionalised in a juvenile correctional centre. Most of the remainder of his life was spent in juvenile and then adult prison.

Read (1982) has also noted that when the Aborigines Welfare Board replaced the Protection Board in New South Wales in 1940 and procedures relating to Aboriginal children were brought under the Child Welfare Act, there was the introduction of the new complaint of being 'uncontrollable'. Aboriginal children were particularly susceptible to being found uncontrollable and as a result being placed in corrective institutions. It would seem likely that the over-representation of Aboriginal young people in the general juvenile detention centres dates from this period. Welfare complaints such as uncontrollable were a significant factor in this process.

Aboriginal people were not passive victims of the policies of child removal. There were individual and community struggles against the Aborigines Protection Board. The removal of Aboriginal children was resisted by parents at every step (Goodall 1982: 73). Indeed, early Aboriginal political organisations in south-eastern Australia, such as the Australian Aborigines Progressive Organisation, drew attention to the forcible removal of Aboriginal children and the role of police as 'guardians' during the 1920s (Markus 1990: 176–7). The struggle concerning the removal of Aboriginal children has been continued by Aboriginal and Islander child-care agencies and Aboriginal legal services.

Meanwhile, individuals have sought compensation through the courts for the psychological, material and cultural damage caused by removal and institutionalisation (Jowett 1993).

A further long-term consequence of the protection period has been its influence on the relationship between Aboriginal people and the police, welfare and juvenile justice authorities. The police played an important role in the administration of the protection legislation (Goodall 1982: 190; Cunneen 1994: 131–2). The fear of police removing children and conducting other duties under the protection legislation has meant that tension, suspicion and conflict continue to characterise relations between police and Aboriginal communities (Anti-Discrimination Board 1982: 125).

When considering the protection legislation, the Royal Commission into Aboriginal Deaths in Custody noted that the policy was designed to achieve the disappearance of Aboriginal people as an identifiable group and that such a policy would today be internationally condemned as genocide (Wootten 1989: 19). Under international law, genocide is defined as those acts committed with the intent to destroy, in whole or in part, a national, ethnic, racial or religious group. Such acts include both deliberate violence and policies aimed at cultural destruction. It is significant that past policies by government towards indigenous young people have been characterised in this manner. It is an issue which must be addressed when understanding the operation of contemporary juvenile justice policy.

WELFARE TO CRIMINALISATION

The removal of Aboriginal children from their families as a result of welfare complaints or protection legislation has fallen into disrepute. Some States have legislated in favour of the Aboriginal Child Placement Principle which requires in relation to welfare matters that an Aboriginal child be placed with members of its own extended family or community, or another Aboriginal family (see, for example, Section 87 of the *Children (Care and Protection) Act 1987* (NSW). However, Aboriginal and Torres Strait Islander young people are still over-represented in child protection (welfare) matters. Most of these matters involve complaints of neglect, and it has been argued that such complaints reflect the poverty of many Aboriginal families (Thomas 1993: 6). The difficulties Aboriginal families have in providing adequately for their children can be attributed to the consequences of colonisation. 'It is manifestly unjust for non-Aboriginal society now to use the consequences of its own crimes against Aboriginal people as the reason for the removal of Aboriginal children' (Chisholm 1988: 333). Indigenous children are also still over-represented in substitute care, and it would be surprising if the links between early welfare intervention and later criminalisation do not continue to exert an influence.

One might have expected a decrease in the incarceration rates of Aboriginal young people with the demise of protection legislation and the more stringent separation of welfare matters. However, indigenous young people continue to be incarcerated in juvenile institutions at extraordinary levels as a result of the processes of **criminalisation** (Cunneen 1994: 133–6). Along with the move towards criminalisation, there has been a shift in the gender focus in the period since World War II, with a change in emphasis from Aboriginal girls to boys. This gendered shift has been intensified by law-and-order campaigns which have focused on Aboriginal males (Goodall 1990a). In addition, there is evidence to suggest that indigenous young people are at greater risk of contact with the juvenile justice system than indigenous adults are with the adult criminal justice system. For example in Western Australia in 1990, approximately 25 per cent of arrested juveniles were Aboriginal young people. In comparison, 14 per cent of arrested adults were Aboriginal people. Indeed 40 per cent of all arrested Aboriginal people were juveniles (Broadhurst, Ferrante & Susilo 1991: 29, 35).

Table 7.2 Aboriginal participation as percentage of total young people in the juvenile justice system, New South Wales, 1990

Participation	%a
Police cautions	6.9
Total interventions (police cautions plus court appearances)	15.3
Prosecutions by way of charge	17.4
Court appearances	16.5
Police bail refusals	23.1
Final bail refusals	21.6
Detention orders	27.2

a   Of the population aged 10–18 years, Aboriginal people comprise 1.8 per cent.

Source: Luke and Cunneen (1993: 258).

Another key finding in various research studies has been that the level of over-representation actually increases as Aboriginal young people move through the system. Aboriginal youth are least over-represented in the least punitive stages of intervention and most over-represented at the point of committal to an institution. In South Australia, where Aboriginal young people comprise 1.2 per cent of the youth population, they account for 7.8 per cent of arrests, 13.9 per cent of referrals to the Children's Court and 28.1 per cent of young people sentenced to detention (Gale et al. 1990: 4–6). Similar processes are evident in New South Wales, as Table 7.2 demonstrates. It shows that Aboriginal young people are over-represented at each stage of intervention, given that they comprise 1.8 per cent of the State's youth population. However, the level of over-representation is highest in relation to the use of custody, either through being refused bail and held in remand or through being sentenced to detention by the court. Conversely, the level of over-representation is least at the formal diversionary stage of a police caution.

CHARACTERISTIC OFFENCES

One explanation for the over-representation of indigenous young people in juvenile justice statistics is that they commit a greater number of offences, including more serious offences. We have already discussed in Chapter 5 some of the difficulties in simplistic interpretations of the relationship between crime statistics and actual offending levels. We now turn to consider some of the specific aspects of Aboriginal offending patterns.

Studies in South Australia (Gale et al. 1990) and in New South Wales (Luke & Cunneen 1993) have compared offences between Aboriginal and non-Aboriginal young people. There were similar results in both studies. The New South Wales data is summarised in Table 7.3 on the following page. For both Aboriginal and non-Aboriginal young people, the greatest emphasis is on property offences including breaking and entering, stealing motor vehicles, shoplifting and other forms of theft (60 per cent of Aboriginal offences and 64 per cent of non-Aboriginal offences). However, there are significant differences between the two groups in terms of the nature of the property offences. Aboriginal young people have a significantly greater proportion of more serious break-and-enter offences and a smaller proportion of shoplifting and minor 'other theft', such as larceny. There are several possible explanations for the difference.

In commenting on the South Australian experience, Gale and her colleagues note that 'it is not clear to what extent Aborigines actually commit more serious property offences or whether other factors and, in particular, police discretion in charging are at work' (1990: 46). The authors cite examples of police discretion in charging, where less serious offences, such as being unlawfully on premises and larceny, could replace the more serious charge of break, enter and steal. Similarly, Cunneen and Robb (1987: 96) found that of all property offences, it was arrests for *break and enter with intent to steal* in which Aboriginal people were most over-represented. In such circumstances there is a range of possible resolutions available to police officers, including the use of diversion or other less serious charges.

Offences such as break, enter and steal also have very low clear-up rates, sometimes as low as 5 per cent of reported crimes. The information on the few offenders who get caught is particularly susceptible to policing practices, reporting levels in particular areas, and the relative sophistication or otherwise of the

Table 7.3 Comparisons of Aboriginal and non-Aboriginal juveniles, major offences, 1990

Offences	Non-Aboriginal %	Aboriginal %
Homicide and manslaughter	0.1	0.1
Armed robbery	0.3	0.1
Sexual assault	0.5	0.3
Drug trafficking	0.4	0.0
Unarmed robbery	0.4	0.4
Grievous assault and malicious wounding	6.1	7.1
Other assault	6.4	10.7
Breaking and entering	14.1	22.0
Stealing motor vehicle/carried in convey	11.1	8.8
Shoplifting	6.0	3.8
Other theft	32.5	25.3
Good order, traffic and rail offences	17.5	19.9
Other drug offences	3.9	1.0
Other offences	0.8	0.5
Total	100.0	100.0

Source: Luke and Cunneen (1993).

offenders. The high proportion of Aboriginal young people in this category of offences may tell us more about *detection by police* than about levels or degrees of criminality.

The issue of reporting and police detection is connected to the issue of environmental opportunities. Gale and her colleagues argue that, even if it could be shown that Aboriginal young people do commit more serious property offences, it would not demonstrate any greater 'criminality' because environmental opportunities and pressures influence the nature of property crime. In particular, urban–rural differences structure opportunities and pressures differently. Simple theft and shoplifting are primarily urban offences particularly associated with large shopping complexes. Similarly, there is increased likelihood of being caught either breaking into or attempting to break into a dwelling in a small country town or remote community.

The second most frequent group of offences is those related to public order. Table 7.3 shows that one in five Aboriginal young people experience formal intervention by the juvenile justice system as a result of these offences. Such findings have been repeated in other studies. In north-west New South Wales, Aboriginal people were greatly over-represented for offences like assaulting police, hindering police, resisting arrest and offensive behaviour (Cunneen & Robb 1987). Similarly, in South Australia a greater proportion of Aboriginal young people were charged with street offences than non-Aboriginal young people (Gale et al. 1990: 48). These charges are also the ones most dependent on direct police intervention, with the potential for selective enforcement and the adverse use of police discretion.

The third significant group of offences involve violence. Aboriginal and non-Aboriginal young people have roughly the same proportion of offences at the more serious end of the scale (murder or manslaughter, armed robbery, sexual assault, grievous assault and malicious wounding). Aboriginal young people have a greater proportion in the less serious 'other assault' category. Similar results are apparent in South Australia, where differences in the proportion of Aboriginal juveniles compared to non-Aboriginal juveniles are related to (the less serious) common assault. Gale and her colleagues argue that the differences might support the argument that poor living conditions lead to a greater degree of violence in Aboriginal communities. Or 'it may reflect nothing more than the well-documented fact that violence in an Aboriginal community is often an open and public event to which police are readily called' (Gale et al. 1990: 48).

Another way of explaining some aspects of the offending patterns of Aboriginal young people is to consider the extent to which the offences are specifically aimed at non-indigenous targets or are responses and resistance to non-indigenous institutions and authorities. A number of researchers in the area have commented upon the fact that some property offences, vandalism, assaults and behaviour classified as offensive can be understood as a form of resistance (Brady 1985, Cunneen & Robb 1987; Cowlishaw 1988; Hutchings 1995). For instance Brady notes that in the community where she did her research, the break-ins by Aboriginal young people were directed at school buildings, European staff houses and the store (Brady 1985: 116). Aboriginal organisations have also noted that resistance has become part of Aboriginal culture. 'What has been described as delinquency could also be regarded as acts of individual defiance. The scale and nature of Aboriginal children's conflict with "authority" is reflective of a historical defiance' (D'Souza 1990: 5).

A further way of explaining offending patterns and the over-representation of indigenous young people in the juvenile justice system is to look at their socio-economic or class position. In general, Aboriginal young people show very poorly on all social indicator scales such as health, housing, education, unemployment, welfare dependency (Johnston 1991: vol. 2). In this sense they are disadvantaged in comparison with non-indigenous youth. Studies which have analysed juvenile offending have also discussed the socio-economic disadvantage of Aboriginal young offenders. In South Australia it was found that, of young people who had left school and were apprehended by police, some 91 per cent of Aboriginal young people, compared to 61 per cent of non-Aboriginal young people, were unemployed (Gale et al. 1990: 56). Similar findings emerged in a study in north-west New South Wales (Cunneen & Robb 1987). Other social factors, such as sole-parent families and residential location, which correlated with poverty were also more prevalent among Aboriginal young people who were apprehended (Gale et al. 1990: 57–58).

However, it is important not to paint a simplistic picture of poverty and social disadvantage among Aboriginal young people. Firstly, there is the need to understand 'social disadvantage' within the context of colonialism, dispossession and the destruction of an Aboriginal economic base. As many indigenous people have stated, Aboriginal and Torres Strait Islander people are not simply a disadvantaged minority group in Australia. They are the indigenous people of Australia whose current *socio-economic status* derives from a specific history of colonisation, and whose *political status* as indigenous people gives them a number of rights and entitlements. We will return to this issue later in the chapter.

Secondly, while in general terms there is a positive correlation between socio-economic disadvantage, poverty and juvenile offending rates, it is simplistic to say that Aboriginal young people actually offend more often and seriously than their non-Aboriginal counterparts because they are more disadvantaged. The *extent* to which Aboriginal young people commit a greater number of offences is difficult to assess because the level of surveillance (primarily policing) plays such a fundamental role in producing the nature and number of offences brought into the juvenile justice system, as well as in selecting young people to be considered as offenders.

We now turn to consider how these selection processes operate in relation to Aboriginal youth.

POLICE DECISION-MAKING

To a large extent, police determine which young people will enter the juvenile justice system, as well as the terms on which they enter. Police must continually decide whether to intervene and how to intervene. All the available evidence demonstrates that their discretionary decisions work against the interests of indigenous young people.

In most States of Australia, police have the power to issue a formal caution against a young person as an alternative to charging them with a criminal offence. If a caution is issued, the young person is not prosecuted and the matter does not proceed to court. Various studies have indicated that Aboriginal young people do not receive the benefits of cautions. Luke (1989) found in a regional New South Wales study that, of those apprehended by police for shoplifting, some 91 per cent of non-Aboriginal youth were cautioned compared to 74 per cent of Aboriginal youth. Similarly, there were differences in the treatment of first offenders, where 49 per cent of non-Aboriginal first offenders were cautioned compared to 29 per cent of Aboriginal first offenders.

A further study by Luke and Cunneen indicated a similar pattern generally across New South Wales. In 1990 some 5.5 per cent of Aboriginal young people were cautioned, compared to 13.3 per cent of non-Aboriginal young people.

Even when young people had no prior record of either court appearance or caution, it was still found that Aboriginal first offenders throughout the State had a greater chance of being prosecuted by police and thus a lower chance of receiving a police caution. This pattern was particularly evident in country areas, where two-thirds of Aboriginal interventions occur (Luke & Cunneen 1993: 262–3). This pattern of differential treatment was maintained when the offence type was held constant. For example, 90.6 per cent of Aboriginal first offenders apprehended for break-and-enter offences were charged rather than cautioned; while 82 per cent of non-Aboriginal first offenders apprehended for the same offence were charged (Luke & Cunneen 1993: 264).

In South Australia, there are no statistics on how many cautions are issued. However, observational studies of police behaviour in Adelaide found that 'case after case emerged which brought into question the equity of police treatment of Aboriginal youth at the point of apprehension' (Gale et al. 1990: 65). There were statements by police officers that cautions were rarely, if ever, used with Aboriginal youth, and the authors found that there were many situations which seemed to warrant a police caution rather than formal proceedings.

If police decide not to caution but to proceed against a young person, there is a range of options available. The specific options vary from State to State. However, the evidence shows consistently that indigenous young people invariably receive the most punitive option available. The use of a summons or court attendance notice, rather than arrest, is a less punitive way of bringing a young person before the courts on a criminal charge. If the police proceed by way of arrest, the young people is detained or has to find bail. In Western Australia, South Australia and New South Wales it has been shown that Aboriginal young people are more likely to be proceeded against by way of arrest and less likely to be summonsed (Broadhurst, Ferrante & Susilo 1991: 33; Gale et al. 1990: 31; Luke & Cunneen 1993: 264).

Because Aboriginal young people are more likely to be proceeded with by way of arrest, they are more likely to face a bail determination. Two issues are important: whether bail will be refused and the young person will be held in custody; or, if bail is granted, what conditions will be attached. In the first instance, Aboriginal young people are more likely than non-Aboriginal young people to be refused bail by police. In an analysis of first offenders in New South Wales, there was a 53 per cent greater likelihood of bail refusal by police when the young person was Aboriginal. In rural New South Wales the likelihood of bail refusal was 129 per cent greater for Aboriginal young people (Luke & Cunneen 1993: 265). The second issue is the nature of the conditions which are imposed when bail is granted. The Royal Commission into Aboriginal Deaths in Custody was particularly concerned with 'unreal conditions' which are imposed and then regularly broken. The result is that young people are recycled through the courts (Wootten 1991: 353). Onerous and oppressive bail conditions include curfews and residential requirements amounting to banishment (Cunneen 1994: 139–41). Such conditions place enormous pressures on young people and their families. In the end, they may simply set up a young person for failure and further intervention.

Several Australian States have utilised formal diversionary systems which rely on children's aid panels as an alternative to the court. Their aim is to divert minor and/or first offenders from the formal processes of the court. Police play a major role in deciding who goes before panels and in the composition of the panels themselves. It has been repeatedly demonstrated that those decisions impact negatively on Aboriginal young people. In Western Australia one in three non-Aboriginal young people were referred to a panel, compared to one in eight Aboriginal youth (Wilkie 1991: 135–6). Until recently in South Australia, a screening panel operated prior to the children's aid panel. The screening panel made the decision as to whether a young person would go to the aid panel or to the Children's Court. Screening panels were more likely to refer Aboriginal young people directly to the Children's Court rather than to the less punitive option of the children's aid panel. The decision of the screening panel was based largely on the initial police decision to arrest Aboriginal young people rather than 'report' (a form of summons) them, and was not dependent on the nature of the offence, number of charges, prior record or socio-demographic variables (Gale et al. 1990: 81–90).

A comprehensive statistical analysis of police use of discretion to proceed by way of arrest rather than utilise less punitive forms of intervention has been produced by Gale and her colleagues. During one twelve-month period, 48 per cent of Aboriginal juvenile appearances were brought about by arrest rather than by reporting. These figures compared with 17 per cent of appearances by way of arrest for non-Aboriginal youth (Gale et al. 1990: 70). The authors analysed the link between the decision to arrest and a range of other legal and socio-economic factors. They concluded that no single factor could adequately account for the disparity in the method of apprehension by police.

It was found that Aboriginal youth with the same social, residential and demographic characteristics as non-Aboriginal youth were more likely to be proceeded with by way of arrest than non-Aboriginal youth. In other words, even where the socio-demographic characteristics were the same between the two groups, the outcomes were different. This was explained, however, by the differing criminal histories: Aboriginal youth were more likely to have multiple charges and a record of prior appearances. According to Gale, this was not necessarily an indication that Aboriginal young people offended differently. However, it did demonstrate the enormous differences in the charges laid and in the frequency with which Aboriginal young people come under official notice (Gale et al. 1990: 75). The variations in charge patterns may indicate police discrimination at the pre-arrest stage. 'What on the surface seems to be a valid police response to a particular person's behaviour may actually conceal discriminatory practices. Indeed, the primary shortcoming of officially recorded crime statistics is that there is no reason to assume that they accurately reflect actual patterns of offending behaviour' (Gale et al. 1990: 78–9).

Ultimately, the authors argue that two sets of factors are the prime determinants of the higher arrest rates of Aboriginal youth. The first set relates to the law. 'When deciding whether to arrest a young person, police may be influenced, whether consciously or otherwise, by the nature and number of offence charges and his or her prior appearance record' (Gale et al. 1990: 76). The second set of factors affecting arrest relates to the lower socio-economic status of Aboriginal young people. The authors argue that unemployment and residential household arrangements influence police decisions as to whether to proceed by way of arrest. Such criteria act to the detriment of Aboriginal youth, because they are more likely to be unemployed and less likely to live in nuclear families. In other words, they are less likely to comply with definitions of social normality.

COURT DECISION-MAKING

Aboriginal young people definitely have a greater chance of being sent to an institution than do non-Aboriginal offenders who appear in court. Similar evidence is available from Western Australia, South Australia and New South Wales, consistently showing that Aboriginal youth receive a greater proportion of custodial sentences than their non-indigenous counterparts (Broadhurst, Ferrante & Susilo 1991: 74; Gale et al. 1990: 107). For instance in New South Wales, 12 per cent of Aboriginal court outcomes resulted in detention compared to 6 per cent of non-Aboriginal court outcomes (Luke & Cunneen 1993: 265).

The key question then is, why does the Children's Court sentence proportionately more Aboriginal young people to detention centres? The simplest explanation would be that Aboriginal young people commit more serious offences. However, the South Australian research showed that differences in penalties remained even when specific charges were analysed. Thus Aboriginal young people were twice as likely as non-indigenous young people to receive a court outcome of detention for break, enter and steal, for assault, etc. It was not the specific offence which determined the penalty (Gale et al. 1990: 109). The major determinant influencing penalty was the young person's prior offending record. However, unemployment and family structure were also relevant, with those who were unemployed and living in a non-nuclear family being more likely to receive a custodial sentence. Research in New South Wales has reached similar conclusions in relation to the importance of prior criminal record. When differences in criminal record were controlled for, there were no significant differences in the percentage of Aboriginal and non-Aboriginal young people given a detention order (Luke & Cunneen 1993: 266).

At the other end of the sentencing scale, it has also been shown that Aboriginal young people are more likely to have their cases discharged. In South Australia 32 per cent of Aboriginal cases were discharged, compared to 27 per cent of non-Aboriginal juvenile cases (Gale et al. 1990: 107–9). The large number of cases which are discharged by the court suggests that many of these young people should not have been sent to court in the first place, but rather should have been given some diversionary option. A further issue of importance is that, although the offence is discharged by the court, the matter is still regarded as proven and the young person obtains a criminal record for the offence (Gale et al. 1990: 107). Ironically, what may appear as a lenient court outcome still contributes to the overall process of criminalisation, particularly since we have identified prior record as a key determinant in the decision of the court to incarcerate.

Children's Court magistrates are guided when sentencing by the social background reports on young offenders which are prepared by welfare and juvenile justice officers. Australian research shows that in about three-quarters of cases the recommendations of these reports are followed by magistrates (Seymour 1988: 332). Specific research relating to Aboriginal young people indicates that social background reports are more likely to be ordered when the young person is indigenous (Gale et al. 1990: 101).

From the late 1970s there has been considerable criticism of the ethnocentric nature of the reports and the psychological tests which were administered (Milne & Munro 1981). The reports gave free rein to prejudices in relation to Aboriginal culture, family life and child-rearing practices through descriptions of 'dysfunctional families' and 'bad home environment' (Gale et al. 1990: 102; Carrington 1993: 48). The following are two extracts from psychological reports on Aboriginal young people.

> Alan is an overweight, aboriginal lad of borderline retarded intelligence . . . He has a rather deprived background with poor parental controls.

> Raymond is a dull, unresponsive lad with poor social and expressive skills (Milne & Munro 1981: Appendix A).

Psychological testing gave an apparent objective measurement of cognitive, educational, social and emotional factors. Yet the tests themselves reflected the norms of the dominant culture and provided 'scientific' evidence that the Aboriginal young person was maladjusted or mentally retarded. In other words, although these 'scientific' tests were not overtly racist, they rested on assumptions about social normality which had the effect of constructing Aboriginal and Torres Strait Islander cultures as abnormal. Milne and Munro (1981: 14–19) analysed the psychological tests and assessments administered to Aboriginal young people entering detention centres in New South Wales, including multiple matrix tests, verbal intelligence tests and verbal interviews. They were critical of a range of factors inherent in the tests, of the procedures which were used, and of the attitudes of those administering the tests.

Much of research on social background reports relates to the period of the late 1970s and early 1980s. There may have been some reduction of the racist assumptions underlying reports—particularly in those jurisdictions which have begun to employ Aboriginal people as juvenile justice officers. However, it is worth considering a recent list of assumptions said to underlie the writing of some pre-sentence reports for Aboriginal adults in New South Wales. These assumptions included: that Aboriginal people have equal access to services, but lack the ability to take advantage of opportunities; that Aboriginal people are lazy and do not want to work; that there is such a person as a 'part-Aboriginal' and that a person must be black to be Aboriginal; that Aboriginal people are shy, reticent and non-communicative; and that Aboriginal people have no culture left (Ozols 1994: 3). It is unlikely that similar assumptions have disappeared from the juvenile arena.

ACCUMULATING A CRIMINAL RECORD

We have indicated the importance of prior record in determining sentencing outcomes. A number of factors are important in understanding the accumulation of prior records among Aboriginal young people. Various studies have shown that intervention occurs earlier with Aboriginal young people. As a result, Aboriginal young people receive a criminal record at an earlier age. For instance, 27 per cent of Aboriginal young people who were cautioned or brought before the courts in New South Wales in 1990 were fourteen years or younger, compared to 19 per cent of non-indigenous youth (Luke & Cunneen 1993: 259, see also Cunneen & Robb 1987: 141; Gale et al. 1990: 56). In Western Australia, Aboriginal over-representation is greatest among younger age groups. Indeed, three out of every four girls under fourteen years arrested by police are Aboriginal, and two out of every three boys under fourteen years arrested are Aboriginal (adapted from Broadhurst, Ferrante & Susilo 1991: 44–6).

Given what we have already established in relation to the adverse use of police discretion and the figures on early intervention, it is not surprising that Aboriginal young people develop extensive criminal records. Police decisions made at the time of apprehension have a compounding effect through the system. The process has been summarised as follows.

> The initial decision made by police at the very gateway into the formal justice system—whether to arrest or summons a child—had significant repercussions for the child's subsequent passage through the system. More specifically, the very fact of being arrested rather than reported by police proved to be one of the main determinants of a referral to Court, with all the negative consequences which that entailed.

The fact of being referred to Court usually resulted in the young person's acquisition of a criminal record, which in turn, was a primary determinant of the Court's decision to sentence him or her to detention (Gale et al. 1990: 6–7).

The most crucial decisions in relation to a young person are often made by the least experienced police officers. Decisions with the most far-reaching effects are made at the lowest levels, where there is the most likelihood of community prejudices relating to race and ethnicity (Gale et al. 1990: 121). In addition to these initial decisions compounding through the system, there is the added momentum that once a young person has come under notice they are likely to be subjected to a high level of surveillance—in other words they become 'known to police'.

Police decisions about Aboriginal young people also need to be put in the much wider context of the relations between Aboriginal and Torres Strait Islander people and non-indigenous Australian society. We have already discussed in this chapter the historical function of policing within a colonial context. It is also important to consider the function of policing within the contemporary context of neo-colonial or post-colonial relations in Australia. We have dealt with this issue at length elsewhere (Cunneen 1994: 128–58) and it is appropriate here simply to refer to the salient features.

From the colonial period, the focus of intervention included both the public and private spheres of Aboriginal life. Indeed, an important part of the colonial experience was the denial to Aboriginal people of a private sphere removed from official scrutiny. Police and others administering welfare policy were imbued with racist assumptions concerning the incompetence of Aboriginal families to care for and nurture their young.

In the period since World War II this historical legacy has been combined with the construction of Aboriginal young people as criminals—as a law-and-order problem. The identification of Aboriginal young people as a 'crime problem' has re-emphasised the role of public order policing. It is the policing of indigenous young people in public places which has led to ongoing complaints concerning harassment and over-policing. There has been the development of punitive legislation, such as the New South Wales *Summary Offences Act 1988* and the Western Australian *Crime (Serious and Repeat Offenders) Act 1992*, which facilitates particular policing styles and which differentially and adversely impacts on Aboriginal young people. In addition there have been continual complaints concerning the use of violence and excessive force against Aboriginal young people by police during arrest and interrogation (Cunneen 1990b).

A further dynamic has been the pressure placed on police in particular areas to take a proactive role in containment strategies. These pressures derive from local business and political interests which have a stake in punitive enforcement strategies, and they may provide some explanation for variations in the level of

Aboriginal over-representation in court appearances between different areas (Chisholm 1984). Certainly, local non-Aboriginal powerbrokers can directly influence the nature of police intervention (Cunneen 1990a; Goodall 1990b).

RESPONSES

The Royal Commission into Aboriginal Deaths in Custody dealt extensively with the issue of Aboriginal and Torres Strait Islander young people in the juvenile justice system. Many of the recommendations put forward were designed to deal with the issues raised in this chapter. They included greater use of summons and diversionary mechanisms, realistic bail conditions, and the establishment of bail hostels. In addition, many of the general recommendations made in relation to police and custodial authorities, if implemented, would have a positive impact on indigenous young people. A fundamental recommendation in relation to young people was that authorities should negotiate with Aboriginal communities on the causes of offending in order to develop suitable responses.

Most States maintain that they are responding to Aboriginal over-representation in the system by implementing the Royal Commission recommendations and by developing a range of programs, including the employment of Aboriginal community workers, the development of Aboriginal community responses, and specific alternatives to custody such as bail hostels (Crawford-Maher 1993: 5). In Victoria, the government response has focused on providing local communities with resources to develop alternatives to incarceration under the Koori Justice Project. Some local programs have included restoration of sacred sites, elders teaching culture and history, and Aboriginal artists providing tuition in music, dance and painting (Ghys 1994).

In recognition of the high numbers of Aboriginal young people in detention centres, some States have introduced Aboriginal and Torres Strait Islander cultural programs for detainees. Queensland, for example, has recently established the Community and Culture Integration Program. Despite the fact that, on average, half the State's inmates have been Aboriginal or Torres Strait Islander, there has been no culturally specific program until recently (Jackomos 1994: 2).

Despite the development of programs in various States, there has been far less movement towards negotiation with communities about suitable responses. In this context it is worth considering what Aboriginal and Torres Strait Islander people have been doing in response to offending by young people. By their nature, Aboriginal responses have tended to be based in communities or regions. One example of a regional response is the Petford Training Farm in northern Queensland, which takes Aboriginal young people (predominantly male) from the communities of Cape York and around the Cairns area. The farm accepts the most serious and chronic offenders—those who have already been institutionalised or who are facing such an outcome. The farm runs courses in animal husbandry, farm mechanics, etc. The program is generally regarded as highly successful (Venables 1988: 8–10).

In many parts of Australia where communities have access to land, outstations have developed. These outstations provide the opportunity for Aboriginal elders to work, away from settlements, with young people convicted of offences. One example of a scheme utilising outstations is the Walgut Kuba Laga scheme on Mornington Island. With support from local police and the visiting magistrate, Aboriginal elders have devised and enforced sanctions for young offenders which are culturally appropriate.

There has been no lack of initiative among Aboriginal communities and organisations to deal with Aboriginal young people within the context of their own communities. What has been, and remains, a problem is that any initiatives are ultimately dependent on non-Aboriginal goodwill. Informal mechanisms without legislative support depend on the co-operation of police and magistrates. Other schemes depend on the funding and referral of juvenile justice agencies. For instance, an innovative Aboriginal-run program for young offenders called the Lake Jasper project was defunded by the Western Australian government along with other schemes (e.g., driver training) which targeted indigenous young people. These funding cuts have occurred at a time when the Western Australian government has proved incapable of reducing the worst incarceration rates of Aboriginal young people in Australia (Jackson 1994).

At a basic level, the problem is that Aboriginal and Torres Strait Islander people have been denied the right to devise and implement their own justice mechanisms.

CONCLUSION

Aboriginal and Torres Strait Islander people have certain rights and entitlements as the indigenous people of Australia. The right to self-determination is one such right recognised in international law. Further rights specifically in relation to indigenous children can be found in the United Nations *Convention on the Rights of the Child*. A fundamental area for the application of self-determination is juvenile justice policy. The development of self-determination in this area must include the right to determine basic questions in relation to law, enforcement strategies and the application of sanctions.

At the moment there is little or no recognition of the principle of self-determination in the delivery of juvenile justice services for Aboriginal young people. To a large extent, the dominant rhetoric is of 'disadvantage'—that is Aboriginal and Torres Strait Islander young people are disadvantaged by the system. The Aboriginal and Torres Strait Islander Social Justice Commissioner, Mick Dodson, has argued that policies and programs which derive from a perception of disadvantage often have the result of reinforcing the powerlessness of the recipients. They are perceived to have been *given* justice rather than receiving their rights and entitlements (Dodson 1993). Clearly, in the context of juvenile justice, the implied right of indigenous people is to develop their own system of social regulation.

In view of the rights of indigenous people, it must be acknowledged that non-indigenous interventions in juvenile justice, both historical and contemporary, have been a dismal failure. Even current programs and policy initiatives have some sense of *déja vu* about them. Two decades ago, the then Commonwealth Department of Aboriginal Affairs organised a national symposium to discuss the care and treatment of indigenous young people in correctional institutions. The symposium recognised that Aboriginal over-representation in institutions was a significant problem (Sommerlad 1977: 5). Contemporary figures seem to indicate that it has got worse. The various States that were represented gave details of 'innovative administrative responses'—many of which amounted to employing Aboriginal people in the relevant departments and liaising more closely with Aboriginal organisations (Sommerlad 1977: 79).

Frantz Fanon (1967) has written about the way the coloniser creates the 'native' as an inferior and subjected being. It is worth extrapolating to consider the extent to which the mainstream juvenile justice system creates the indigenous juvenile delinquent. Certainly, there are discriminatory practices which criminalise indigenous young people. In addition, Aboriginal young people are identified as a law-and-order problem. Continual representations of indigenous youth as criminals legitimises intervention and reinforces assumptions concerning the homogeneity and uniformity of 'Aboriginal youth' (Palmer & Collard 1993: 22). The only credible way of breaking out of the destructive relationship between juvenile justice agencies and indigenous young people is to facilitate the move to control by Aboriginal and Torres Strait Islander communities.

8 young women and the role of gender

The purpose of this chapter is threefold. Firstly, we want to analyse specific issues relating to girls and juvenile justice. We are aware of the risk of marginalising girls' issues by this approach—after all, the entire spectrum of discussion in a book on juvenile justice must acknowledge that clients and personnel consist of males and females. However, in terms of *specific* issues affecting girls there is some merit in dealing with the discussion separately. Secondly, we want to pose the broader question of how gender is related to juvenile justice. A discussion of gender inevitably involves a consideration of masculinity. Finally, we want to consider the extent to which masculinity and femininity as social and psychological constructs determine the nature of the interaction with juvenile justice agencies.

These questions have become increasingly important over the last two decades as feminist criminologists have challenged the male-centredness of the criminological enterprise. Feminists have made women visible as victims and offenders within criminology. Feminists have challenged criminology with the demand to consider gender relations as necessarily implying a focus on masculinity as well as femininity (Gelsthorpe & Morris 1990: 3–4).

From the point of view of criminological research generally, it is important to acknowledge that criticism relates to not only the subject of analysis, but to the method of analysis as well (White 1990). For example, it has been pointed out that a specific focus on young men, or young women, is not necessarily the main issue. Gender bias resides at the level of explanation, as well as at the substantive empirical level. Furthermore, greater attention needs to be directed not only at the nature of 'femininity' or 'masculinity' in explaining system discrimination or the gendered patterns of crime. We must also examine the relationship of each social construct to the other, how 'masculine' practices shape existing male behaviour toward young women, and how 'femininity' is actively used and shaped by girls in negotiating their way in a male-dominated social world.

Although they are beyond the scope of the present work, we also view as very important further analysis of the material constraints and opportunities available to either sex as shaped by wider social processes. Issues of parental control, the use of public space, the means by which different groups of young people communicate with each other, income and employment opportunities, and availability of sex-specific services all have an impact on youth behaviour and attitudes (see, for example, White 1990, 1993a; Carrington 1989, 1993). An understanding of gender demands both an analysis of the ideological construction of 'difference' between the sexes based upon biological features, and an examination of the real, material differences in power relationships, economic resources and cultural forms.

One indication of these material differences is provided in Table 8.1, which shows the different participation of females and males at various levels of juvenile justice and welfare intervention. The figures come from New South Wales. They represent common findings in relation to differences between males and females. Boys are about six times more likely to have a proven criminal charge before the courts. In relation to criminal matters, the participation of girls decreases further into the system. Thus, they represent 22 per cent of police cautions, 14 per cent of proven criminal matters and 6 per cent of custodial outcomes. Representation for welfare matters is roughly even for boys and girls— both for proven matters and for committal to care.

Table 8.1 Police cautions and Children's Courts determinations, New South Wales, 1990

Determination	Female		Male		Total
	n	%	n	%	n
Police cautions	557	22	2 009	78	2 566
Proven criminal matters	2 117	14	12 540	86	14 657
Custodial outcome for criminal matter[a]	49	6	720	94	769
Proven welfare matters	526	49	556	51	1 082
Committed to care for welfare matter	255	48	277	52	532

a Custodial figures relate to 1992–93 from New South Wales Department of Juvenile Justice (1993: 1–3).

Source: NSW Bureau of Crime Statistics and Research (1990: 51, 54, 61).

EARLY FEMINIST RESEARCH ON YOUNG WOMEN

Understanding the different position of young women and young men in the juvenile justice system requires analysis which allows for the specificity of experience of each group. The fact that the system is by and large oriented toward young men has fundamentally shaped its institutions, programs and objectives along masculine lines. This has a number of implications with regard to how we explain the presence of young female offenders in the first place (given the overall gender bias of the system), and how the state has constructed and responded to female youth crime.

Early feminist research was concerned with a number of key issues in the analysis of young women and the juvenile justice system. A major issue was the apparent preoccupation by juvenile justice agencies with the sexuality of girls and young women and with so-called 'inappropriate' female behaviour. The process was referred to as the **sexualisation of delinquency**. The analysis was based upon an examination and critique of traditional notions of 'a woman's place' in society. Femininity as a social construct defined women primarily in terms of their location in the private sphere of the home; their dependent relationship to men as daughter, wife or mother; their social role as child-carer, housekeeper and sexual object; and their emotional state as 'naturally' caring, passive and excitable. Young women who did not conform to the ideals of chastity before marriage, subservience to the male figure, and convention (defined in terms of biological and social roles) were particular targets for state intervention.

Issues surrounding the regulation of 'femininity' were linked in feminist analysis to the question of whether girls and young women were subjected to more punitive intervention than boys by juvenile justice agencies, including welfare personnel, police and magistrates. It was argued that girls were more likely than boys to come into the juvenile justice system as a result of welfare complaints or status offences, such as being exposed to moral danger. A variety of studies during the 1970s and 1980s by Chesney-Lind (1974), Shacklady-Smith (1978), Casburn (1979), Sarri (1983) and others sought to demonstrate the apparent differences in treatment. There have been several parts to the argument of differential treatment. Firstly, it is argued that girls' sexual behaviour is scrutinised by juvenile justice agencies in a way that boys' sexual behaviour is not. Secondly, it is argued that other non-sexual behaviours or offences by girls are either overlooked or redefined as status offences relating to moral danger. Thirdly, there is a preoccupation with defining and maintaining the boundaries of what is *appropriate* behaviour for girls. An example of the research is that of Chesney-Lind (1974) who found that 70–80 per cent of young women compared to 1–10 per cent of young men were given medical examinations prior to their appearance in the Children's Court. Doctors' reports commented upon the apparent sexual experience of the girls even though this may have been unrelated to the offence. In summary, the early research in the area indicated that there was a preoccupation by authorities with the sexuality of girls; girls' behaviour was sometimes redefined as sexual and girls were more likely than boys to come into the juvenile justice system for status offences.

One initial point of intervention is the police. Generally, studies of police behaviour have not examined the role of gender in police decision-making. However, evidence from England and Wales showed that girls were more likely than boys to receive a police caution and be diverted (Morris 1987: 96). Alder cites American research which suggested that the sex of an individual affected police decision-making (Alder 1994: 160). It is important to recognise, however, that differential treatment can reflect the commission of less frequent and less serious offences by girls than by boys.

Gelsthorpe noted that police dealing with juveniles in an English police station viewed boys' and girls' offending patterns differently and along stereotypical lines: girls engaged in shoplifting and boys engaged in car theft. An analysis of offences at the station revealed that boys and girls shoplifted equally and that girls were involved in a wide range of offences (cited in Alder 1994: 161). It has been suggested that girls who do commit offences outside the boundaries of defined 'feminine behaviour' can expect to receive greater disapproval and more harsh treatment (Youth Justice Coalition 1990: 26). Alder cites other American research which suggested that police officers respond to young women on the basis of their image, rather than the offence they have committed. The demeanour of a young person very much influences police use of discretion (see Chapter 10). And it is apparent that assumptions concerning appropriate demeanour and image are mediated by gender-based expectations.

In Australia, Hancock noted that police reports on juveniles were more likely to explicitly refer to sexual history in the case of girls (29 per cent) than to boys (1 per cent). The sexual and moral activities were cited in police reports in 40 per cent of female court appearances and 5 per cent of male court appearances. Alleged promiscuity was seen as one reason for intervention (Hancock & Chesney-Lind 1982: 112). Alder notes that overseas research indicates that the overall assessment of 'immorality' is determined by a range of factors beyond alleged sexual experience (Alder 1994: 165). The work by Hancock draws attention to social variables such as attitude and co-operation with authority, 'credibility' and home situation, as well as 'moral reputation' (1980: 10). The activities that were commented upon in police reports for complaints of 'exposed to moral danger' included under-age drinking, hitch-hiking, living away from home, or being in the company of undesirable persons. Hancock also noted the importance of the relationship between class and gender. 'Those females who are most likely to be affected by a moralistic/welfare definition of the charge and thus presented on a "protection application" are working class females whose behaviour is more likely to bring them to police notice . . .' (Hancock 1980: 11).

A further area of concern has been the nature of punishment used in the case of young women. This has included not only the use of diversion but also sentencing by the courts. Alder (1984) has noted that, while girls appear to be disproportionately involved in diversion programs, they tend to be diverted for minor forms of misconduct. An unanticipated consequence of the expansion of diversionary schemes has been to draw more girls into processing by the juvenile justice system for non-serious matters. Diversion has occurred for matters which would not normally have been dealt with formally by the juvenile justice system in any case.

There have been at least two aspects to the question of sentencing. Firstly, there has been a questioning of the sentencing rationales used for young women. Morris (1987) cited an English study of the use of secure detention for girls which showed that, during a twelve-month period, of thirty-two girls placed in an institution, eight were there for 'delinquent' behaviour and the rest for truanting, neglect, moral danger and other status offences. The major reason for the secure placement was absconding. The reason the social workers sought a secure environment was because they believed protection was needed for the girls (Morris 1987: 95). The issue of 'protective custody' will be discussed further below.

Secondly, it has been argued that girls receive harsher sentencing outcomes than boys for status offences, and less severe sentencing outcomes for delinquent or criminal matters. However, it has also been noted that these findings have often been made without adequate controls (Morris 1987: 97). Research in this area requires the use of control variables, such as offence type, prior record, bail, and mode of intervention (summons, arrest, etc). Research in Australia which has used control variables found that girls were less likely to be arrested, less likely to be sent to the Children's Court, and more likely to be discharged (Wundersitz, Naffine & Gale 1988).

Parker, Casburn and Turnbull (1981) argued that girls in Britain were treated differently by magistrates when charged with the same offence. The difference in treatment usually resulted in greater intervention, such as the use of supervision orders rather than fines. Similar findings have been made in Australia (see Wundersitz, Naffine & Gale 1988). Datesman and Scarpitti (1980) found that girls were given more severe dispositions for status offences (especially for repeat offenders), and boys were given more severe dispositions for criminal matters. Hancock (1980) found similar results in Victoria when analysing welfare matters and specific criminal offences such as break, enter and steal. In the research by Datesman and Scarpitti, however, the discrepancies were less apparent for black girls: they received more severe sanctions than white girls for criminal matters and less severe sanctions than white girls for status offences. The research appears to indicate that issues of race and ethnicity impact on sentencing decisions as much as gender.

In Australia, Carrington (1993: 25–7) has argued against simplistic interpretations of the data by suggesting that both girls and boys who appear before the Children's Courts on welfare matters are likely to receive harsher dispositions than those who appear on criminal matters. Two issues need to be explained: why is the means by which a young person is brought before the court so important, and why are welfare cases treated more harshly? Carrington suggests that, because welfare matters are more likely to be guided by social and psychological discourses which justify early and long periods of intervention, the outcomes are more likely to be punitive.

A further issue which has been explored is the extent to which young women appear before the courts either for welfare or criminal matters. Much of the early feminist work rested on the observation that girls were more likely to appear in Children's Court on a welfare complaint or status offence rather than a criminal charge. While acknowledging variations between States, during the 1970s a large proportion of girls brought before the courts were there as a result of welfare complaints. In fact, in some States such as New South Wales and Victoria, at least until the mid-1970s, the majority of girls in court were there for welfare-related matters (Hancock & Chesney-Lind 1985: 238).

However, the 1980s showed a clear decline in the use of welfare complaints against girls and an increase in the number of criminal matters. The vast majority of girls who now appear in court do so as a result of a criminal charge. As shown in Table 8.1, in 1990 in New South Wales girls were about four times more likely to appear in the Children's Court on criminal matters than on welfare matters (or care and protection orders, as they are now more frequently called). Increases in the number of cases going to Children's Court nevertheless warrant careful consideration. For example, due to a crackdown on fare evasion and misbehaviour on Public Transport Corporation property in the early 1990s there was a dramatic rise in the number of criminal cases brought before the Victorian Children's Court. Many of these cases were due to the inability of young offenders to pay hefty on-the-spot fines for various offences. The main impact of this prosecutorial zeal was felt among young women, as evidenced in figures which showed that PTC cases made up a higher proportion of Children's Court criminal cases against females than against males, and the prosecution of young women rose sharply to more than one-half of all cases in 1991 (O'Grady 1992).

It is worth considering the extent to which the decline in welfare complaints was influenced by feminist intervention into juvenile justice and welfare policy. Certainly, by the early 1980s, lawyers, social workers, academics and others working in the area were highly critical of the use of welfare complaints, such as uncontrollable or exposed to moral danger, against girls and young women. For example, Marrickville Legal Centre, which had a specialist children's legal section, opposed the use of 'uncontrollable' complaints against girls in a published policy paper (Miller 1983). The paper stated in part:

> Girls are subject to controls on their behaviour that are not applied to boys, especially in relation to their sexual development. Further, girls are more often the victims of sexual abuse within the family than boys. In our experience these two factors feature predominantly in the case histories of girls on 'uncontrollable complaints' (Miller 1983: 1).

The later part of the 1980s saw administrative and legislative changes in many Australian States which separated welfare from criminal matters, and the withdrawal of complaints such as uncontrollable and exposed to moral danger. In New South Wales the Community Diversion Program in 1985 aimed to provide alternatives to incarceration (such as community service orders) and to separate welfare matters from criminal matters. Specifically in relation to girls, the diversion program was to encourage greater use of police cautions; discourage juvenile justice officers from recommending incarceration for minor offences; and discourage the setting of unrealistic bail conditions which could not be met by girls (Saville 1993: 293–4). Howe (1990) outlines the similar changes in Victoria. However, there are still important concerns relating to the incarceration of young women, and some of them are precisely the concerns that policy and legislative reform were supposed to have remedied. These will be discussed below.

A further issue which has been raised by feminists, but still not adequately addressed, is the relationship between unemployment and young women's involvement with juvenile justice agencies. The failure to address the issue itself reflects the assumption that employment and unemployment relate primarily to males. However, Alder (1986: 211) cites Australian research which indicated that young women were more concerned about unemployment than young men. Certainly, the impact of the changes in the labour market during the late 1970s and 1980s and the limitations on job opportunities have affected young women as well as young men. Alder's interviews with young women indicated that unemployment impacted on identity, on the ability to live independently of parents, and on the sense of hope and expectations for the future. While there was no simple relationship between unemployment and criminal activity, some of the young women interviewed by Alder had resorted to property offences such as shoplifting, while others saw drug and alcohol abuse as a means of coping (1986: 219–21).

More recent work has shown that the link between unemployment and crime needs to be considered as a gender-specific issue (Naffine & Gale 1989). Perhaps a more fruitful approach is to consider the survival strategies utilised by young women. The concept of survival strategies incorporates the interstices between the experiences of sexual and physical abuse, homelessness, inadequate welfare support, poverty, criminalisation, and unemployment and lack of job opportunities (Bargen 1994). Comments by young women in the juvenile justice system both in Australia (Alder 1993) and in the United States (Chesney-Lind & Shelden 1992) have stressed their need to establish independent lives, with economic independence, adequate long-term housing, and less dependence on social services. These comments imply a recognition of the potentially destructive outcomes of criminal or semi-criminal survival strategies which force young women into the net of juvenile justice.

CHALLENGING ESSENTIALISM

One of the most important changes to earlier feminist interpretations of juvenile justice has been the demand that issues of race, ethnicity and class be seen as intersecting with gender. Challenges to feminist essentialism developed during the 1980s and can be seen, for example, in the work of Eisenstein. She criticised the 'false universalism' which 'in spite of its narrow base of white middle class experience, purported to speak about and on behalf of all women, black or white, poor or rich' (1984: 134). Connell (1987: 59) also discussed the problems with a 'categorical' theory of gender. Gender essentialism gives primacy to the category of woman and presumes a shared interest of all women. In simple terms, women are the oppressed group and men are the oppressors. The effects of class, race or ethnicity are seen as subsidiary to the central category of sex. It should be noted that gender essentialism equally presumes the shared interest of all men as oppressors.

In the Australian context, it has been the omission of Aboriginal young women which has been the most obvious point of neglect in feminist analyses (Carrington 1993: 15). In the previous chapter we discussed the gendered forms of intervention in relation to Aboriginal young people. It is also worth considering that there is still a paucity of empirical data which considers specifically the issues relating to Aboriginal young women—although we know they continue to constitute a large proportion of institutional populations.

Similarly, with some exceptions (Hancock 1980; Carrington 1993), social class has not received the level of consideration it deserves in the contact between young women and juvenile justice. Some research has shown a positive correlation between appearances by girls and indicators of social disadvantage. More girls from working-class communities appear before the Children's Courts than from more affluent areas (Carrington 1993: 15). And, as noted above, Hancock's study indicated that class was related to police decisions about girls. There is a high incidence in our prisons of unemployed women, those with few formal educational qualifications and those institutionalised for low-level welfare fraud; this provides some indication of the class background of women who are likely to have ongoing contact with the criminal justice system.

One of the theoretical issues raised initially by Connell (1987), and taken up by Carrington (1993) specifically in relation to juvenile justice, is that essentialist notions of gender cannot be overcome simply by adding or incorporating class and race issues if these structures are also treated in a categorical or essentialist manner (Connell 1987: 59; Carrington 1993: 17). For instance, an understanding of the relationship between Aboriginal girls and juvenile justice and welfare agencies demands an analysis of the historically specific practices of those agencies. Whether the nature of the relationship overlaps or not with what happens to non-Aboriginal young women is an empirical question to be answered on the basis of research. It cannot be assumed by asserting the primacy of the social category of gender. As we have seen (Chapter 7), the fact that four out of ten Aboriginal girls compared to one out of ten non-Aboriginal girls are likely to have formal contact with juvenile justice agencies during their adolescence suggests a qualitatively different level of intervention.

Essentialist notions of gender also affect how we conceptualise men and masculinity. Judith Allen (1990) for example argues against the sex/gender distinction, (the distinction between the sex 'male' and the gender 'masculinity') because such a distinction removes analysis from men as a group. She asks 'What is it about men, not as working-class, not as migrant, not as underprivileged, but as men that induces them to commit crime?' (1990: 39). On the face of it, this is a powerful argument. However, other writers in the area, such as Connell (1987), argue that theories based on the sexual dichotomy of male/female cannot grasp the historicity of gender relations. In other words, gender is a historical formation open to change.

To put it simply, we can say that gender is, demonstrably, a learned role; it is not fixed according to biology, insofar as its actual behavioural content *varies* from society to society. The evidence of both historical analysis and cross-cultural study is that 'gender' (however it is defined in any particular society) can likewise be *altered*. Some indication that gender is open to change is provided in the various political struggles between progressives and conservatives over the specific relations, behaviours and attitudes that ideally should be associated with maleness and femaleness. Often the activist interventions from the Right and the Left include attempts to acquire social resources precisely in order to shape particular gender conceptions and behavioural patterns, either by maintaining, or by transforming, mainstream social institutions (for an example, one need only think of the debates over the definition of 'the family' throughout 1994).

History is also important if we are to understand class and other social relations, which may impact on a person as much as, or more than, their gender at a given moment. These arguments have particular application to juvenile justice. For example, as discussed in the previous chapter, the intersections between race, gender and juvenile justice have changed during the twentieth century in Australia. The earlier focus of government was on the removal of (mainly) Aboriginal girls through a protection and welfare approach. There is a contemporary law-and-order focus primarily on Aboriginal boys through the process of criminalisation. Another area demanding concrete historical and social research is the way specific cultural groups of young women are over-represented in detention centre figures. For instance there has been the relatively recent growth in numbers of Indo-Chinese and Pacific Islander girls who are incarcerated.

A move away from gender essentialism also opens up the terrain to a discussion of masculinities. We will return to this point later in the chapter, but note now that it is probably fair to say that 'criminological theory has not yet begun to recognize the hegemonic masculinity of its central concepts nor, therefore, to revise its deep-seated androcentrism' (Sumner 1990: 27). Certainly, in discussions of juvenile justice, masculinity by and large remains unproblematised. The issue of masculinity is invisible.

GIRLS IN THE JUVENILE JUSTICE SYSTEM

We have indicated some of the broad explanations as to how and why girls come into contact with juvenile justice agencies. A critical focus has been on the treatment by juvenile justice agencies of young women, particularly in arguments about the way the system apparently sexualises girls' behaviour to facilitate intervention. We have also indicated the importance of social class, race and ethnicity in determining the likelihood of intervention. Some of these broad social relations, like class and race, also apply to boys and their contact with juvenile justice agencies.

We also need to understand what other factors increase the likelihood that some girls within this broader framework will be drawn into the juvenile justice net. There is a range of social conditions that increase the likelihood of contact with juvenile justice agencies, such as inadequate accommodation, family breakdown and abuse, and unemployment. These social conditions may impact differently upon girls and young women compared to boys. For instance, homelessness and the strategies developed to deal with it may be different for girls and boys.

Certainly, Australian studies have outlined the connections between violence, family break-up, negative contact with welfare agencies and police, and the move from welfare needs to eventual criminalisation (Women's Co-ordination Unit 1986). The following is a summary of the key issues.

- In the past, girls have been more likely than boys to come before the court the first time for welfare reasons rather than for criminal charges. Although the use of welfare complaints has decreased, the link between welfare and criminalisation is still strong.
- Girls are sometimes charged with a minor criminal offence when police are been called to respond to a domestic conflict.
- Girls in state care who rebel against the institutional regime may be reported to the police by staff responsible for their care, charged with a criminal offence and transferred to a detention centre.
- Girls who are state wards are forty times more likely to be detained in custody than other girls. Boys who are state wards are seventeen times more likely to be detained than other boys.

- Girls who are state wards are frequently unable to meet the bail conditions regarding an approved place of residence and, by default, remain in detention.
- Studies have found that girls charged with criminal offences have a history of being abused at home.
- A large proportion of the girls before the courts for criminal matters are dependent on drugs (adapted from New South Wales Standing Committee on Social Issues 1992: 53–4).

It has been noted that the lack of safe and supportive accommodation is an important factor in bringing girls before the courts on both welfare and criminal matters (Women's Co-ordination Unit 1986). The New South Wales Standing Committee on Social Issues (1992) noted that life on the streets for homeless girls is more dangerous than for boys, and there is greater vulnerability to drug abuse and self-destructive behaviour. A large proportion of girls came into the juvenile justice system because of welfare-related issues which themselves arose from abuse or neglect at home (New South Wales Standing Committee on Social Issues 1992: 35). It was estimated that between 80 per cent and 90 per cent of girls in detention centres had been abused. A similar proportion was dependent on drugs (New South Wales Standing Committee on Social Issues 1992: 139). Drug dependency has also been related to recidivism and, for a number of girls released from detention, death from drug overdoses. Between May 1990 and January 1991, six young women died from drug overdoses after leaving juvenile justice custody in Sydney. Four of the six were Aboriginal (Bargen 1994: 122). The inability of detention centres to deal with drug dependency has been a focus of concern.

Much of the recent policy development in relation to girls has focused on the special needs of female offenders once they are in the system. It has been noted that young women in custody live in an environment which is heavily dominated by a male culture: over 90 per cent of detention centre inmates are male, the majority of the staff are male, and there are few women in senior management positions. There are few positive female role models for girls in custody. Furthermore, there has been no staff training on the special needs of young women (New South Wales Juvenile Justice Advisory Council 1993: 189).

Various committees and inquiries have considered issues relating to girls and young women in the juvenile justice system. Recommendations have centred on:

- specific counselling for sexual and other forms of abuse
- specific counselling for drug and alcohol dependencies
- assistance with accommodation
- assistance with finding employment

- pre-release and post-release schemes specifically for young women
- more women with specialist training to staff detention centres specifically catering for girls.

Given the above discussion, it is important to consider the profile of girls who are in detention centres. The following summary is based on a survey of twenty-five girls held in New South Wales detention centres on 13 April 1993 (Cain 1994a: 28–38) as well as a preliminary survey of 469 young women admitted to custody in New South Wales over an eleven-month period between 1992 and 1993 (Cozens 1993: 2).

Of the twenty-five girls in detention centres on 13 April 1993, nine were on remand and sixteen had been sentenced. The girls were held in custody for a range of offences, including assaults (6), malicious wounding (5), armed robbery (1), assault and rob (1), robbery (1), drug trafficking and possession (3), break and enter (1), motor vehicle theft (1), receiving stolen goods (1), escapes (2), and breach of previous court orders (3).

It appears that offences against the person (crimes of violence) are the major reason for incarceration. As explained previously (Chapter 5), however, it is difficult to make any statement concerning the seriousness or otherwise of these offences simply on the basis of the legal categories employed. Another issue of importance is that static census surveys taken on a single day overestimate the number of persons serving longer sentences (presumably for more serious offences). These surveys give no indication of the volume of traffic through detention centres. In contrast, the Cozens survey covering an eleven-month period showed that 39 per cent of girls detained had been charged with break and enter or other theft offences; the second-largest category was offences against good order (23 per cent); and the third category was offences against the person (17 per cent) (1993: 15). The relevance of this data is that it shows that crimes of violence account for a relatively small proportion of those incarcerated. The majority of girls are detained for property or good order offences.

Detention figures show that ethnicity is an important issue. Ten of the twenty-five girls were recorded as coming from an Anglo-Australian background, seven were Aboriginal and eight girls were from non-English speaking backgrounds. The Cozens survey also indicated a significant proportion of girls from 'Island' background (4.9 per cent) and 'Asian' background (4.3 per cent) (1993: 2).

All of the sixteen girls sentenced to detention had prior criminal convictions, while seven of the nine on remand had previous criminal convictions. Eleven of the twenty-five girls in detention centres had been previously sentenced to detention. We can make some conclusions concerning process from this information. At any one time, there are few girls in detention who have not been previously convicted of an offence, and almost half have been previously institutionalised. As a group, these young women have experienced contact, and in some cases extensive contact, with juvenile justice agencies.

Previous contact with authorities in relation to welfare matters is also of some importance. Seven of the twenty-five girls had first appeared in court in relation to welfare matters. Three had been institutionalised as state wards. The Cozens survey indicated that, in detention centres, girls were twice as likely as boys to be state wards (9.3 per cent compared to 4.6 per cent).

Cozens identified a number of broad issues arising from the survey of girls in detention centres. Firstly, there were 'links between the welfare needs of young women, the progression into crime and the difficulties of escaping the juvenile justice system' (1993: 9). The issue of wardship and early intervention on welfare matters is still apparent. Proportionately more females than males in custody are likely to be wards, and at least for some girls their first contact with the Children's Court is through a welfare complaint. However, these girls are not the majority. It needs to be recognised here that in the future fewer girls will have been first detained as a result of a welfare complaint. The separation of welfare and justice administration and the removal of welfare complaints such as 'uncontrollable' and 'exposed to moral danger' from the statutes have led to a relative decline in this form of intervention. This change does not necessarily mean that girls will cease to be institutionalised; rather we are witnessing a long-term transformation in the mode of intervention. The transformation is from welfarisation to criminalisation.

Thus it seems apparent that increasingly young women's contact with the justice system will be through the criminalisation process. It is possible to see how criminalisation replaces welfare intervention through the following processes: bail refusal, conditions relating to bail and probation, and the use of offences against good order. It should be noted that at least some of the issues, such as bail, were already the subject of concern during the 1980s. It has been suggested that detention centres may be used inappropriately for young women who are homeless. Certainly, Cozens estimated that 25 per cent of young women held in remand did not in fact receive a sentence of imprisonment (1993: 9). Others have estimated that as many as 68 per cent of girls refused bail are not subsequently sentenced to detention (Youth Justice Coalition 1990: 281).

It has been noted that young women are more likely to be refused bail than young men (Youth Justice Coalition 1990: 281). Generally, there is a higher proportion of young women in detention centres who have been remanded in custody than is the case for young men. The New South Wales departmental figures indicate that 40 per cent or more of girls in custody are there on remand. The suggestion is that custodial remand is being used essentially as a substitute welfare measure and is seen in terms of protecting the interests of the young women. In this sense, one can see the continuities with the previous use of welfare matters (and their overlap with criminal matters) to incarcerate girls for 'their own good'.

The conditions which apply to bail and to probation and parole orders also need to be considered within the context of the continuities with earlier welfare intervention. These conditions typically include to be of good behaviour, to accept supervision from juvenile justice officers, to attend school or counselling as directed, to reside where approved, and not to attend to certain areas (such as Kings Cross, etc.). Breach of these conditions is a further criminal offence and may well lead to further incarceration.

It was noted above that 23 per cent of girls in custody during 1992–93 were held for offences against good order; comparatively, 12 per cent of boys were there for the same offence category. Offences against good order include both public order offences, such as offensive behaviour, offensive language and prostitution, and offences against justice procedures, such as breach of court orders and conditions. To the extent that these figures can be interpreted as showing process, there seem to be two related issues here: the criminalisation of welfare needs, and the use of incarceration within the framework of protection. Certainly, feminists considering these issues have shown that authorities—welfare officers, police and magistrates—continue to use custody as a means of 'protecting' girls from perceived risks associated with lifestyle (Moore 1994; Bargen 1994).

In terms of policy, it has been noted for many years that, unless there are community-based preventive and supervisory services available for girls, the unnecessary use of custody will continue (Women's Co-ordination Unit 1986). For girls in need of assistance because of homelessness, abuse or drug and alcohol problems, the choice facing agencies will be either neglect or enforced containment (Moore 1994: 5).

DEVELOPING PROGRAMS FOR YOUNG WOMEN IN CUSTODY

We have discussed some of the issues arising from the use of detention for young women. Many of the inquiries have specifically identified the special needs of young women in detention centres. A recent research project summed up the problems:

> Those girls interviewed by the Youth Justice Project were among the most distressed and resentful of all our respondents. A higher proportion of girls than boys in our sample had serious drug problems, for which there was little or no treatment available. Of the six girls from one detention centre interviewed for the Project, two girls had mutilated themselves ... There were a series of disturbances in this centre

during our period of research ... Ambulances and the police Tactical Response Group had been called in on [one] occasion (Youth Justice Coalition 1990: 314).

In response to the criticisms concerning girls in detention centres, there has been greater consideration of the nature of custody by juvenile justice authorities. In New South Wales a specific program has been developed, which recognises that the majority of girls in custody 'have been abused, subjected to discrimination and that systemic issues have impacted upon their lives' (Yasmar Juvenile Justice Centre 1994: 3). The detention centre established for girls aims to strengthen the girls' self-concepts and to empower them to manage their futures in a non-destructive manner. To achieve its objectives, the centre concentrates on providing a stable and therapeutic environment. To date there has been no evaluation. However, the program has been criticised for over-emphasis on individual change—despite the official recognition of structurally oppressive conditions. Indeed, the techniques being utilised, such as psychotherapy, are premised on the individual and her ability to effect change.

Moreover, the same level of resources has not been provided for non-custodial girl-specific support to achieve diversion from custody. Such programs might include day-attendance centres, short-term supportive accommodation and open custody programs (Moore 1994: 142). The resources are still focused on the custodial setting.

In Victoria, the CSV (Community Services Victoria, now Health and Community Services) released a specific policy on young women which, like the New South Wales policy, recognised structurally oppressive conditions. The policy was to 'help young women become independent in ways which recognise the inequalities which have shaped their development as children and young women and have impact on their ongoing opportunities for independent adulthood' (quoted in Alder 1993: 305). According to Alder (1993: 306–8), those who implement such a policy must understand and challenge several issues specific to young women, particularly the following.

- The workforce is still segregated along gender lines, so that it is difficult for young women to achieve economic independence.
- There are fundamental social assumptions about femininity which undermine achieving independence.
- Young women who have been institutionalised face particular stigmatisation.
- The previous sexual abuse of many girls who are institutionalised has to be sensitively understood and resolved in some form for the young women involved.
- There needs to be a sufficient range of services for young women despite their relatively small numbers in the juvenile justice system.

GENDER RELATIONS AND MASCULINITY

We have already mentioned that discussions of juvenile justice fail to address gender issues in a way that considers masculinity. We want to show how notions of masculinity are useful in discussing offending behaviour as well as the response by juvenile justice agencies. For instance, Brake (1985) comments that young men tend to see themselves in terms of masculinity, whereas young women are *judged* on their femininity. This implies a complex relationship to the social world around them, and significant differences in how young women and men engage with each other as well as with mainstream social institutions.

The idealised male sex-role is to be tough, competitive, emotionally inexpressive, public, active and autonomous. The specific content of these characterisations varies, however, depending upon the cultural, class, and ethnic background of the young men we are talking about. Thus, in stereotypical terms, a 'working-class male' might construe masculinity in terms of brute strength, physical attributes, competency in using one's body and machines (such as cars), and peer group solidarity. By way of contrast, a 'middle-class male' might exhibit masculinity through expressions of intellectual agility, a detached 'professional' attitude, performance of mental labour, and assertion of the importance of individual autonomy. The picture gets more complex once we start to explore the variety of masculinities that are shaped by cultural, national and ethnic backgrounds and histories (e.g., Greek, English, Aboriginal, Torres Strait Islander, Vietnamese, Chinese).

It has been shown already that boys make up the overwhelming majority of young people brought before the Children's Courts on criminal matters. During most of the twentieth century, those theories which attempted to explain male delinquency with respect to notions of masculinity tended to assume that gender relations were 'natural'; as a consequence, they often focused attention on the mother as a cause of male offending. This is because delinquency was seen to reside in the formation of masculinity itself: if young men were not socialised the right way, then they would not express their manhood in the appropriate manner. Some theorists such as Bowlby concentrated on explaining delinquency through maternal deprivation: delinquent behaviour could be understood as a form of compensation for inadequate mothering. Others explained forms of masculinity and delinquency as a compensation for too much mothering (Miller 1958). Delinquency and toughness became an expression of protest against maternal domination. Delinquents were thought to come from families where there was a weak or absent father—where the mother was effectively the household head. One can see that these theories, which on the face of it contradict one another, are based on tacit assumptions about the 'natural' family with a mother at home and a father as head. Deviations from the norm are held to cause delinquency. Such theories, although they attempt to explain male delinquency, still accept dominant gender relations (Cunneen 1985).

One approach to understanding masculinity is the notion that there is a **hegemonic masculinity** which is constructed in relation to various subordinated masculinities as well as in relation to women (Connell 1987: 183). The concept of a hegemonic masculinity is useful: it recognises that there is no one masculinity, but that there is a dominant masculinity which prescribes particular behaviour as normal and devalues other forms of behaviour. In reality, ethnic differences, generational differences, class patterns and sexual preference come into play in the construction of masculinities; however, these are subordinated to the dominant definition of what it is to be a 'man' (see Segal 1990; Connell 1987). Hegemonic masculinity emphasises male domination (and women's subordination), the sexual division of labour (in both the private and public spheres), and heterosexuality as the dominant, and exclusive, categorisation of male sexuality (rather than seeing heterosexuality and homosexuality as part of a sexual continuum).

The idealised male sex-role as defined in and by hegemonic masculinity is essentially built upon a contempt for women, and gays and lesbians, and which emphasises success in terms such as wealth, power and status, rather than in terms of meaningful and open relationships. In practice, being a man may involve a range of strategies designed to shape the behaviour of oneself and those around one in accordance with the ideal. For example, the activities of young men often parallel those of the criminal justice system in that they constantly police the behaviour of young women, both in terms of sex and sexuality and more generally with regard to what are deemed to be acceptable feminine behaviours (Nava 1984). Hegemonic masculinity is dependent upon, and implicated in, the enforcement of particular masculine *and* particular feminine modes of behaviour and social interaction.

The application of these theoretical insights has been almost totally lacking in considerations of juvenile justice and juvenile offending, although they have been useful in exploring the class and gender biases of the law in relation to the experiences of working-class men in court (Naffine 1990). Yet they promise insight into the nature of some types of male offending. For example, we could explore the specific nature of young men's offending behaviour (defined narrowly in terms of official violations of the law, rather than with regard to issues of sexism *per se*). We might examine the gender differences in the use of public spaces such as the street (where traditionally males have had a dominant presence), or look at the gendered dynamics of the so-called private sphere of the home (where there is differential regulation of girls' and boys' behaviour by parents). In each case, there are clear implications regarding opportunities, material resources, choices and group affinities, all of which can have an impact upon patterns of offending (White 1989, 1990).

For present purposes, however, we wish to illustrate the explanatory potential of such analysis by discussing three examples. The first issue is homophobia. A 1985 phone-in concerning violence against homosexuals revealed that the majority of attacks on gay men were carried out by teenage boys or young men. A recent Victorian survey of more than 1000 lesbians and gay men revealed that 70 per cent of lesbians and 69 per cent of gay men reported being verbally abused, threatened or assaulted in a public place (see also Lesbian and Gay Anti-Violence Project 1992 for discussion of New South Wales). One in five gay men reported actual physical assault in public places. The typical perpetrators were gangs of young men (GLAD 1994: 18–19). Overseas literature also stresses the participation of young males in assaults on gays (Comstock 1991). In Sydney, a number of murders of gay men have involved male juveniles. For example in 1990, eight young men aged between sixteen and eighteen years were responsible for the bashing and death of Richard Johnson in a Sydney park.

Interviews with attackers note their inability to accept and understand sexual attraction and affection between men (Herek & Berrill 1992). Connell has noted that this fact raises 'disturbing questions about the role of violence and homophobia in the construction of masculinity' (1987: 12). Those responsible for the deaths of gay men have often claimed they were simply 'out for some fun'. In this sense, we can see that homophobic assaults receive some social approval through the dominant definition of masculinity which devalues and disapproves of homosexuality.

A common way in which young men are brought before the courts is for offences related to motor vehicles, including theft. As we indicated earlier (Chapter 5), young males make up a large proportion of all people apprehended for motor vehicle theft. In previous work, we have drawn attention to the relationship between the expression of masculinity and the theft of vehicles (Cunneen 1985: 84–6; White 1990: 135). Cars and motorbikes need to be seen as symbolic objects of masculine power, linked to fantasies of material and sexual domination and success. They are powerful cultural symbols which define aspects of what it is to be a man. Motor vehicles are also commodities which are produced and consumed in the market-place. Time, space and patterns of social life are also predicated to a large extent on the private ownership of motor vehicles. For those without a wage, access to the commodity may be available only through theft. In this brief summary, we can begin to see the links between the symbolic and social values of particular commodities and how they are intertwined with the subjective meanings attached to gender. We would argue that it is not possible to understand why young men are so often criminalised through offences related to motor vehicles without an understanding of masculinity.

On the one hand, our subjective understandings of the world are structured through gender. On the other hand, it is necessary to consider how state agencies and the forms of regulation in which they are engaged are gendered. Such an analysis in the area of juvenile justice is an examination of gender-specific control of boys and girls within an institutional setting. Kersten (1989) has argued that there is a salvationist attitude by the staff towards the boys in relation to homosexuality. While there is scope for employment and sport, caring and emotional needs remain unmet. Certain taboos are prevalent, including speaking about problems or serious discussions about relationships unless they are defined as being within a *therapeutic* environment. While there is a taboo on physical touching, a certain level of violence is permitted. Kersten also noted that the use of space reflected the images of an aggressive masculinity, with posters of macho figures and pin-up girls. Without any challenge to this form of masculinity, it is likely that those young men who have been institutionalised will go onto to further criminalisation.

It has been argued that the social practices which construct gender relations do not express natural patterns or reflect natural differences between boys and girls. What these practices do is establish the social marks of gender. They weave a structure of symbol and interpretation around what it is to be a boy or a girl (Connell 1987: 79–80). We have only sketched the way in which a theory of the construction of masculinity can help our understanding— both of the nature of offending, and of the ways in which the juvenile justice system itself operates within the parameters of the dominant gender relations. Of course, we add that it is not a necessity that men and women working in the area of juvenile justice must reproduce the dominant conceptions of masculinity and femininity—they may be in a position to challenge those relations.

CONCLUSION

This chapter has shown some of the transformations which have occurred in feminist thinking about young women and juvenile justice over the last two decades. The concern has shifted from a focus on welfare complaints and juvenile justice agencies' preoccupation with girls' alleged sexual misconduct. There is still concern about the links between welfare and criminalisation, however; increasingly, this is within the context of the failure to deal adequately with the oppressive conditions which young women experience. The response of juvenile justice is still focused on detention. Furthermore, there has been a challenge to simplistic categorisations which ignore the importance of class, race and cultural difference.

To describe the operation of the juvenile justice system as sexist or patri-archal is to over-simplify the processes which are in operation. There is a range of social processes which mediate the treatment of male and female young people. These include race and ethnicity; class and economic background; family arrangements; and demeanour, style and membership of subcultural groups. In the case of young women, we need to specify how these social attri-butes are simultaneously constituted with gender. Furthermore, we must think about what individual factors are important. After all, many girls from working-class backgrounds never come into contact with juvenile justice agencies. Individual considerations must include abuse, homelessness, and drug and alcohol problems.

There is also a range of organisational and administrative factors which influence the processing of offenders. Gender relations are mediated by the work practices of social workers, police, court staff, etc. They also contribute to the constructions of those work practices. For instance, to what extent does the police definition of 'proper' police work influence their treatment of young women?

Studies which simply compare the treatment of girls with that of boys have been criticised for their theoretical limitations. These approaches assume equal treatment: the treatment of males is the norm against which the treatment of young women is measured. As feminists have noted, even if it were found that there was no difference in treatment, such studies avoid the more difficult polit-ical question of how young people *should* be treated, as well as the theoretical problems of explaining why juvenile justice agencies operate the way they do (Cain 1989).

It is apparent that there has also been a growing demand to deal adequately with masculinity in the context of juvenile justice. The vast majority of young people who appear before the Children's Courts are young men. Yet, by and large, masculinity remains the invisible social relation—uncommented upon and unproblematised. The chapter has shown some specific instances where the-ories of masculinity can contribute significantly to our understandings of juvenile justice.

part three

the state, punishment and crime prevention

The purpose of this chapter is to describe and analyse the institutions of juvenile justice. What are these institutions? It is accepted in everyday language to talk about juvenile justice or the juvenile justice system. The implication is that there is a system which is, to a greater or lesser extent, coherent in terms of policy or practices. In a formal sense, there certainly is a system created by the body of legislation and regulations which govern interactions between institutions and young people of a certain age.

However, it would be simplistic to imagine that there are no competing interests, indeed no *different* interests in the way juvenile justice agencies deal with young people. If the so-called system has any competing interests within it, there are important implications in terms of political change and policy development. What is seen as a progressive policy change at one level may be thwarted and undermined at another.

A further factor is that the system is not closed. While the age of a young person defines jurisdiction of parts of the juvenile justice system, these boundaries are somewhat fluid. Young people accused of serious offences may be transferred to the adult courts. Under particular circumstances, young people may be transferred to the adult prison system. Conversely young adults may be kept in the juvenile detention system although they are no longer a 'young person' (over seventeen or eighteen years depending on the State). There are close links with the welfare system in terms of historical development, personnel, clientele and operational practices.

We can discuss the institutions of juvenile justice by asking some central questions.

- What is the legislative framework?
- Who are the key players?
- What are the mechanisms of accountability and regulation?
- What are the principles of the system?
- What are the effects of the system?

In the following sections we will look at these questions to understand how juvenile justice in Australia operates at an institutional level.

THE LEGISLATIVE FRAMEWORK

Young people are subject to the criminal law and to a range of other laws. When we talk about juvenile justice legislation, we primarily mean the legislation which establishes a separate system for dealing with young people. This legislation varies between States and there are differences as to precisely what is covered in each jurisdiction. However, generally speaking, juvenile justice legislation covers:

- the principles applicable to dealing with young people
- the definition of a young person or child
- the way police may proceed against a young person through the use of arrest, attendance notices and summons, including any preference for attendance notices or summons over arrest
- what diversionary schemes are available (such as cautioning, panels or family group conferences) and how they should be utilised
- any special considerations for young people in regard to being released or detained through bail or custody
- how the Children's Court is established as having special jurisdiction over children
- what criminal matters the Children's Court can determine and which matters must go before a higher court
- the mechanisms for appealing against a decision by the Children's Court
- the sentencing options available to the court
- any special requirements relating to restitution and compensation
- the establishment of detention centres and their operations.

Juvenile justice legislation may be split between a number of Acts, and not all legislation necessarily covers each of the points listed above. In Queensland most of the law specific to juveniles can be found in the *Juvenile Justice Act 1992* and in South Australia in the *Young Offenders Act 1993*. In contrast, in New South Wales there are several pieces of legislation, including the *Children (Criminal Proceedings) Act 1987*, *Children (Community Services Orders) Act 1987*, *Children (Detention Centres) Act 1987* and the *Children's Court Act 1987*. The key juvenile justice legislation current in Australia is shown in Chart 9.1.

As well as being subject to specific juvenile justice legislation, young people are also subject to general criminal laws and to laws relating to criminal justice procedure, such as the Crimes Act or Criminal Code in force in various States. Indeed, most of the offences for which a young person is likely to come before

Chart 9.1 Key legislation on juvenile justice, Australia, 1995

State	Act
Victoria	*Children and Young Persons Act 1989*
New South Wales	*Children (Criminal Proceedings) Act 1987*
South Australia	*Young Offenders Act 1993*
ACT	*Children's Services Act 1986*
Queensland	*Juvenile Justice Act 1992*
Western Australia	*Children's Court of Western Australia Act 1988*
	Young Offenders Act 1994
Northern Territory	*Juvenile Justice Act 1983*
	Juvenile Justice Amendment Act 1987
Tasmania	*Child Welfare Act 1960*

the Children's Court are violations of the law under the Crimes Act or Criminal Code. Young people are also subject to the law governing public order under the various Summary Offences Acts and Police Offences Acts in different States, and a sizable proportion of young people brought before the courts is there for violations of public order governed by this type of legislation.

Legislation covering criminal justice procedures also impacts on young people. Legislation of this nature covers the issuing of search warrants, commitment warrants and summons. Young people are also subject to the legislation covering bail in each State, which sets out the criteria for bail and any presumptions for or against bail. Juvenile justice legislation in some States modifies the requirements of the general Bail Act in its application to young people, for instance specifying special conditions relating to the release of young people.

Finally, young people are also subject to general sentencing laws such as the New South Wales *Sentencing Act 1989*. Sentencing legislation sets out requirements in relation to fixed terms, minimum terms and additional terms of imprisonment, as well as the relationship between parole periods and imprisonment. While arguably the New South Wales legislation has been primarily aimed at adult offenders with the rhetoric of 'truth in sentencing', it has also been applied to young offenders. In both cases, the result of the legislation has been increased time in institutions.

We mentioned above that not all juvenile justice legislation covers each of the areas specific to the administration of juvenile justice. In other words, in some States there are serious gaps in the legislation. In general terms, the Youth Justice Coalition (1990: 67–8) has argued that principles setting out consideration of young people's families are often omitted. There is often inadequate recognition in legislation of the following points.

- A child's family should participate in decision-making and their views should be taken into account.
- Consideration should always be given to the wishes of the child.
- Decisions should be made that correspond to a child's sense of time.

- The special vulnerability of children entitles them to special protection during investigation.
- Special consideration should be given to the cultural background of the young person.

There are also considerable variations in the legislation concerning the extent to which police procedures in dealing with young people are set out in law. In some States the process by which police should give cautions, or the criteria which should be used in deciding which children should be cautioned for particular types of behaviour, are not articulated in the legislation. As a result, the administration of such schemes is left to Police Instructions or Standing Orders which do not have the force of law. Similarly, the entitlement of a young person to consult a solicitor before questioning, the notification of parents that a young person has been arrested, and the entitlement of parents to consult with their child often have no basis in legislation. While some of these matters are dealt with in some States through Police Instructions or Standing Orders, they are not obligatory by law (Warner 1994).

Gaps in the legislative framework also raise the issue of the extent to which juvenile justice legislation is consistent with Australia's international obligations in relation to the treatment of young people. The two major United Nations instruments relating to juvenile justice are the *Standard Minimum Rules for the Administration of Juvenile Justice* (the Beijing Rules), and the *Convention on the Rights of the Child* (CROC). Australia helped to develop the Beijing Rules and is a signatory to CROC. The latter deals with juvenile justice issues in Articles 37 and 40, covering a range of matters relating to the rights of young people accused of an offence, their trial, sentencing and punishment. However, juvenile justice legislation in general does not provide any legislative base to enforce the rights which are spelt out in these instruments.

The *Convention on the Rights of the Child* specifies a wide range of rights of children. For example, Article 37 (b) states that:

> No child shall be deprived of his or her liberty unlawfully or arbitrarily. The arrest, detention or imprisonment of a child shall be in conformity with the law and shall be used only as a measure of last resort and for the shortest appropriate period of time.

Article 40 (b) stipulates that every child accused of having infringed the criminal law has at least the following guarantees:

> i) to be presumed innocent until proven guilty according to law;
>
> ii) to be informed promptly and directly of the charges against him or her, and if appropriate, through his or her parents or legal guardian, and to have legal or other appropriate assistance in the preparation and presentation of his or her defence;

iii) to have the matter determined without delay by a competent, independent and impartial authority or judicial body in a fair hearing according to law, in the presence of legal or other appropriate assistance and, unless it is considered not to be in the best interest of the child, in particular taking into account his or her age or situation, his or her parents or legal guardians;

iv) not to be compelled to give testimony or to confess guilt, to examine or have examined adverse witnesses and to obtain the participation and examination of witnesses on his or her behalf under conditions of equality;

v) if considered to have infringed the penal law, to have this decision and any measures imposed in consequence thereof reviewed by a higher competent, independent and impartial authority or judicial body according to law;

vi) to have the free assistance of an interpreter if the child cannot understand or speak the language used;

vii) to have his or her privacy fully respected at all stages of the proceedings.

These provisions provide benchmarks by which we can evaluate the legislative and administrative operation of the juvenile justice system in this country (see Crane 1993; Alston, Parker & Seymour 1992).

The Youth Justice Coalition (1990: 70–1) has identified three characteristics of juvenile justice legislation in Australia. They are few rights, wide discretion and few criteria. In general, juvenile justice legislation does not identify the **rights of young people** before the system. At best, implicit rights are created through legislation which imposes conditions and requirements on certain behaviour by officials—for instance, the requirement of a magistrate to give reasons for the imposition of a detention order. However, the recognition of some implicit rights is far weaker than a legislatively enacted charter of rights which list the entitlements of a young person.

The second characteristic identified by the Youth Justice Coalition is **wide discretion**. For example, legislative requirements relating to the administration of juvenile detention centres allow wide discretion in relation to visits, phone calls, mail, etc. Such wide discretion undermines the notion that young people have any rights to certain conditions and makes it difficult to challenge official decisions.

The third characteristic is **few criteria**. In general the legislation does not stipulate the criteria which should be used when important decisions about young people are being made. The lack of criteria is evident from the beginning of involvement in the system, when police are required to decide the important issue of who will benefit from a diversionary option rather than criminal proceedings, through to the end of the system where segregation and transfers in detention centres can be used capriciously.

THE KEY PLAYERS

We began the discussion of this chapter with the question of whether there is a 'system' of juvenile justice. To a certain extent, each State's legislation imposes a legislative framework in which the major agencies operate. The major agencies involved in juvenile justice are clearly the police, the courts, and the family or community services department with responsibility for offender supervision. Yet there are also many other players in the field. These range from small community-based organisations, such as an Aboriginal-run bail hostel dependent on government funding, through to the State Cabinet which must pass any proposals for legislative change.

Not only are there many players in the field, but there are also many interests at work in the way juvenile justice operates. The Youth Justice Coalition (1990: 74) has identified some of them as:

- the party political interests of government and opposition
- the personal political interests of responsible ministers
- the personal and professional interests of senior bureaucrats
- the organisational needs of the agencies involved
- the interests of associations representing the industrial interests of people working in the field (for example, police associations)
- the interests of other connected agencies (for example, prisons, schools)
- the interests of lobby groups (for example, church groups, youth justice coalitions)
- the interests of major media and local media organisations.

The list illuminates some of the powerful vested interests that can be involved in juvenile justice. The political interests of government and opposition may coincide to bring about progressive change, or—more likely in the current climate—their interests may coincide to push for more punitive intervention, with both groups attempting to be seen as tough on juvenile crime. As we identified in Chapter 5, the media also plays a powerful role in identifying presumed problems of juvenile offending. The personal and political interests of ministers with responsibility for various aspects of juvenile justice are also important. Reforms to procedures introduced by departments have been almost immediately abolished by ministers when they have perceived backlash from the public or the media. Similarly, senior bureaucrats may see their own personal prospects fulfilled more quickly if they control the organisation in a particular manner. Overall, the articulation of these different interests helps us to understand that the interests of the young person, their family, and the victim may indeed be of a minor nature in the broader picture.

The Police

The State police services play a major role in juvenile justice through the apprehension of young people who have allegedly committed offences. Apprehending young people is a significant component of police work. As we have previously noted (see Chapter 5), some 26 per cent of offences cleared by police involved juveniles. Beside the obvious aspect of police work in catching criminals, police are involved in many other aspects of juvenile justice. Police play a role in diversion schemes by selecting the young people to be involved, and in States where there are schemes utilising police cautions they administer diversion. Police are involved in determining bail and in prosecuting cases before the Children's Court. They are involved in detaining young people in custody if they have been refused bail, and in escorting young people to detention centres.

Police also collect information on juvenile offending and provide information to the community and the media about juvenile crime. They formulate policy regarding their own role with young people, as well as responding to policy initiatives from other departments. Police services play a part in police training and in determining the nature of information new recruits receive about juvenile offending and young people. Police services also allocate resources and services, prioritising attention to particular forms of juvenile crime or prioritising resources to specialist youth officers.

Community Services

Departments of community services in various States have the key function of administering juvenile justice services (support services, non-custodial programs, detention centres, etc.). There is usually a division within the relevant community services department which administers juvenile justice. There are some exceptions to this: in the Northern Territory, juvenile justice comes under the Department of Correctional Services, and in New South Wales there is a separate Department of Juvenile Justice. The functions of these departments include the preparation of court reports, the supervision of young people placed on a probation order or some other supervisory order by the court, and the provision of specialist counselling services to young offenders. The departments of community services also have responsibility for establishing and administering detention centres for young people who have been committed to an institution.

The departments of community services collect and disseminate information relating to the number of young people appearing in court and young people who end up in detention. The departments have a key role in developing policy on responses to juvenile offending. Finally, although welfare and juvenile justice matters are separated in virtually all States of Australia, the links between welfare and justice are strongest in these departments. Welfare functions such as child protection and family support operate from the same offices that administer community-based programs for young offenders.

Other State Bodies

The departments of attorneys-general also play a key role in juvenile justice administration. These departments are responsible for the administration of the Children's Courts as well as the higher courts, and allocate staff and resources to the courts. The departments are also active in other areas of relevance to juvenile justice through preparing legislation and developing policy on criminal proceedings. Finally, the departments may be involved in prosecutions of children in the higher courts through directors of public prosecution.

Other State bodies include legal aid commissions, which provide legal representation for some young people; law reform commissions, which provide reform proposals that may impact on young people; judicial commissions, which monitor sentencing and provide education and training for magistrates and judges; bureaus of crime statistics, which publish crime data; and victims' compensation tribunals, which provide compensation to victims of crime—including juvenile crime.

Most other State departments have either a direct or indirect role in relation to juvenile justice in terms of prosecutions, policies and programs. They include school education, technical education, health, industrial relations and employment, state railways, youth affairs, housing, public works, sport and recreation, treasury and cabinet. Often these departments are not recognised for the role they play. For instance, treasury departments advise on departmental budget allocations, including the money which is allocated for juvenile justice. Another example is the State rail authorities, which are involved in prosecutions of young people for offences committed against railway regulations.

The Commonwealth Government

The Commonwealth government plays an important but often unrecognised role in juvenile justice. The Commonwealth provides money for jointly funded services, and money in the form of general and tied grants to state governments. The level of provision of this funding can directly affect a range of services, from legal aid to emergency accommodation.

Commonwealth policy on youth employment, training, higher education, income support (including allowances for the unemployed and young homeless people), and so on directly affects the well-being of young people and their opportunities for growth and development. The nature and level of income support and social services can determine the lifestyle and immediate conditions of existence for many young people. These in turn have major consequences with regard to the causal factors underlying juvenile offending.

In addition to playing a crucial role in social provision, the federal government has a major contribution to make in the ratification, promotion and monitoring of international treaties and conventions. In the specific area of juvenile justice, it has been suggested that the Commonwealth government can play a much stronger role in defending and enhancing the rights of young people. For example, the National Children's and Youth Law Centre has proposed that a Charter of Rights for Children and Young People should be enacted in Commonwealth legislation, and that the federal government should actively intervene in instances where State governments have passed laws which ignore or run contrary to the provisions contained in instruments such as the *Convention on the Rights of the Child.*

Local Government

Local governments play an important but often neglected role in juvenile justice. There are various facets to the relationship. On the negative side, local governments are victims of juvenile crime, particularly in regard to the vandalism of public property. As a result, we have seen local governments demand more punitive approaches to young people, including attempts to impose local curfews (Simpson & Simpson 1993). Local governments have also played a role in the direct regulation of public space through the use of by-laws. In several States of Australia, local government has the power to introduce alcohol-free zones and to regulate the use of public places and shopping centres. These regulations may bring local government officers into a direct policing role in relation to young people.

On the positive side of the relationship, local government is also a provider of services and facilities. The provision of services for young people can be used by progressive local government bodies as an important crime prevention tool. Rather than seeing young people as a problem, progressive local governments use part of their resources to provide facilities for young people, and treat them as part of the local community which this tier of government represents.

Non-government Organisations

There are many community-based organisations which play a role in juvenile justice. Some provide general services to young people but, because of their nature, a large proportion of their clientele has had contact with juvenile justice agencies. Youth refuges which provide emergency accommodation are one example. Some service clubs are also involved in the supervision of young offenders who undertake community service work.

Some community legal centres, such as Marrickville Legal Centre in Sydney, have lawyers which specialise in juvenile justice. There are also a few community legal centres which work solely with young people, such as the Youth Legal Service in Perth and the Youth Advocacy Centre in Brisbane.

The National Children's and Youth Law Centre is an important advocate for justice for young people and children. The centre is active in a wide range of research projects, legal test-cases involving children's rights, and co-ordination of a network of youth legal and advocacy services. A central aspect of the centre's work has been to lobby for the establishment of a National Commissioner for Children to act as a watchdog for children and to monitor and report on the implementation of children's rights in Australia. As mentioned above, the centre has also advocated national legislative protection of the rights of children and young people. In relation to this, it has recently undertaken a joint project with the Australian Youth Foundation to develop a draft Charter of Rights for Children and Young People.

There are Youth Affairs Councils (or their equivalent) in each State, and a national body, the Australian Youth Policy and Action Coalition. Their purposes are to lobby governments and to express the interests and opinions of young people to elected representatives and state officials on a wide range of issues. Often these non-government youth organisations provide support to, or work in tandem with, specific juvenile justice lobby groups such as the Youth Justice Coalitions in various States (for example, New South Wales and Western Australia).

There are also many religious groups which provide a range of services, from specific programs for young offenders (such as wilderness camps) through to accommodation services and assistance to police by attending interviews with young people (for example, the Salvation Army).

Many of the community organisations which provide services for young people receive their funding through the State and/or federal governments.

ACCOUNTABILITY AND REGULATION

The agencies that play a role in juvenile justice can exert enormous power over young people. If young people are convicted of an offence, they receive some form of sanction which, at worst, can deprive them of their liberty. Even without such an extreme outcome, the police, courts and community services personnel can exert significant control over the lives of young people once they have entered the system. It is important to ask, therefore, whether there is adequate review of and accountability for the decisions made by juvenile justice agencies. Are decisions made fairly? And, if not, how are these decisions reviewed?

The accountability and regulation of juvenile justice agencies operates through a range of different mechanisms. There are legal forms of regulation through legislation, the courts, and disciplinary and complaint bodies, and the setting of standards with which agencies must comply. There are non-legal forms of accountability through management structures, public participation in advisory and consultative bodies, and the provision of research and evaluation. We will explore these different methods of achieving accountability in the sections which follow.

Review and Complaints Mechanisms

How accountable are juvenile justice agencies for the decisions they make in regard to young people? Both young people and the community in general have the right to expect that juvenile justice is administered fairly, responsibly and appropriately. One way of achieving such administration is through adequate mechanisms for review and complaints.

In practice, a number of review mechanisms specific to juvenile justice have been identified (Youth Justice Coalition 1990: 110–19). These include the following.

Management review

New managerial techniques, such as program budgeting, corporate planning, performance contracts and program evaluation, have been adopted by agencies working in juvenile justice. However, the major impact has been that of economic rationalism with its particular focus on budgeting, accounts and economic responsibility. For accountability to operate through managerial techniques, far greater attention needs to be paid to issues of access, equity and citizenship.

Inspections

One way of achieving accountability is through inspections of the closed institutions of juvenile justice: detention centres and police stations. Some States have moved to establish lay visitors' schemes in police stations, and some have official visitor schemes in institutions. In addition, in some States the Ombudsman's Office makes regular visits to detention centres.

Case planning

Jurisdictions vary in the extent to which they use case planning with individual young people who are either in detention or under the supervision of the community services department. Case planning can allow some participation by young people and parents, as well as making it more likely that there will be ongoing reviews of what is happening to an individual young person.

Complaints

In theory at least, young people can complain about matters relating to their treatment. Such complaints can be directed to a number of people: the responsible government minister, the officer-in-charge of the institution or police station, visitors' schemes where they exist, the Ombudsman's Office, or the police complaints tribunal. The mechanisms available for complaint vary from State to

State. However, a central problem is providing young people with the confidence, necessary information and opportunity to make complaints where appropriate. It is a recognised failing that organisations established to handle complaints, such as Ombudsman's Offices, do not deal adequately with issues affecting young people.

Quasi-judicial review

Some States at various times have established review boards for the purpose of reviewing and making decisions about the release on parole of young people in detention (for instance the Training Centre Review Board in South Australia). In general, though, young people have not had the type of review boards which operate in relation to adult offenders.

Judicial review

In general, young people have not had access to courts to review matters in relation to the way detention centres operate. The decisions in detention centres in relation to transfer, segregation and punishment have not been open to the scrutiny of the courts to the same extent as equivalent matters in the adult sphere.

Professional regulation

The extent to which personnel working in the juvenile justice system are regulated by legislation or professional bodies varies. Lawyers, magistrates and police face some regulation through professional bodies, tribunals and commissions, although there are frequent and consistent criticisms concerning their usefulness. Personnel working in detention centres and non-custodial environments usually have no professional regulatory body.

It is clear that there are specific problems relating to the mechanisms for achieving regulation and accountability in the sphere of juvenile justice. Even where there are specific measures for complaints, there are substantial problems in enabling young people to utilise what is available.

Establishing Standards

It has been acknowledged that standards have not been used widely as a way of ensuring consistency in the operation of juvenile justice agencies in Australia. However, developments in the United States show that national standards can be of use in promoting common approaches to operational matters. The development of national standards seems particularly applicable to Australia, given the eight different State and Territory juvenile justice systems.

Much of the United Nations involvement in juvenile justice has been about setting standards (see Crane 1993). The *Standard Minimum Rules for the Administration of Juvenile Justice* (the Beijing Rules) provide that:

- a comprehensive social policy be in place to ensure the well-being of juveniles
- reaction to juvenile offenders always be in proportion to the circumstances of both the offenders and the offence
- police officers dealing extensively with juveniles be specially instructed and trained
- detention pending trial be used only as a measure of last resort and for the shortest possible period of time
- placement of a juvenile in an institution always be a disposition of last resort and for the minimum necessary period
- necessary assistance such as housing, vocational training and employment be provided to facilitate the rehabilitative process.

The United Nations has also published *Draft Rules for the Protection of Juveniles Deprived of Their Liberty*, relating to detention centres. As the Youth Justice Coalition (1990: 106–9) has noted, minimum standards have been increasingly used in other areas of social policy in Australia, including hospitals, aged care and residential care in child welfare.

In the area of juvenile justice, standards could have a range of functions, establishing criteria for evaluating, reviewing and funding programs and services. They would also help to establish consistency in approach within and between different jurisdictions.

Community Input

A structure to ensure community input into juvenile justice policies and operations is a formal advisory mechanism. In general these types of mechanisms have not been established in the juvenile justice area. One exception is the New South Wales Juvenile Justice Advisory Council. However, even this group is heavily dominated by institutional interests, including representatives from the police, Children's Courts and Department of Juvenile Justice. Young people are not represented through any of their peak bodies, nor are young offenders represented. Recent South Australian legislation also established a Juvenile Justice Advisory Committee. The majority of the six members are experts nominated by the Minister, including an established position for a judge. Two members of the six could be said to be community representatives, with one of the two nominated as an Aboriginal person. Both the community representatives are also appointed by Ministers.

With the move to embrace community policing as a central objective of Australian police services, there has been a considerable expansion in consultative processes. Mostly these initiatives have relied on consultative committees in the local area. There has been no national information available on the nature, location or priorities of these committees, but there has been some indication of their inability to incorporate youth issues. Certainly the Youth Justice

Coalition (1990: 221–3) has noted that consultative committees have not been successful in dealing constructively with young people. The committees have often targeted young people as a crime problem, rather than attempted to incorporate them into a community consultative mechanism.

As can be seen, the existing advisory mechanisms offer little scope for community input into juvenile justice administration. There is virtually no opportunity for young people's involvement.

Research and Evaluation

Research and evaluation can be important tools for ensuring accountability in juvenile justice. Unless we know how the system is operating and to what effect, it is extremely difficult to hold agencies accountable for what they are doing.

Generally, research in and evaluation of juvenile justice have been poor. There have been some exceptions, such as South Australia's relatively sophisticated information base. Some of the research which has used this information shows the need for reliable monitoring (see Gale et al. 1990). However, the despairing note sounded by the Youth Justice Coalition is typical of the rest of Australia: 'The situation in relation to planning, research and evaluation in the juvenile justice area is so underdeveloped that it must be questioned whether those responsible for the system really want to know what is going on' (Youth Justice Coalition 1990: 95).

Sound research and evaluation are important for a number of reasons. Policy must be based on an understanding of whether programs are effective or not, and on an understanding of existing problems within the system. Without adequate information, policy development is susceptible to political interference and can be replaced by crisis management. Research and evaluation inform the public, parliament and media how particular programs are working or can be expected to work. Finally, research and evaluation enable departmental resources to be allocated effectively.

THE PRINCIPLES OF JUVENILE JUSTICE

We have outlined the legislative framework of juvenile justice, the key players, and the issues of accountability and regulation. It is also necessary to consider the philosophy and principles underlying juvenile justice systems. Earlier we discussed the usefulness of 'ideal types' as a method of understanding various theoretical strands in criminology (see Chapter 2). Ideal types have also been used for considering the model adopted by juvenile justice systems.

We reiterate that an ideal type is an analytical tool rather than a statement about what actually exists or ought to exist. Juvenile justice has often been seen as alternating between models of 'justice' and 'welfare'. Although juvenile justice as it has developed historically has never actually conformed to either the justice or welfare models, these ideal types have been invoked in order to conceptualise changes within the system, and to measure the system against the principles elaborated in either model.

The welfare and justice models are usually considered as being at opposite ends of the spectrum and representing quite different approaches to dealing with young people. But in practice, particularly in Australia, the juvenile justice system represents aspects of both models. What then are the features of these different models of juvenile justice?

The welfare model

- Behaviour is regarded as arising from a range of factors outside the control of the individual.
- The emphasis is on 'needs' over 'deeds'. That is, the offender is more important than the offence.
- Rehabilitation is the primary goal in sentencing.
- The needs of the young person must be treated through appropriate intervention.
- Treatment can occur outside the formal justice process through diversion, but still involves professionals and experts.
- The protections of criminal justice procedures are not required because the focus is on rehabilitation rather than punishment.

It is clear that the focus on a welfare approach has close connections with the theories of positivism which we outlined earlier (Chapter 2), as well as incorporating some aspects of the mainstream theories (Chapter 3).

The justice model

- Emphasis is on the offence rather than the offender.
- The model promotes due process: that is, the rules applicable to the adult courts concerning prosecution and criminal procedure are applied to young people as well.
- Young people are seen as responsible for their actions, and offending is seen as the result of a choice.
- The model promotes 'just deserts' in sentencing: that is, it focuses on the responsibility of the young person for the offence and on a punishment that 'fits the crime'.
- Rehabilitation is seen as a secondary goal in sentencing.

We can see the similarities between the justice model and the classical theory of criminology previously outlined, which also stresses individual responsibility for offending behaviour (Chapter 2). Indeed, the emphasis on justice in the approach to juvenile justice can be seen as part of the resurgence of neo-classicist approaches to law and order (see Chapter 4). To some extent, this move has been at the expense of those promoting rehabilitation. However, as we discuss later (Chapter 11) the *actual* effect on sentencing practices is not so clear.

Much of the impetus towards a justice approach arose in the United States during the 1960s, where there was a disillusionment with the failures of rehabilitation (Freiberg, Fox & Hogan 1988: 4). There were calls for a greater concentration on retribution and deterrence, as well as concerns about the degree of discretionary power and the failure to consider the rights of due process for young people. Labelling theorists also had an impact with their argument that the agents of juvenile justice could themselves expand and confirm the likelihood of criminal careers (Freiberg, Fox & Hogan 1988: 4). There was also a number of United States Supreme Court decisions between 1966 and 1970 in *Kent, Gault* and *Winship* which insisted that due process rights were applicable to young people. (*Kent v United States* (1966) 383 US 541; In *Re Gault* (1967) 387 US 1; In *re Winship* (1970) 397 US 358).

The Australian Experience

As we noted in the first chapter, Children's Courts in Australia never moved as far to the welfare model as in the United States. However, there were substantial differences between the adult and juvenile courts in Australia, not the least being the court's power to deal with both criminal matters and welfare matters, and to use welfare-style interventions in relation to a criminal offence. From the late 1970s through to the early 1990s there has been a move to separate welfare from justice matters in most jurisdictions. South Australia was the first State to achieve the separation, in 1979. This separation has been accomplished in some jurisdictions by separate legislation governing criminal matters and welfare matters, such as the New South Wales *Children (Criminal Proceedings) Act 1987* and *Children (Care and Protection) Act 1987*. Other jurisdictions have made use of a single piece of legislation, such as the Victorian *Children and Young Person's Act 1989* which establishes separate decisions of the Children's Court in the Family Division and the Criminal Division—effectively separating welfare from crime. Tasmania is the only Australian State to continue to operate a system that mixes welfare and criminal matters.

The current Tasmanian legislation is an example of the old-style welfare legislation. When contrasted with new justice legislation it provides a window on the broader changes which have been occurring in juvenile justice. The philosophy is clearly stated in Section 4 of the Tasmanian *Child Welfare Act 1960*:

> As far as practicable and expedient, each child suspected of having committed, charged with, or found guilty of an offence shall be treated, not as a criminal, but as a child who is, or may have been, misdirected or misguided, and that the care, custody and discipline of each ward of state shall approximate as nearly as may be to that which should be given to it by its parents.

192 THE STATE, PUNISHMENT AND CRIME PREVENTION

The Tasmanian legislation is subject to many of the general criticisms that have been levelled against welfare-model legislation. The court's assessment of the welfare needs of a young person may result in a far longer sentence than an adult would have received for the same offence. The court can determine that the young person appearing for a criminal matter is in need of wardship and thus declare them a ward of state until their eighteenth birthday. The legislation allows for indeterminate sentencing by magistrates. The release of the young person is dependent upon the discretion of the department (Stokes 1992: 11).

The problems with the welfare approach can be summarised as follows.

- There is a failure to protect the rights of the young person.
- The issues of neglect and offending are intertwined.
- There is no proportionality between the offence and the sentence.
- Indeterminate sentencing is permitted.
- There is excessive administrative discretion.

Much of the recent juvenile justice legislation developed in other parts of Australia sets out to a greater or lesser extent the principles under which juvenile justice and the Children's Court operate. And, with the exception of Tasmania, it is possible to see the shift which has occurred towards a justice-oriented approach.

For example, the South Australia *Young Offenders Act 1993* notes in Section 3 the following statutory policies of juvenile justice.

- Young people should be made aware of their obligations under the law and of the consequences of breach of the law.
- The sanctions imposed against illegal conduct must be sufficiently severe to provide an appropriate level of deterrence.
- The community, and individual members of it, must be adequately protected against violent or wrongful acts.

The legislation refers to responsibility, deterrence and community protection, which are seen as components of a justice approach. Similarly, the Queensland *Juvenile Justice Act 1992* sets out the principles of juvenile justice in Section 4. Subsection (e) states that 'a child who commits an offence should be . . . held accountable and encouraged to accept responsibility for the offending behaviour'. Again, accountability and responsibility are hallmarks of a justice approach.

However, legislation provides some special considerations for young people. For instance, Subsection (e) of the Queensland legislation goes on to state that the child should be punished in a way that provides opportunities to develop in responsible, beneficial and socially acceptable ways. Similarly, the South Australian legislation in Section 3(1) states that the object of the act is to secure for youths who offend against the criminal law the care, correction and guidance necessary for their development into responsible and useful members of the community, and the proper realisation of their potential (for a similar discussion of the Victorian and New South Wales legislation see Naffine 1993).

Thus there is clearly still a preference for rehabilitation and special considerations of care and guidance. Currently, juvenile justice legislation is moving towards a more justice-oriented model, but it has retained a commitment to welfare-related principles as well. How these essentially contradictory moves relate to practice is, of course, a separate issue.

THE EFFECTS OF THE SYSTEM

The justice versus welfare debate has come to be regarded by many as a limited way of conceptualising events in the juvenile justice arena. Many commentators in Australia and overseas have argued that the debate about welfare or justice is essentially sterile because it fails to explain either how the system operates or what effects it has. Pitts (1988) has noted that both the justice and welfare models are ultimately attempts to ensure the social conformity of young people; they disagree only on how to achieve this objective. One method advocates conformity through the punishment of the rational actor, thus deterring future aberrations; the other promotes conformity through various approaches which rest on social engineering and rehabilitation to the existing social conditions and norms.

It is difficult to match the claims of either a justice or a welfare model with the real operation of juvenile justice. The large institutions which have dominated most of the twentieth century have been sites of petty oppression rather than rehabilitation. Specifically in relation to Aboriginal young people, the welfare approach saw large-scale social disorganisation imposed on young people and families. Far from any notion of rehabilitation, the system was deliberately and actively destructive.

Similarly, the justice-based model, which emphasises responsibility, accountability and due process, has offered punishment as a panacea. The emphasis has been on greater punishment of young offenders, rather than ensuring the other supposed benefits of a justice model which include proportionality in sentencing and the protection of legal rights. As we note further in Chapter 11, most young people plead guilty in court and generally they are not in a position to assert their various rights. Clarke (1985) has noted that the 'back to justice' movement in Britain was, by and large, an anti-welfare movement which saw an attack on social workers by police, magistrates and lawyers. In this sense at least, the shift occurring in juvenile justice from the 1970s onwards fitted closely with attacks on the welfare state in general.

During the 1980s in Australia there were considerable changes: the separation of juvenile justice and child welfare jurisdictions, and the introduction of new policies. However, these changes were not a simple shift between two dichotomous models. Some were aimed at progressive reforms, such as reducing the number of children in institutions, of those going to court for first and minor offences, and of those committed to institutions without having received community-based sanctions, and reducing sentencing disparities (Youth Justice Coalition 1990: 43). As Luke (1993) indicates, in New South Wales during the early 1980s there was a strong emphasis on decarceration, led by a Left-wing Minister in the Labor Party. Indeed, his senior adviser on juvenile justice issues had been a founding member of the Prisoners' Action Group (a group advocating the abolition of prisons). The search was for 'practical ways of achieving a sustainable decarceration and greater equality of treatment between rich and poor, black and white' (Luke 1993: 151). Yet these progressive changes were relatively short-lived, and there was a noticeable swing to the Right by the late 1980s.

Finally, we would like to consider three alternative ways of conceptualising the operation of the juvenile justice system through notions of 'corporatism', 'governmentality' and 'social class'. Pratt (1989) has argued that the justice/welfare dichotomy does not account for the changes which are occurring in juvenile justice. Pratt argues that the significant changes are:

- an increase in cautioning and disposal of matters prior to court
- the growth of co-operation between a range of agencies, with a focus on greater efficiency and crime prevention
- the development of alternatives to custody (non-custodial programs are intermediate between detention and an unsupervised order)
- a decline in the autonomy of professionals and the judiciary through attempts to control discretionary power
- an increase in the role of the voluntary sector, particularly in providing intermediate treatment and programs
- the development of juvenile justice technology which has increased the level of planning
- bifurcation in policy for 'hard-core' and 'minor' offenders: young people who are defined as recidivist and dangerous are dealt with punitively, mainly through adult sentencing structures and regimes, while those defined as minor offenders are dealt with through pre-court diversionary options.

Pratt developed his argument in relation to changes in Britain, and it is clear that not all of the characteristics he identifies apply in Australia. Indeed, some Australian jurisdictions have been criticised for not implementing changes such as cautioning and pre-court disposal, the use of planning, etc. However, the importance of Pratt's approach is that it attempts to move beyond the justice/

welfare conceptualisation. He argues that the current changes can be considered within the context of **corporatism**. Pratt argues that corporatism is a characteristic of advanced welfare states, whereby the 'capacity for conflict and disruption is reduced by means of the centralisation of policy, increased government intervention, and the co-operation of various professional and interest groups into a collective whole with homogeneous aims and objectives' (Pratt 1989: 245). He argues that these are precisely the types of changes which are occurring in juvenile justice, through increased administrative decision-making; centralisation of authority, decision-making and planning; greater involvement of non-government agencies; greater sentencing diversity; and high levels of control in some sentencing programs.

The second conceptualisation of the juvenile justice system which we wish to consider is the application of Foucault's ideas of governmentality and power. **Governmentality** refers to the collection of institutions, knowledge, procedures and practices which allow the exercise of power over and through the population. According to Rose (1989), childhood is the most intensely governed part of personal existence; in other words the process of governmentality has a particular application to children and young people. There has developed around children a complex of laws, agencies and practices which determine delinquency and pathology. According to Rose, the most powerful outcome of the study of 'delinquency' is that it has been used to define 'normality'. 'Knowledge of normality has not in the main resulted from studying normal children . . . It is around pathological children—the troublesome, the recalcitrant, the delinquent—that conceptions of normality have taken place' (Rose 1989: 131).

Government of the child through education, child welfare and juvenile justice is important because it is concerned ultimately with the management and regulation of the self in contemporary society. According to Rose (1989: 1) our 'personalities, subjectivities and relationships are not private matters . . on the contrary they are intensely governed'. The process of governmentality begins in childhood: through various institutions, public power targets and regulates the personal and subjective characteristics of the population. Children and young people are intensely governed through a range of agencies, among which juvenile justice is important because of its role in detecting pathology and abnormality. It is clear that this view of the function and effects of juvenile justice is far removed from any debate about justice or welfare. Like Pratt's argument above, Rose is considering juvenile justice within the context of a regulatory practice. What is important is the way in which juvenile justice regulates young people and children, not what guiding principles might be invoked to explain its existence.

Finally, we want to consider Clarke's (1985) analysis of the juvenile justice system in terms of **social class**. Clarke argues that the 'presentation of juvenile justice as a site of an opposition between principles of justice and welfare is ill-conceived, and leads to potentially dangerous political consequences' (1985: 407). It is not helpful to consider two abstract principles; what needs to be analysed is the way in which juvenile justice essentially criminalises working-class young people, and manages those young people defined as being delin-quent through a patchwork of processes and programs which draw on a range of philosophies and principles. In particular, Clarke argues that concentration on the 'rule of law' masks class inequalities. Equality before the law as due process rests on assumptions of the formal equality of citizens. However, the class inequality of young people who are criminalised undermines the formal equality. Furthermore, there is a class bias in the selection of activities which are prohibited by the law and policed, in particular those activities which are regu-lated in public places. Finally, the process of the law acts against working-class young people. Despite notions of equality, the actual use of discretion through-out the juvenile justice system acts against the interests of young people from working-class backgrounds.

This discussion of the work of Pratt, Rose and Clarke shows that there is a trend to move beyond the conception of the juvenile justice system as a body of agencies working within a framework of ideas constrained by notions of welfare or justice. All three writers are keen to argue that juvenile justice must be *theor-ised* in terms of practices as well as ideas. All three writers have a concept of political power and a particular view of the function of institutions and the state. For Pratt, the role of the state is to regulate and manage conflict and dis-sent. For Rose, power and regulation operate through discourses and institu-tions. For Clarke, the state, through juvenile justice, is essentially concerned with class control.

CONCLUSION

We began this chapter by asking whether there was a juvenile justice system and showed that those whose function is to administer juvenile justice differ in their interests. We considered the role of legislation in providing a legal framework for the operation of juvenile justice.

We identified the key players in juvenile justice at the level of each State, as well as the Commonwealth and the non-government sector, and we looked at the various systems of accountability and regulation of those who administer juvenile justice. Finally, we considered the formal principles and philosophies underlying juvenile justice and the debates which have occurred about justice and welfare approaches. For many, though, the debate between justice and wel-fare has been sterile and does not really come to grips with the broader functions of juvenile justice within the social fabric.

One way of moving beyond such debates is to consider the role of the state and institutional power. Clearly at this level we are talking about a 'system' of juvenile justice which regulates, controls and manages dissent and conflict. Yet the operation and effects of the 'system' cannot be deduced from an a priori structuralist position. We need to know precisely how, under particular historical conditions and economic and social circumstances, the institutions of juvenile justice are operating. We turn, then, to an analysis of the players in the field, beginning with the police.

10 policing the young

The police are the gatekeepers of the criminal justice system. The formal contact young people have with the system—as victims or offenders—usually begins with some kind of contact with police officers. The nature of this contact can have far-reaching consequences. For example, a young person who does not co-operate with the police might find themselves being brought further and further into the criminal justice system. On the other hand, simple compliance with everything the police demand of the young person may in fact constitute a violation of legal and human rights.

The aim of this chapter is to survey the relationship between young people and the police in Australian society; to explore the roles and activities of the police in relation to different groups of young people; and to assess the major issues surrounding police–youth contact. We begin by examining the different roles of the police in society, the media images of police in relation to their actual practices, and the range of powers the police have to deal with young people. This is followed by a discussion of the nature of police–youth contact, police harassment, and groups of young people who constitute the main targets of police intervention. The chapter concludes with a discussion of community policing and the types of reforms needed to improve relations between police and young people.

ROLES

What do the police actually do? Surprisingly, this question rarely receives systematic or thoughtful consideration in references to the police in conversation or media stories regarding their work. Certainly the predominant image of the police is as 'crime fighters'. The police are often presented in the media as the 'thin blue line' in the 'war on crime'. Yet, in fact, the success of the police in these terms is very limited indeed.

For example, in 1988 the head of the Australian Institute of Criminology pointed out that the ratio of police to population in Australia had increased by almost 30 per cent in recent years; that the annual expenditure in police departments had increased by 60 per cent; that a new tier of policing in the form of the National Crime Authority had been added; and that extensive new powers had been extended to the police, such as the ability to tap phones (Chappell 1989). The picture that emerged was one of increased staff, increased funding, more departmental bodies, and enhanced powers. Yet in the same period, there was an increase in the rates of commission of serious offences, and a decrease in the rates of clearance of these crimes by the police. So, whatever the resources allocated for crime fighting, the evidence suggests that perhaps a different measure of effectiveness might be needed to evaluate the overall role and tasks of police in our society.

One way to approach the roles of the police is to briefly summarise the mission statements of various departments (for recent statements and further information, see Bryett, Harrison & Shaw 1994). The police in New South Wales, for example, see their role as providing, with the assistance of the people:

- protection of life
- prevention of crime
- enforcement of the law
- maintenance of peace and good order
- protection of property
- management of traffic.

In Queensland, there is a commitment to preserving the security and well-being of the populace, preventing crime, and maintaining peace and good order. In South Australia, the service is designed for the protection of life and property and the maintenance of peace. In Victoria, the police see themselves as part of the community and acting for the community in maintaining law and order, with honour and dignity, in the tradition of peace, order and good government through:

- protecting of life and property
- preserving the peace
- preventing crime
- enforcing legislation
- helping those who need assistance
- maximising safety for road users.

In Tasmania, the police are to serve the people by protecting life and property, enhancing community safety, reducing the incidence and fear of crime and violence, and detecting and apprehending offenders.

As these different mission statements show, we ask a lot of the police. Consequently, they perform a wide variety of functions, and crime fighting is only a minor part of their overall role.

In summary, we can say that the police are engaged in: the prevention and detection of crime; the apprehension and prosecution of offenders; the maintenance of law and order at such events as parades, marches, funerals, and football games; the handling of sudden deaths, as in traffic accidents; the co-ordination of searches and rescues; community crime prevention programs, working with various groups on an ongoing basis; law-related education, as in schools and police–youth recreational programs; a range of service functions, such as traffic regulation and control; the surveillance of perceived dangerous people in the community; the protection of dignitaries; and the list could go on.

Chart 10.1 Police task orientations

Task	Comments
Law enforcement	• crime fighting through detection, investigation, prosecution • involves dealing with those who have committed a crime • a minor proportion of police time • most investigation done through specific departments such as criminal investigation branch (CIB)
Order maintenance	• police role is to restore disruptive situations to normality • often does not involve arrest of individuals • includes public order surveillance, intervention and monitoring of specific groups in particular locations • may involve riot squads • linked to policing of 'domestic violence' and of major public events
Crime prevention	• proactive programs and strategies designed to prevent crime and to address the fear of crime • includes working closely together with local government, non-government agencies and institutions such as schools • includes providing information on how to secure one's property and person against potential threat
Social services	• police operate 24 hours a day • may be called upon to offer social welfare, psychiatric and other services • counselling abused women and children • finding lost children • dealing with potential suicides and sudden deaths • providing information to the public on a variety of matters
Traffic management	• ensuring the smooth flow of traffic • regulating traffic laws and driver habits • managing drink driving campaigns and enforcement • often handling license allocation and provision • participating at traffic accidents and in accident prevention schemes • supervising evacuations from crisis areas

Figure 10.1 summarises the main tasks undertaken by the police. The figure shows that law enforcement is only part of a wide range of functions. Perhaps we need new criteria for assessing the overall performance and roles of the police in society.

As we shall see, the different task orientations of the police can subject them to contradictory demands. For example, calls to 'clean up the streets' for law enforcement or public order may go against the more benign objective of providing for the general welfare of young people in city centres. Or, regardless of the motivation, the mix of different functions and the coercive powers available to the police may cause young people to perceive any kind of intervention in their lives as threatening or unwanted.

PRACTICES AND IMAGES

Most of us know little about the police. Our main images and experiences of the police are shaped by the media (both in news reports and fictional dramas). These present a skewed picture of who the police are and what they actually do on a day-to-day basis. Common media portrayals of the police include the following.

- *The Rogue Cop:* the 'Dirty Harry' type of police officer, who breaks the rules in order to get the 'bad guy' and thus to protect the rest of us from predatory crime.
- *The Boy Scout:* the 'Mountie always gets his man' type, the kind who does things by the book and who speaks nicely to everyone during investigations.
- *The Crazy Cop:* this character is a bit twisted, like Riggs in the *Lethal Weapon* movies, but is essentially OK and has the special kind of craziness needed to handle serious street crimes, terrorism and drugs.
- *The Super Hero:* these police possess a whole range of special physical qualities and technological aids, as seen in the *Batman* movies and the 'Police Rescue' television series.
- *The Sleuth:* the officer who uses brains, rather than brawn, in order to outwit the criminal mind, and who generally is more sophisticated or educated than your average street cop; for example, Columbo and Inspector Morse.

All too often, the idea conveyed to us about police work is that violence is intrinsic and absolutely necessary to the job. Furthermore, while the police engage in a wide range of activities, in our image of the police the crime fighter predominates; indeed, this also tends to be the view that police have of themselves (see Beyer 1993). Thus, within police departments there is often an informal division of police tasks into 'real' police work and that of the 'plastic cops'. The first emphasises the use of force, intervention and the muscled arm of the law; the second, dialogue with members of the community and the peaceful resolution of conflict.

The emphasis on the police as crime fighters dictates the terms of discussions about the impact of the police, what they ought to be doing, and how their effectiveness is to be measured. Traditionally, different strategies of policing have aimed to improve basic crime-fighting measures. Recent decades, for example, have seen attempts to streamline police performance and make it more effective by:

- patrolling at saturation level in high crime areas
- decreasing police response time by getting to the crime scene faster
- employing technology, such as two-way radios, motorised patrols, computerised data systems and advanced software for data retrieval
- using administrative measures such as prioritisation of calls
- replacing random patrols with directed patrols to pre-determined destinations and times
- screening cases as a means to write off unsolvable cases
- increasing police powers, such as fingerprinting.

The evidence concerning police effectiveness, measured solely in terms of crime fighting, shows that such measures have had little impact on overall crime rates and offence patterns (Vernon & Bracey 1989). It has become clear that the criminal justice system, including the police, only marginally affects crime; as a result, partly due to pressures emanating from the grassroots level, there has been a major debate about the police function in recent years. These discussions have tried to identify the best policing methods and to relate these to the varying objectives for the police. Invariably, the discussions have turned to the strengths and weaknesses of reactive and proactive methods.

- *Reactive policing:* Police activity is driven by demand and the emphasis is on responding to problems or incidents. Goals are expressed in terms of activities, not achievements or defined outcomes. No attempt is made to influence the environment; rather, the idea is simply to respond to a situation and return to base.
- *Proactive policing:* Police activity results from planned courses of action, which are designed to prevent criminal or anti-social events from occurring. Here the police seek to influence the environment in which criminal activity is likely to take place, in order to prevent its occurrence.

Although at times these strategies are viewed as opposing each other, in many circles they are viewed as complementary strategies with different aims. One's view of these methods rests on one's preference for traditional policing or problem-centred policing. The **traditional** style of policing emphasises reponse to individual incidents, with a focus on the incident and the specific offender and victim. This approach is reactionary and police-centred.

By way of constrast, **problem-oriented** policing encourages the identification of recurring problems and the causes of anti-social behaviour and crime. The approach analyses underlying problems—for example, ongoing conflict between police and young people in a particular locale—and devotes time and funds to determining causes and solutions. This perspective encourages co-ordination between police and other public sector agencies. Hence, it is not simply police-centred as in the traditional style of policing, but seeks to broaden its activities to incorporate public participation.

Within the various police departments and service divisions, there are strong conflicts over the definition of what is real, positive, effective policing. Indeed, there are deep divisions within political parties and the public at large and among police officers themselves as to what constitutes 'a good cop'. Traditionally, this concept has been associated with the notion of exerting authority, a masculine street presence, and the fighting of crime. Problem-centred and community-based policing presents a different image, preferring to concentrate on deep structural issues of crime and the responses to it, and doing so in ways which do not intimidate or alienate community members. Attempts to change the face of policing have included, for example, employment of greater numbers of women and people from other than English-speaking back-grounds.

POWERS AND METHODS

There are different models of policing, stressing different approaches and strate-gies, but in the end what counts are the actions of the police on the beat and in direct contact with members of the public. In the course of their dealings with young people, the police have a range of choices in terms of how to proceed. These are outlined below. Importantly, what the police do in practice involves a high degree of discretion.

Police procedures for dealing with young people include the following.

- *Assistance:* advice to young people; general information; street directions; traffic regulations and responsibilities; anti-theft suggestions; information about safety and personal security.
- *Informal caution:* casual dealing with young people with no formal charges laid; may take young people home or phone parents/guardians; minor inter-vention; may be recorded administratively on caution sheet at station or in police notebook; includes warning or telling young people to move on.
- *Formal caution:* formal record of caution administered at police station and authorised by senior police officer; parent or guardian must attend or be

notified to contact station within a set period; can be administered whether or not the young person is arrested for an offence; may be linked to a screening panel, children's aid panel or police cautioning panel.

- *Interrogation:* common-law rules of voluntariness and discretion apply; presence of adult witnesses is required when juveniles are interviewed; questioning may take place in the absence of adult in some instances (e.g., safety of others, serious offence); cautions and legal advice should be offered; generally police have no power to involuntarily detain suspects or witnesses solely for the purpose of questioning or investigation, or to hold them pending inquiries.

- *Search:* there are common law and statutory powers to search for certain classes of suspected persons, to search persons who have been arrested, and to search for specific articles and material relevant to the investigation of crime; search without a warrant applies only in cases where, on reasonable grounds, the arrested person is believed to have committed a serious indictable offence.

- *Summons:* the usual procedural option is a summons (citation notice or attendance notice), calling for the alleged offender to appear on a specified date before a magistrate's court; in the case of less serious offences, the legislatively preferred option is by way of charge and summons.

- *Arrest:* the decision to arrest and place in custody is meant to be used in exceptional circumstances (e.g., serious or violent offence); parents or guardians are informed of charges laid at police station; reasonable force may be used; person arrested is entitled to know on what charge or on suspicion of what crime they are being arrested.

- *Fingerprinting:* usually subject to statutory provisions and restrictions; court order may be required, depending upon the age of the young person; in some cases the young person must be in custody or on a charge of an indictable (serious) offence before fingerprints can be taken.

- *Custody:* once arrested, a young person must be taken before a justice as soon as practicable unless bail is granted; bail may be refused on grounds of seriousness of offence, welfare or protection of child; every person taken into custody must be released, granted bail or taken before court; in some jurisdictions, time limits are set by legislation (for example, in Victoria a young person can be held in custody and questioned for up to twenty-four hours).

- *Complaints:* there are no special procedures where the complainant is a juvenile; complaints may be made to another member of police force or Office of the Ombudsman.

The exercise of police discretion is influenced by a range of institutional and occupational factors. In the specific case of young people, discretion is based partly upon broad departmental policies and guidelines, and partly on the officer's perception of the event and individual in question. According to the police, the decision to deal with a young person one way or the other is determined by the seriousness of the offence, and the degree of co-operation displayed by the young person (Alder et al. 1992).

But the general attitude and appearance of the young people obviously play a part in shaping police perceptions and decisions. The police develop expectations regarding the potential threat or trouble posed by certain groups of young people. This leads them to pre-empt possible trouble by harassing those young people whose demeamour, dress and language identify them as being of potential concern. Indeed, distinctions are often made between the 'respectable' and the 'rough', the 'haves' and 'have-nots', and police action is taken in accordance with these perceptions (James & Polk 1989; Smith 1975; Conway 1992).

In aggregate terms, then, we know that such 'personal' discretion is in fact social in nature. That is, the same people tend to receive the same kind of treatment, positive or negative, depending upon overt social characteristics and social background. For example, a report prepared by the Federation of Community Legal Centres in Victoria (Biondo & Palmer 1993) pointed out that police mistreatment of the young was more prevalent amongst unemployed young people and students—i.e., the more marginalised youth in terms of income. Charges of police mistreatment and harassment also predominate among groups such as Aborigines and Torres Strait Islanders, young homeless people and young people who use the streets (White & Alder 1994).

Recent work in Australia has also pointed to the emerging issue of the specific, and often negative, relationship between the police and young people from so-called Asian backgrounds (which include, for example, Vietnamese, Cambodian, Laotian, Malaysian, ethnic Chinese, and many other national groups). The tension between police and these young people is fostered by a range of stereotypical images pertaining to the young people (e.g., ethnic gangs) and the police (e.g., repressive figures associated with authoritarian regimes). Police officers lack adequate training in dealing with people from non-English-speaking backgrounds, particularly refugees and recent migrants (Chan 1994). The differential policing of young people from other than English-speaking backgrounds is captured in the following finding from a recent New South Wales study (Youth Justice Coalition et al. 1994: 32):

> Young people from other than English backgrounds are particularly visible because of their language, clothes and skin colour. This extra visibility combines with a fear of youth gangs (fuelled by periodic media stories) and ethnic stereotypes. Consequently, these young people are likely to be approached and questioned by police for no valid reason. In these situations the police may believe that they are simply reflecting community concern and responding to pressure to do something about 'ethnic gangs'.

The particular vulnerability of these young people—to economic disadvantage, racism and social dislocation—is a matter of urgent concern. The style and manner of policing in relation to their activities and attitudes likewise warrants further research and continual assessment.

In regard to specific operational processes, we also know that arrest rates, use of summons, granting of bail and issuing of formal cautions depend heavily upon police decisions, and these in turn are greatly influenced by the social background of the young person. As we have seen (Chapter 7), young Aboriginal people are many more times likely than non-Aboriginal young people to be dealt with harshly by the police. The nature of the initial intervention by the police has, of course, major consequences for those caught up in the criminal justice system. Again, young Aboriginal and Torres Strait Islander people are systematically disadvantaged by the agents of the state, as reflected in disproportionate arrest and imprisonment rates (Johnston 1991; Cunneen 1992).

CONTACT WITH YOUTH ON THE STREET

In Australian society there is a high level of contact between young people in general, and the police. For instance, 80 per cent of the young people involved in the National Youth Affairs Research Scheme (NYARS) survey reported that they had been stopped by the police, and 50 per cent said they had been escorted back to the police station. Most of the contact occurred in public places, and 70 per cent of the young people reported they had just been 'hanging out' when stopped by the police. Some 37 per cent of the respondents said that they were just walking when approached by the police (Alder et al. 1992). Hence, those aged fifteen to seventeen experience a lot of interaction with the police.

The NYARS research project included interviews with police officers. They revealed that most contact with youths occurred in the early evening shifts, not at night, and that the most frequent location of contact is in malls, shopping centres and other public spaces. The police registered considerable concern about the activities of young people. In terms of particular groups of youths, it was reported by the police that they experienced most difficulties with street kids, gangs and young Aboriginal and Torres Strait Islander people. They listed the characteristics of their contacts with them as follows.

- *When:* early evening shifts, late afternoon
- *Where:* malls, shopping centres, train stations
- *Who:* young men more often than young women; unemployed; students
- *Special cases:* street kids, gangs, Aboriginal and Torres Strait Islander people.

The relationship between the police and young people is frequently marred by tension and conflict. As a number of recent reports and studies make clear (Youth Justice Coalition 1990; Cunneen 1990b; Alder et al. 1992; Watkins 1992; White & Alder 1994), the issues of harassment, intimidation and violence lie at the heart of many of the complaints young people make about the police in Australia today. Conversely, the chronic disrespect for the law and its officials on the part of many young people, and the abuse of police by young people, have also been ably documented (Alder et al. 1992).

To a certain extent, the issue of police harassment is related to the nature of police work in general. As recent reports point out, the use of violence is often seen as a routine part of policing, and any misconduct or over-stepping of boundaries in the use of police powers is protected by the police code of silence (Cunneen 1990b; Fitzgerald 1989). Media images of the 'tough cop', and the age and sex of the officer also contribute to the adoption of a certain style of policing. As a recent Victorian report noted:

> It is our view that many young people at eighteen and a half [the minimum age for recruitment] are too immature to properly undertake the responsibilities and powers that go with the provision of police uniform and weapons, including guns. It is our perception that this is particularly true of young men who too often bring to the job the desire to test their manhood through physical confrontation with others. The fact that the police force is overwhelmingly male contributes to a culture within the police force whereby physical strength and confrontation is glorified and other perspectives which include alternative methods of conflict resolution are undervalued or dismissed. (McCulloch & Schetzer 1993: 15).

A culture of violence involving police and young people is fostered by the actual experience of physical force in their interactions. For example, the NYARS report determined that the police felt that there was little respect for them among sizeable portions of the youth population. It also found that, almost unanimously, police said that they had been assaulted and harassed by young people in the course of their work. The nature of the harassment varied from verbal taunts, being shouted and sworn at, to outright assault, including kicks and punches (Alder et al. 1992). Such reports indicate a high degree of antagonism between police and young people, and 82 per cent of the police reported that they had had to apply force to a young person at some stage. Furthermore, a majority of the police officers interviewed admitted feeling that sometimes too much physical force is used in dealing with young people.

For their part, the young people interviewed in the study reported a high degree of physical and verbal abuse directed at them by the police. They reported that police–youth contact was unfair, and often physical. In the literature on relations between police and youth (see Youth Justice Coalition 1990; White &

Alder 1994), a common theme is 'why pick on me?' Young people complain of the use of 'name-checks' (asking of name and address); of constantly being stopped and questioned; and of lack of explanations for such treatment. All these contribute to feelings of frustration and unease in the police–youth relationship. In such circumstances it is not unusual for emotions to boil over into physical confrontations.

Some groups of young people experience particularly aggressive 'rough treatment'. For example, the 1992 ABC television documentary 'Cop It Sweet' depicted on-the-job racism directed toward young Aboriginal people and people from Asian backgrounds. An earlier report by the Human Rights and Equal Opportunity Commission on Aboriginal juveniles and the police found that the majority of Aboriginal juveniles in detention centres in New South Wales, Queensland and Western Australia had suffered violence at the hands of the police (Cunneen 1990). The study found that:

- 85 per cent of the juveniles reported being hit, punched, kicked or slapped by police
- 63 per cent reported being hit with objects by the police (e.g., police baton, telephone books)
- 32 per cent reported police revolvers drawn and/or fired
- 81 per cent said that they had been subjected to racist abuse by police officers.

Clearly, by approaching their work in such an aggressive manner the police have set in train a dynamic of fear, lack of respect, and resistance on the part of many young Aboriginal people. Resentments and negative feelings result, which may fuel continuing conflict and antagonism.

Another occasion for harassment occurs when young people challenge the arbitrary use of police power. Research shows that police tend to treat more favourably those young people who exhibit co-operation and compliance in their dealings (O'Connor & Sweetapple 1988; Alder et al. 1992; O'Connor 1994). Alternatively, some young people who attempt to claim their legal rights are branded as 'troublemakers' or 'smart arses', and consequently suffer. This was certainly so in the case of Joe Dethridge, a seventeen-year-old who had his jaw broken by the sergeant in charge of the Fremantle police station in 1992. Dethridge and a friend had been picked up by two plainclothes police officers for no specific reason other than 'hanging around'. Partly because they challenged the right of the police to intervene without apparent good cause, extra-special treatment was meted out at the police station (White 1993c). Both young men were roughed up, in separate incidents, and Joe Dethridge in particular was to suffer for months afterwards for confronting the power of the police. Unfortunately, not only is violence part of the repertoire of the police, but occasionally it is used to silence the critics of police conduct.

Existing patterns of police mistreatment and misconduct raise major questions about the style and nature of policing in relation to young people. In instances of alleged misconduct, it is interesting to examine the role of police unions. Customarily, police unions come to the defence of any accused member, regardless of the offence; hence, it is often difficult for victims to obtain justice for abuse of police powers or harassment. Police unions are involved in both proactive and reactive campaigns in the media. At election time, for instance, they often produce political statements demanding more resources, funding and police powers. In specific cases, they mobilise media attention against so-called do-gooders concerned with human rights, or assert the interests and rights of individual police officers over and above the prescriptions of the law or ethics of the office (White & Richards 1992; White 1993c). It is rare indeed to find any police union acknowledging the need for an independent, fully accountable complaints tribunal, much less greater community participation in and control over police work.

COMMUNITY POLICING

Not all interaction between young people and the police is negative, nor does it occur exclusively on the street. 'Community policing', broadly defined, is now an important part of most police departments. Sometimes this term refers to a particular style of policing; more often, it refers to particular types of police practices or specific policing projects. Many of these are linked to programs designed specifically for young people.

The precise nature of community policing is variable, ranging from crime prevention to legal information and safety measures. For example, Blue Light Discos provide young people under the age of seventeen with an opportunity for a night out in a secure environment under the supervision of off-duty police officers. The Police Schools Involvement Program in Victoria is an example of police commitment to developing a better relationship with young people. The long-term aim of such programs is to reduce the incidence of juvenile involvement in criminal behaviour (see James 1994). Information about the criminal law, road safety, and the rules and regulations of bicycle riding are some of the topics covered in such schemes. Police youth clubs, which offer sporting activities and are intended, at least in part, to nurture citizenship in young people, are another example of community-based intitatives (James 1994).

In a number of jurisdictions there have been efforts to create specific youth-centred sections or positions within the police department. In New South Wales, for example, the General Duties Youth Officer Program is designed to integrate crime prevention into routine operational police work. The program is flexible, and officers can choose the level and style of their participation. As in the Victorian Police Community Involvement Program, the general approach is one of 'problem-solving' (McDonald 1991; Beyer 1993). The intention is that officers act in accordance with a charter which specifies that:

- participating police act as protectors of, and advocates for young people
- officers act to divert young offenders away from the criminal justice system wherever possible
- patrols adopt a multi-agency approach to youth crime prevention
- participation in the program is dependent on the General Duties Youth Officers working to a performance-based work contract (McDonald 1991: 116).

While the police who are involved in such duties and programs are enthusiastic about their success (see Beyer 1993; McDonald 1991), there has been little independent evaluation of these schemes to make an accurate appraisal of their strengths and weaknesses (James 1994). Community policing generally is still marginalised within the context of overall policing. Furthermore, there is often an overt resistance to such policing from operational police who view crime fighting and increased police powers and numbers as the real issues in responding to youth crime (White 1991; Beyer 1993).

The concept of community policing is somewhat vague and subject to very different interpretations (McKillop & Vernon 1991). Nevertheless, it does appear to open the door to a form and style of policing which is less coercive and more responsive to the needs of some young people. It promises to be 'more effective, more humane, less stigmatising and much cheaper in the long run than policies directed at crime fighting' (Beyer 1993: 108). However, big questions remain: the central objectives of some types of community policing initiatives are framed within the logic of crime control, rather than peace-keeping; they are preoccupied with young people as 'threats' and 'outsiders' who are to be excluded from any notion of community or joint decision-making; and there is a lack of independent accountability structures (for both day-to-day operational matters and the handling of complaints).

A further problem confronting the police as a whole is that the diversity of their functions can cause contradictions in specific goals and objectives. For example, positive participation of police in schools (e.g., road safety classes) may be counterbalanced by coercive functions relating to the control role (e.g., apprehending truants). In a similar vein, the police may be called upon to play several roles at the community, school and street levels, each of which may undercut the success of the other (White 1993b). The police experience contradictory demands with regard to protecting private property, facilitating the flow of pedestrian and road traffic, fighting crime, and providing for the general welfare of young people. Taken together, and including the wide variety of community policing initiatives, it may well be that the widespread disenchantment with the police among young people arises from the sheer frequency (as well as the nature) of police intervention in their lives.

The frequency of contact can be described as over-policing, and it is necessarily related to the phenomenon of under-policing. That is, it is often the case that the victims of crime in our society belong to the sections of the population that are targeted by the police for continual intervention. As Hogan (1991: 86) comments:

> The impact of crime is unequally distributed across the community: it is the vulnerable and marginalised who are most likely to be victimised, and upon whom being victimised has the most effect. They are the least able to protect themselves from crime (insurance, security), to isolate themselves from it geographically (moving away) and to ameliorate its damage (fewer financial resources). Moreover, this criminal victimisation tends to compound the other ways in which those people are disadvantaged by other social factors.

In essence, these two dimensions—over-policing and under-policing—are flip-sides of the same problem: the non-accountability of police to the communities which they are meant to serve.

From a policing perspective, early intervention among selected groups is seen as pre-empting or preventing the commission of an offence and deterring potential criminal activity. However, as discussed above, the expectations that police have are often based upon particular social and ethnic stereotypes, which in turn are usually associated with unemployment, poverty, social marginalisation and political vulnerability. In such circumstances, the police may appear as an alien force who intervene unnecessarily, unfairly and all too frequently in the lives of these young people.

Police are a group in society that wields enormous power. What they do has significant and lasting impacts on particular groups of young people and their families and communities. How the police use and abuse their power, therefore is of crucial importance for community relationships as a whole. This again raises many of the issues underpinning any critical analysis of the notion of community policing. In particular, the relationship between young people and the police can be framed in terms of these questions: whether policing is in the interests of young people; whether it is being done in a manner which acknowledges their particular social problems; and whether young people themselves can and should have a say in the nature of the policing which occurs in their midst.

Chart 10.2 outlines several different ways in which community policing might be construed, and the alternative practices which could be adopted depending upon the approach one chooses. The 'community' itself is very diverse in nature. As a result, community policing sometimes does not acknowledge or reflect the social divisions and power differences which exist in

Chart 10.2 Dimensions of community policing

Dimension	Comments
In the community	• different types of police presence across a range of social institutions • police youth clubs, blue light discos; police in schools, Constable Care cartoon figure • general duties police officer • Neighbourhood Watch • beat level policing • generally marginal to overall police role
Of the community	• orientation and tasks shaped by opinion-makers and the more powerful in the community • police have a pivotal role in defining who is to be subject to their methods and surveillance • emphasis on crime control and imposing order on certain sections of the community • analysis needed of different social interests and distribution of power within the 'community'
By the community	• conservative versions involve police–community consultative committees, where control and expertise are in hands of police • often policy and control over operational strategies and practices are not in hands of community • links to more representative recruitment and training procedures • more radical versions tied to self-determination at a community level
For the community	• adoption of a community problem-solving approach • identifiable links to 'community' rather than 'police' interests • emphasis on peace-keeping • dealing with offences against certain groups, such as domestic violence and racial discrimination • involves participatory decision-making structures and independent accountability mechanisms

some localities or, conversely, does so in a manner which is unjust, racist and inequitable (see, for example, Cunneen 1989). In some instances, such as some Aboriginal communities, it is more desirable to implement community policing which in effect provides for communal self-determination of locally based programs (Airo-Farulla 1992). The style of policing, the targets of policing, and the control over policing are crucial issues which must be addressed if tensions and conflicts between young people and police are to be overcome.

THE CONTEXT OF REFORM

It is important to locate police–youth relations within the context of wider economic, social and political processes. As we have seen, the position of young people in the political economy has declined markedly in recent years. The immediate and long-term prospects for many young people continue to look bleak as the 1990s come to a close. The consequences of a deep and extensive recession will continue to reverberate throughout the social order for some time. This in turn will be accompanied by persistent tensions and contradictions in the role, functions and practices of the police.

In Australian society, the police are called upon to perform a range of different roles. If we examine these functions in class terms we find that, beyond the routine activities linked to traffic management and welfare, the police are primarily concerned with the protection of private property and the maintenance of public order. The general targets for police intervention are the poor, the unemployed, Aborigines, striking workers, and demonstrators. In general, it is the less powerful sections of the population, such as people with mental health problems (Hearn 1993), who are most vulnerable to police action.

The policing of young people is an intertwining of different images and styles, of different groups of young people, and of different types of police officers. Values such as 'respect for authority' can influence the nature of the relationship. The ways in which youth subcultures form and take part in the world can be seen as a problem by the formal agencies of social control (see White 1993a). The creation of a large, visible youth underclass in the last decade brings with it images of anarchy, desperation and profound alienation—and political pressure to do something to protect respectable citizens from the perceived threat posed by the dispossessed. Regular moral panic directed at certain groups (e.g., ethnic youth gangs) and certain issues (e.g., violence, drugs) keeps attention on working-class street crime and not only legitimates but sustains demand for a strong police presence in the affairs of young people.

It is this general social context which makes it difficult to produce significant reform in the area of police–youth relations without changes to the wider social structure. The history and traditions of policing have been bound up with policing the working class (see Farrell 1992), and in particular those sections of the working class identified as the criminal classes. In periods of sustained economic hardship and social upheaval, the primary class role of the police tends to be reasserted, with the focus on containing and managing the effects of economic transformation. Operationally this is manifested in a major extension of police powers. For example, recent legislation in South Australia, specifically the *Young Offenders Act 1993*, has greatly expanded the discretionary power of police to determine what constitutes a minor offence, and enables them actually to impose sanctions themselves in cases which are so defined (Simpson 1994).

Economic recession is associated with survival crime and anti-social behaviour; and the police have a significant role to play in the criminalisation of the poor for activities stemming from lack of economic control. Simultaneously, progressive policing reforms are likely to collapse in the face of a conservative backlash—the law-and-order lobby tends to become stronger when the incidence of violent and property crime is believed to be high. The role of the police is thus necessarily tied up with structural economic trends and the class-related ebb and flow of electoral politics.

Without significant changes in structural features of society, such as a reorientation of economic goals and redistribution of community resources, it is likely that police work will continue to take the form of controlling young people, rather than exhibiting the more progressive aspects of community policing as identified in Chart 10.2. Nevertheless, even if the wider context does not change in the immediate or foreseeable future, there are reforms which are practicable and worthwhile to pursue here and now (Youth Justice Coalition 1990; Hall 1994). In particular, any agenda for change should centre on the question of rights, especially given the potential importance of the United Nations *Convention on the Rights of the Child* and allied legal instruments.

There are a number of areas where reform is needed if youth–police relations are to be constructed on more equal and positive terms. These are summarised below:

Police training

- greater attention to the nature of youth livelihood, the social construction of youth, youth studies research on the needs and position of young people in society
- training in particular skills, such as interpersonal communication, which will make it easier to work with young people
- alternative dispute resolution techniques, an emphasis on mediation and peace-keeping, concern with providing a public service
- critical discussion and evaluation of the lack of effectiveness and limits of crime fighting as a model for policing
- provision of continual in-service as well as pre-service training and education so that police are kept up to date with developments in the world of young people.

Community policing

- greater integration of community policing styles into operational policing
- extension of community participation in and control over day-to-day activities, with more involvement by young people
- adoption of proactive and problem-solving approaches
- establishment of collective methods to deal with persistent problems (rather than by targeting selected individuals for action), and a focus on the on-going relationship and disputes between young people and the police in particular neighbourhoods.

Law reform

- acknowledgement and implementation of the provisions of the United Nations *Convention on the Rights of the Child*
- greater checks on police powers such as 'name checks' and the use of 'move on' powers
- provision of adequate legal safeguards in areas such as police interrogation, use of independent youth advocate, fingerprinting and body searches
- improvements in the provision of legal aid for young people, and greater flexibility in court proceedings to take into account relationship between the police and the young person.

Police accountability

- constant monitoring and evaluation of police performance from the point of view of young people via questionnaires and consultations
- provision of an independent complaints authority to deal with matters of police mistreatment and misconduct
- development of mechanisms which ensure constant community feedback on general issues, not only individual complaints
- use of independent lay visitors to police lock-ups
- assessments of police performance using criteria which reflect the immediate needs of community, rather than traditional law-enforcement statistics.

To this list could be added a number of youth-specific or youth-centred proposals. For example, we might mention attempts to provide young people with knowledge of their legal rights, their position in the law and their obligations in relation to police action directed at them. However, as several studies make clear (O'Connor 1994; Warner 1994), the crucial issue is not knowledge of youth rights—it is the actual exercise of such rights in practice that counts. With regard to this, the main obstacle is the nature of policing itself, which systematically ignores or disregards the spirit of the law in relation to youth rights. Consequently, reform must in the first instance be directed at the institutions of law and order (see also Naffine 1993).

CONCLUSION

This chapter has provided an overview of issues pertaining to police–youth relations in Australian society. The study of this relationship shows that there are a number of competing perspectives regarding what constitutes good policing, both within police departments and in the wider community. The ways in which individual police interact with young people can have a major influence on their personal relationship with them. For example, police in schools and various officers in community police squads often report a close, friendly relationship with the young people with whom they have contact over a period of time. However, it is clear that the general relationship between young people and the police is of great concern. This chapter has attempted to explain some of the dynamics which underpin this general relationship, and to explore some of the alternative measures which could be adopted to improve police–youth relations.

11 courts and the sentencing process

For many young people, apprehension by police inevitably leads to an appearance in the Children's Court. We have already discussed the history of the establishment of separate courts to hear matters involving children (Chapter 1), and the types of offences for which young people appear in court (Chapter 5).

In this chapter we discuss the jurisdiction of the Children's Courts—what type of offences the court can hear and other matters about the power of the court. We also look at how the courts make decisions about sentences, what options are available and what principles are applied. Finally, we consider the use of incarceration as the most punitive sentencing option.

THE JURISDICTION OF THE CHILDREN'S COURT

The jurisdiction and status of the Children's Court varies between States and Territories. In some States it is presided over by a magistrate, in others by a specialist judge from the District Court. Most States have specialist Children's Courts operating in the major cities. In other areas the local magistrate can convene a Children's Court when necessary.

The Children's Courts have major jurisdiction over offences committed by young people. These include all **summary offences** (minor offences usually heard in a magistrate's court), although traffic offences may be excluded. The hearing in a Children's Court is summary, that is, before a magistrate and without a jury. The public is excluded from the court, and there are prohibitions on the printing of the names of young people before the court. For most **indictable offences** (serious offences usually heard before a judge and jury in a higher court, such as car theft and break and enter), the young person can elect whether to have the matter dealt with by the Children's Court or in a higher court by a judge and jury. The court itself may decline jurisdiction and refer the case to a higher court. For serious indictable offences such as homicide, where the offence might result in a sentence of life imprisonment and there is a prima facie case to answer, the young person is tried in the Supreme Court.

In Queensland, Western Australia and South Australia, the Children's Court is headed by a judge. Other jurisdictions have a children's magistrate or senior children's magistrate. In the jurisdictions where a judge heads the Children's Court, the judge is able to hear and determine more serious matters than in jurisdictions where a magistrate heads the court. The available maximum penalty is usually greater if the young person is sentenced by a judge rather than a magistrate.

In jurisdictions where the Children's Court is headed by a judge, the judge also acts as a review court for matters determined by the magistrates. In other States, appeals from decisions by the Children's Court go to the higher courts.

The age of criminal responsibility is an important requirement governing juvenile justice legislation. In most Australian jurisdictions, the age of criminal responsibility has been raised above the seven years set by the common law. For example in New South Wales it was raised to eight in the 1930s, and then to ten in the mid-1970s. There are still variations between States, but the trend has definitely been upwards. The age of criminal responsibility is ten years in most States. Children under this age cannot be charged with a criminal offence. It should be noted that, whatever the age chosen for the attribution of criminal responsibility, there is some degree of arbitrariness. The reasons for raising the age of criminal responsibility to ten were that few children under this age appeared on criminal matters, and that those who did were better dealt with as welfare or care and protection cases. Because the age is partly arbitrary, it is open to political challenge. During the height of law-and-order campaigns there have been calls by extremist groups to *lower* the age of criminal responsibility back to seven or eight years (Cunneen & Robb 1987: 231).

The Children's Courts are often seen as the pinnacle of the juvenile justice system. A young person who has been charged by the police with a criminal offence is brought before the court, where guilt or innocence is established and a penalty imposed. However, in reality the Children's Courts play a relatively minor role in testing evidence and determining the innocence or guilt of the defendant. Most children plead guilty to the offence with which they have been charged, or to a lesser offence after negotiations with the prosecution. Although there are difficulties in obtaining accurate information, Naffine, Wundersitz and Gale (1990) estimated on South Australian data that there was a guilty plea in 87 per cent of Children's Court appearances. In a further 7 per cent, no plea was entered because the police decided not to proceed with the prosecution and the matter was withdrawn. In the remaining 6 per cent of cases a formal not-guilty plea was lodged and the matter was contested. It would appear that these figures are typical of Children's Court appearances in other Australian jurisdictions. As shown in Table 11.1, some 9 per cent of cases in the New South Wales Children's Court were not proven—some of these were withdrawn by the prosecution, and in others the defendant pleaded not guilty and the prosecution subsequently failed to prove its case beyond reasonable doubt.

The high rate of guilty pleas has important implications for the administration of justice in the Children's Courts. Naffine, Wundersitz and Gale (1990) have stated the position thus:

> If children plead guilty as matter of course, then there is no adjudication and the court's function is simply to decide what to do with offenders. Indeed, with the plea of guilty, the child abandons many of the standard rights and protections implicit in due process . . . [the child] fails to take advantage of the presumption of innocence and the right to have the prosecution prove its case beyond reasonable doubt (Naffine, Wundersitz & Gale 1990: 196).

By pleading guilty, the young person gives up the right to challenge the prosecution's case and to have a lawyer present a defence and argue for their innocence. For the purposes of this discussion, however, the most important point is the role assumed by the court. If young people plead guilty, then the major role of the court is to decide on a penalty. The court is not reviewing evidence and how it was obtained, nor is it playing a significant role in monitoring or remedying any abuses of young people's rights (O'Connor 1994: 92–3). The key

Table 11.1 Court outcomes, Children's Court, New South Wales, 1992–93

Court outcome	Male		Female		Total	
	n	%	n	%	n	%
All matters						
Proven matters	9 710	90.7	1 681	91.8	11 391	90.9
Unproven matters	995	9.3	151	8.2	1 146	9.1
Total matters determined	10 705	100	1 832	100	12 537	100
Proven matters						
Prison sentence	10	0.1	0	0.0	10	0.1
Detention order	710	7.3	49	2.9	759	6.7
Community service order	667	6.9	59	3.5	726	6.4
Probation—supervision	1 047	10.8	156	9.3	1 203	10.6
Probation—no supervision	599	6.2	92	5.5	691	6.1
Fined	1 548	15.9	242	14.4	1 790	15.7
Recognizance—supervision	493	5.1	113	6.7	606	5.3
Recognizance—no supervision	1 769	18.2	369	22.0	2 138	18.8
Dismissed with caution	1 645	16.9	392	23.3	2 037	17.9
Dismissed	951	9.8	175	10.4	1 126	9.9
Other	271	2.8	34	2.0	305	2.7
Total proven matters	9 710	100	1 681	100	11 391	100

Source: Adapted from New South Wales Department of Juvenile Justice (1993: 137–9)

function of the Children's Court is to decide on an appropriate penalty for the young person.

CHILDREN'S COURTS AND DECISION-MAKING

How do magistrates and judges make a decision on a penalty appropriate to a young person before them who has been convicted of an offence? What are the relevant factors to be taken into account, what are the options available, and what external factors affect the court's decision?

In the discussion which follows, we consider three areas of importance to sentencing: the sentencing options which are available and their hierarchy; the principles of sentencing; and the role and content of presentence reports.

Sentencing Options and Hierarchy

Any decision by Children's Court on what to do with a young person convicted of an offence is limited by the sentencing options which are available to the court. These sanctions (or dispositions) vary from one Australian jurisdiction to another. In general, the options are set out in the legislation which governs juvenile justice in the particular State.

Sentencing hierarchies have been established in some recent juvenile justice legislation (for example, New South Wales and Victoria). Such a hierarchy sets out the available penalties in order of severity. Sentencing hierarchies have been introduced to guide the court in selecting an appropriate penalty and to provide a greater degree of consistency in sentencing. Some legislation (for example, in New South Wales and Victoria) prevents the court from imposing a sentence at one level unless it is satisfied that a sentence at a lower level of the hierarchy is inappropriate. Such requirements are intended to oblige magistrates to justify the use of severe penalties, to promote the use of non-custodial options, and to reinforce the use of detention as a sentence of last resort.

A typical sentencing hierarchy ranges from the most punitive disposition (detention) to the least intrusive—dismissal with or without conviction. Although the actual sanctions vary from one State to another, we can construct a general picture of what is available to the Children's Courts and place them within a hierarchy.

The sanctions available to the court, in order of decreasing severity, may include:

- detention in a youth training centre (in some jurisdictions and particular cases, imprisonment in an adult gaol may also be an option)

- community service order or attendance centre order (the maximum hours vary between 100 and 500, depending on jurisdiction)
- probation (usually up to two years)
- fine and recognisance
- fine (usually with a maximum of $500 per offence, although the maximum is $2000 in some jurisdictions)
- good behaviour bond or recognisance (usually up to two years)
- undertaking to observe certain conditions
- dismissal.

Later in this chapter we will discuss the more severe sentencing option of incarceration and the next chapter discusses in detail various community-based sanctions. For the present, it is important to see in general terms the types of penalties which can be applied to a young person who is convicted of an offence.

Sentencing Principles

The existence of various sentencing options in itself does not tell us very much about why a particular sanction might or might not be used. How does a magistrate decide whether a particular young person should receive a community service order or a period of detention? What are the most important factors to be taken into account: the nature of the specific offence, the prior record of the young person, the protection of society, the prospects of rehabilitation, or the likelihood of re-offending?

There are a number of general principles applicable to the sentencing of young people which we outline below.

Responsibility

Responsibility refers to the fact that an offender is liable to some form of punishment or sanction for an offence. There may be mitigating factors which reduce the level of responsibility, such as the following.

- *Intent:* for example, was the offence the result of intention or recklessness?
- *Excuse:* for example, self-defence, provocation
- *Impairment:* mental or physical conditions which might reduce responsibility
- *Motive:* for example, was the offence an act of maliciousness or an act of conscience?

These mitigating factors are common to both adults and juveniles and can be taken into account by the magistrate when deciding on an appropriate penalty.

However, of particular importance to young people is the notion of reduced responsibility because of age.

Reduced responsibility

It is commonly accepted in sentencing that juveniles are to be treated differently from adults because of their immaturity and level of development. It is regarded as unjust and unrealistic to hold young people to the same standards as adults. Such a view is partly reflected in the different sanctions which are applied to young people and the notion that young people are particularly vulnerable and need protection.

Proportionality

It is an accepted principle that the severity of the sentence should be commensurate with the seriousness of the offence. In other words, the sanction which is applied by the court needs to take account of the seriousness of the crime and the blameworthiness of the offender: the punishment should fit the crime. Such a principle can affect both the upper and lower limits of the punishment, but tends to be concerned with preventing excessive sentences.

Equality

The principle of equality refers to consistency in punishment—that like cases are treated alike. Disparity in sentences is seen as undermining a fair and equitable legal system. Unequal sentences are sometimes a problem within particular jurisdictions; some research, has shown for instance, that specialist Children's Courts in the city are less likely to impose detention orders than country courts (Luke 1988).

Specificity and determinancy

Specificity refers to the precise nature of the sanction. It is accepted that the offender should know precisely the nature of the sentence that is being imposed. Determinancy refers to the duration of the sentence and that the offender knows the duration in advance.

General and specific deterrence

Sentencers may regard a particular sentence as sending a message to the community concerning the seriousness of an offence and the likely punishment, thus *generally* deterring other potential offenders. A sentence might also be regarded as designed *specifically* to deter the particular young person from reoffending. General and specific deterrence is often argued in conjunction with community protection. The view that there is a need to protect the community from particular types of offences may lead to a sentence involving some element of deterrence.

Frugality

The sentence imposed should be the lowest that is appropriate. The court should select the least restrictive sentencing option and time period, while taking account of the seriousness of the offence, the role of the young offender and their age and prior record.

Rehabilitation

The chance of rehabilitation of the offender should be considered by the court when determining sentence. With young people, this normally requires consideration of their needs in relation to guidance and development.

Even a cursory analysis of these general sentencing principles shows the difficulties that could be encountered in practice. How does a court decide what relative weight to place on rehabilitation or deterrence? How does holding young people responsible for their actions sit with notions of reduced responsibility because of age and immaturity? What weight should be given to protecting the community compared to the likelihood of a young person undergoing rehabilitation? Generally, juvenile justice legislation in Australia has articulated the sentencing principles applicable to the Children's Court within the relevant legislation. South Australia was the first State to do this in 1979 and most States have now followed this practice. We list the major sentencing principles from Section 109 of the Queensland *Juvenile Justice Act 1992*.

In sentencing a child for an offence, the court must have regard to:

- the general principles applying to the sentencing of all persons
- the general principles of juvenile justice
- special considerations (see below)
- the nature and seriousness of the offence
- the child's previous offending history
- any information about the child that the court considers appropriate including a presentence report
- any impact of the offence on the victim
- the fitting proportion between the sentence and the offence.

The special considerations referred to in the legislation provide that:

- the child's age is a mitigating factor on any penalty to be imposed
- a non-custodial order is better than detention in promoting the child's reintegration into the community
- rehabilitation of a child is greatly assisted by the child's family and opportunities to engage in educational programs and employment
- a child who has no apparent family support or opportunities to engage in

educational programs and employment should not receive a more severe sentence because of the lack of these opportunities

- a detention order should be imposed only as a last resort and for the shortest possible period.

The sentencing principles set out in the Queensland legislation incorporate the general principles referred to previously, as well as attempting to delineate those principles which are specific to young people. While it is important that such principles are to be found in the legislation, they tend to be extremely generalised and representative of a variety of goals. Their generalised nature limits the assistance they provide in actual sentencing. A more fundamental problem is the extent to which magistrates and judges take the principles into account when sentencing. To illuminate these problems, it is worth considering a specific case that went to the New South Wales Court of Criminal Appeal and was decided on 22 April 1991 (*R v GDP* (1991) 53 A Crim R 112).

P. was a fifteen-year-old boy who, with two friends, caused extensive damage to a car yard and construction company in the western suburbs of Sydney, to the value of more than $1.5 million. P. was arrested by police, and made admissions in two records of interview. P.'s charge could have been determined in the Children's Court; however, the court used its discretion to commit P. to stand trial in the District Court. P. pleaded guilty and was sentenced to twelve months' detention. A successful appeal was lodged in the Court of Criminal Appeal and the sentence was reduced to twelve months' probation.

Justice Matthews in her judgment made a number of points concerning the principles of sentencing young people. She noted that P. was a first offender and had received a favourable court report, school report and psychiatric report. He had rehabilitated himself to a substantial degree since the original offence by not re-offending and by returning to school. Justice Matthews found that original judge who imposed the custodial sentence had been wrong on two accounts. Although the sentence of twelve months' detention was within the range of appropriate penalties, given the seriousness of the offence, it did not take into account the youth of the offender nor his prospects for rehabilitation. The sentencing judge had stated that the ordinary principles of sentencing applied to young offenders in the same way as they did to adult offenders. Judge Matthews in the Appeal Court found that this was not the case, and that different principles apply in the sentencing of young people. Secondly, the sentencing judge had failed to distinguish the comparatively minor role played by P. in the offences. P. received the same sentence as one co-offender but had played a substantially lesser role.

In *R v GDP*, the Court of Criminal Appeal stated that general deterrence was not a substantial consideration in sentencing young people and that rehabilitation must be the primary aim, particularly where there was positive evidence of the prospect of rehabilitation. The court in reaching this decision was re-affirming a principle that has been repeated on other occasions in the higher courts, giving rehabilitation primacy over punishment and deterrence.

Presentence Reports

Presentence reports are taken into account by magistrates when they are sentencing young people. These reports have been a feature of the Children's Courts since they were established, and in many jurisdictions they are mandatory if the court is considering committing a young person to an institution. Presentence reports are known under a variety of names, depending on the jurisdiction (social background report, assessment panel report, court report, etc.). Essentially, they supply social background information on the offender in order to assist the court to determine the most appropriate way of dealing with a young person.

There is legislative guidance as to the nature of material in a presentence report, but the extent of guidance varies between States. In Victoria, the legislation refers to information on the circumstances of the offence, any prior offences, family circumstances, education, employment, recreation and leisure activities, and medical and health matters (Freiberg, Fox & Hogan 1988: 110). In various jurisdictions, presentence reports have been prepared by assessment panels, police, departmental psychologists, juvenile justice staff and welfare officers. They have also included reports from probation officers, schools, employers and doctors. The Queensland sentencing principles in Section 109 of the *Juvenile Justice Act 1992* allow virtually any material to be presented as long as it is deemed relevant by the court.

Research from most States in Australia has shown that presentence reports have a significant influence on sentencing decisions. Magistrates in general follow the recommendations put forward in the reports (Freiberg, Fox & Hogan 1988: 112–13; Carrington 1993). One particular study in Western Australia in the early 1980s found that 68 per cent of presentence report recommendations were followed in their entirety and a further 15 per cent were substantially followed. Furthermore, magistrates expressed a desire that presentence reports contain information on possible sentences (Freiberg, Fox & Hogan 1988: 113).

The scope of the reports is generally ill defined and they can bring before courts information which would otherwise be excluded because of irrelevancy or evidentiary rules (Freiberg, Fox & Hogan 1988: 105). Because of this, there has been considerable debate over the information in presentence reports and the effect they have on sentencing. Broadly speaking, it is claimed that presentence reports contain information which is fundamentally ideological in nature, and rest on particular assumptions concerning the causes of offending. These assumptions work against the interests of indigenous young people and those from working-class backgrounds and ethnic minority groups. The gender assumptions work against the interests of young women.

For example, when discussing family structure, many psychologists' reports have highlighted non-nuclear family arrangements (such as 'the young person lives with her aunt'). Such statements are based on an assumed model of normality—the nuclear family. They give the impression that non-nuclear families are abnormal, that they are disrupted and dysfunctional, and therefore that the children are disturbed (Milne & Munro 1981; Ozols 1994; Gale et al. 1990; Carrington 1993). Similarly, issues of control and supervision within the family are a theme in presentence reports. Reports often highlight what is assumed to be inadequate supervision with statements like 'little effective control or supervision', 'supervision lax', 'few limits'. Again there is an implicit assumption about normality and abnormality in child-rearing practices. Social and cultural differences are ignored and what are assumed to be the failings of individual parents and children are stressed (Milne & Munro 1981: 11). Finally, the level and depth of family interactions and attachments are described with statements like 'seems to be little interaction between family members', 'unresponsive, non-verbal'. These models of communication and interaction derive from white and middle-class families and have the effect of making the relationships of young offenders appear pathological or abnormal.

Many of the assumptions underlying presentence reports can be understood within a framework of the ideology of cultural deprivation. That is, members of working-class and minority families are assumed to be lacking, in comparison to the middle-class norm. The young offender is thought to come from a social situation which leads to 'deficiency' in physical, cognitive and linguistic experience. The importance of this view in relation to sentencing is that presentence reports embodying these assumptions are likely to provide the rationale for intervention. Given that most magistrates themselves are white males coming from middle-class backgrounds, the presentence reports are likely to reflect the cultural assumptions of the sentencer. Perhaps, then, it is not surprising that magistrates in the majority of cases follow the recommendations which are put forward.

It is apparent that the court puts together a sentence based on an amalgamation of inputs, including the formal requirements of the sentencing hierarchy and sentencing principles, with the information presented in court reports. Such a process is probably more pronounced with use of punitive sentencing options such as detention. Clearly a range of factors is involved, including the nature and seriousness of the offence and the age and prior record of the defendant. There is also the influence of other, less tangible, factors, such as conceptions of social normality, which find their way into the sentencing process and work to the disadvantage of certain young people. When the court is considering issues such as 'the likelihood of rehabilitation', there is the most room for assumptions about social class and cultural difference to affect decision-making.

THE UTILISATION OF SENTENCING OPTIONS

We have outlined the sentencing options available to the Children's Court in general terms and discussed various aspects of sentencing. A key issue which remains to be examined is the actual use of these sentencing options. How often is detention used? What are the most commonly used sentencing dispositions? Table 11.1 (page 219) shows the court outcomes for one State, New South Wales, during 1992—93, giving sentencing options for criminal matters which were proven before the Children's Court. It also shows the analysis by sex of the use of sentencing options. Sentencing outcomes are different between the sexes, with girls generally receiving less punitive options. This issue was explored at greater length in the previous chapter. Table 11.1 shows the comparative percentages of matters which were proven and matters where the court found the offence to be unproven. Overall, some 9 per cent of matters that come before the Children's Court are found to be unproven.

The major sentencing option utilised by the Children's Court is a dismissal, which is used in almost 28 per cent of cases. In most of the dismissals, the court also issues a caution to the offender. The use of dismissals in over one in four cases may indicate the trivial nature of the offence and/or the court's desire not to further stigmatise the young person. Certainly the offence categories where dismissals were most frequently used were for shoplifting, stealing, property damage and offensive behaviour.

In almost 24 per cent of matters a recognisance (or bond) is used, and in a minority of these cases some form of supervision is ordered. The third most frequent sentencing outcome is probation, which accounts for almost 17 per cent of outcomes; in the majority of these cases there is supervision. Fines are used in 15.7 per cent of cases. Finally, community service orders and the use of detention comprise 6.4 per cent and 6.7 per cent of sentencing outcomes.

YOUNG PEOPLE'S EXPERIENCE OF THE CHILDREN'S COURT

We have already noted that a young person's experience of the Children's Court is usually that of a defendant who has pleaded guilty to an offence. If young people do not avail themselves of the fundamental right to the presumption of innocence, it is important to ask what level of legal representation they have received. In principle, young people who appear in court have a right to legal representation. In practice, however, this right is limited by the ability to access services and by the quality and availability of services. Young people are generally represented in court in one of the following ways: by a duty solicitor who operates at the particular court; by a legal aid solicitor or one funded by legal aid; by a specialist community legal service (for example, the Youth Legal Service in Western Australia or Aboriginal Legal Service); or by a private solicitor.

O'Connor (1994: 88–91) has noted five barriers to accessing appropriate legal representation.

- *The cost of legal representation:* Young people are rarely in a position to pay for private representation and are therefore dependent on the services of legal commissions or community legal centres. Generally, however, the needs of young people are peripheral to such organisations.
- *Young people's lack of legal knowledge:* Although there have been some projects aimed at providing legal education for young people (for example Streetwize Legal Comics), it is generally not a high priority.
- *Youth workers' lack of legal knowledge:* Young people often depend for legal information on youth workers who in some cases are ignorant of legal rights (see also Underwood, White & Omelczuk 1993).
- *Limited availability of services:* Even if young people are aware of their rights, actually accessing services can be difficult, particularly if young people require legal assistance while in police custody.
- *Problems with duty solicitor schemes:* Most young people have access to legal services through duty solicitors. We discuss this issue further below.

In Queensland, interviews with young people have identified a number of problems with the duty solicitor schemes. Duty solicitors tend to deal with guilty pleas and bail applications. Young people stated that it was common for them to plead guilty either to 'get things over and done with' or because the duty solicitor had recommended that they do so (Youth Advocacy Centre 1993: 38). The young people also identified these major problems: limited time with the duty solicitor; poor communication by the solicitor; and lack of clarity concerning the role of the solicitor. Young people felt they were not properly represented in court (Youth Advocacy Centre 1993: 39).

Young people's experience of the court processes is shaped by the fact that most young people have pleaded guilty to the offence for which they are appearing. As a result the court is experienced as an institution primarily concerned with sentencing. In a Queensland study, the majority of young people interviewed 'indicated that they believed if they did not plead guilty immediately they ran the risk of being remanded in custody, with the consequent process taking far longer than admitting the crime' (Youth Advocacy Centre 1993: 41).

If young people experience court as essentially a system for imposing punishment, then it is important to consider what understanding they have of the court's processes. Interviews with young people show that the court is seen as an alien world; it is a rapidly conducted and poorly understood process, which imposes significant decisions upon their lives (Youth Advocacy Centre 1993: 41). Young people have indicated that they are unclear about the process which is occurring and the meaning of the outcome, in some cases completely misunderstanding the nature of a sanction (O'Connor & Sweetapple 1988).

Given these experiences, it is difficult to see how the court processing from guilty plea to sentence is of benefit to the young person. There appears to be alienation and a poor understanding of what is occurring, even to the point of misunderstanding sentences. For a small but not insignificant group of young people the court process ends with a sentence to detention. More than any other sentencing option, the deprivation of liberty and the use of incarceration remains the most controversial of juvenile justice interventions.

THE USE OF DETENTION

Throughout Australia there are provisions for incarcerating young people in an institution separate from adult offenders. These institutions are variously known as youth training centres, detention centres, juvenile justice centres, etc. Apart from rare cases in which young people are sent to adult prisons, a detention order is the most severe of the sentencing options available to the Children's Court. For this reason, it is necessary to consider in more detail how the use of detention works in practice.

In some jurisdictions there are certain legislative requirements when the court is considering sentencing a young person to a period of institutionalisation. As we noted above, a presentence report must be considered. The court must be satisfied that no other sentencing option is appropriate. If the detention order is made, the court must state its reasons for the order in writing (see for instance the Western Australian, Queensland and New South Wales legislation). Some jurisdictions also define the purpose of detention in their legislation. For instance, in the New South Wales *Children (Detention Centres) Act 1987*, Section 4 of the legislation stipulates that young persons subject to remand or a detention order should take their place in the community as soon as possible as persons who will observe the law, and that 'satisfactory relationships' should be maintained between the young person and their family.

The establishment, operation and procedures relating to detention are spelt out in some general juvenile justice legislation. For example, Part 6 of the Queensland *Juvenile Justice Act 1992* covers:

- the establishment and management of detention centres
- the appointment, functions and powers of official visitors
- such matters as initial reception, medical treatment, visitors, leave of absence, transfer to prison
- complaints and complaint handling
- offences relating to detention centres.

The relevant legislation provides the formal aspects of the operation of detention. It does not tell us much about the practices of detention, about who is incarcerated, or about the extent to which detention is utilised. One way of considering the use of detention is to compare the rates of incarceration between different jurisdictions. The rates vary considerably between States. In Chapter 7 we analysed the different incarceration rates between Aboriginal and non-Aboriginal young people, and the fact that there were significant differences between States in the use of detention. Overall, the jurisdictions with the highest juvenile incarceration rates at the beginning of 1993 were Northern Territory (89 per 100,000), Western Australia (52 per 100,000) and New South Wales (45 per 100,000). Victoria had the lowest rate, about one-third that of New South Wales (Atkinson 1994: 25).

Most young people in detention centres are there because they have been sentenced by the courts. However, one feature of the juvenile justice system is the relatively large number of young people held on **remand**. These are young people who have been refused bail by the court and are in custody awaiting the determination of their case. One profile of juvenile detainees found that 28 per cent of those in detention were on remand. The average age of the remand population was also younger than that of the young people sentenced to detention, with one-third under sixteen years (Cain 1994c: 32).

Other key characteristics of the young people in detention relate to gender and indigenous status, which we have touched upon in earlier chapters. Ethnicity is also an important aspect of detention, particularly in New South Wales and Victoria where significant numbers of young people from non-English-speaking backgrounds are incarcerated. For instance, in June 1992 almost 20 per cent of young people in New South Wales detention centres were from non-English-speaking backgrounds (New South Wales Department of Juvenile Justice 1992: 55).

The services provided to young people with mental illness and intellectual disability within the juvenile justice system also require more discussion and research. A New South Wales report on young people with intellectual disability, for example, found that more resources were needed for staffing, identification processes, training programs, post-release support services, data collection, information exchange, and so on (New South Wales Department of Family and Community Services 1988). In addition to resource questions, the report raised a number of substantive policy issues, such as the issue of segregation (which was not considered justifiable on the grounds of either possible numbers or effective programming).

Another important issue is the nature of offences for which young people are sentenced to detention. The offence types which lead to a detention order are shown in Table 11.2, using figures from New South Wales. It shows that the major offences for which a detention order is imposed by the court are break,

Table 11.2 The use of detention and the nature of offence, Children's Court, New South Wales, 1992–93

Offence	Detention order	
	n	%
Homicide	1	0.1
Serious assault	52	6.9
Assault	55	7.2
Sexual offences	2	0.3
Other against the person	3	0.4
Robbery and extortion	55	7.2
Fraud	12	1.6
Break and enter	204	26.9
Motor vehicle theft	93	12.2
Shoplifting	8	1.1
Other stealing/theft	54	7.1
Possession stolen goods	40	5.3
Property damage	30	3.6
Justice offences	97	12.8
Against good order	15	2.0
Serious driving	4	0.5
Drug offences	33	4.3
Other	1	0.1
Total	759	100

Source: Adapted from New South Wales Department of Juvenile Justice (1993: 126–30).

enter and steal (26.9 per cent), justice offences (12.8 per cent) and motor vehicle theft (12.2 per cent). If we combine the offence categories into broader definitions—offences against the person, offences against property, and other offences—it is apparent that 65 per cent of detention orders are given by the courts for property offences. Offences against the person comprise 15 per cent of offences. Those related to driving, drugs and good order comprise another 7 per cent, and the remaining 13 per cent are justice offences (mainly escaping custody or breaching probation, bail, recognisance or community service order). These figures raise serious questions concerning the appropriateness of incarceration for property offenders.

SERIOUS OFFENDERS AND REPEAT OFFENDERS

In recent years there has been considerable controversy concerning repeat and serious offenders and appropriate policy responses to them. A number of States have introduced specific legislation to deal with repeat offenders or have special provisions to deal with serious offenders. In Queensland, the legislation has particular provisions for young people convicted of a serious offence (defined as an offence for which an adult would be liable to imprisonment of fourteen years or more). In such circumstances the young person can be sentenced to detention for up to ten years. In cases of offences which carry life sentences for adults, such as murder or rape, the court can order the detention of the young person for up to fourteen years.

In Western Australia the *Crime (Serious and Repeat Offenders) Sentencing Act 1992* allowed for youths who had been classified as serious repeat offenders to receive a minimum of eighteen months' detention if they had been convicted of a prescribed offence. Release of the young person was dependent upon the determination of a Supreme Court judge. In other words, the sentence is indeterminate. This legislation has now been allowed to lapse through a sunset clause, but will be substantially reintroduced in a section of the *Young Offenders Act 1994*. The problems of legislation designed to achieve incapacitation and deterrence are discussed further below. For now it is important to consider how repeat offender legislation itself offends against certain sentencing principles. Broadhurst and Loh (1993: 57) have noted four principles in particular that are ignored by such legislation.

- *Special consideration for young people:* Adults and juveniles are treated alike on the basis of their previous offending history and a mandatory sentence is imposed.
- *One punishment for each offence:* By imposing a mandatory sentence on the basis of previous offending history, in effect the court is sentencing the young person afresh for past offences.
- *Proportionality:* The sentence imposed for the final offence which activates the legislation is mandatory and bears no proportion to the seriousness of the offence.
- *Prohibition of preventive detention:* Young people subject to the legislation are sentenced on the basis of likely recidivism and the protection of society from the offences they would be likely to commit.

From the available evidence, it appears that most young people who end up in detention centres are in fact repeat offenders, irrespective of any specific legislation aimed at incarcerating recidivists. A study by Asher (1986) of seventy-five incarcerated young people in Victoria found that most of them had had considerable previous experience with the juvenile justice system. Some sixty-five of them had three or more previous convictions, and more than three-quarters had previously been placed on bonds or probation (Asher 1986: 68). A study in Queensland found that over 80 per cent of young men in one detention centre had been previously incarcerated (Youth Advocacy Centre 1993: 9). In New South Wales it was found that 8 per cent of young people in detention centres on control orders (not on remand) had no prior convictions and 51 per cent had ten or more previous proven offences (Cain 1994c: 36).

A recent study that considered sentencing found that only a very small proportion of young people sentenced to detention had no previous court appearance (0.6 per cent). Conversely, about 30 per cent of young people appearing with six or more previous appearances were sentenced to detention (Luke & Cunneen 1993: 266).

THE RATIONALE FOR DETENTION

Reasons given for the use of detention include incapacitation, deterrence, punishment, rehabilitation, and the protection of society. Theories of incapacitation argue that control of delinquency can be achieved by identifying repeat offenders and incarcerating them. The argument is that once chronic offenders are locked up the juvenile crime rate will be reduced significantly. However, it is difficult to predict who will be a repeat offender. A cohort study by Wolfgang, Figlio and Sellin (1972) showed that a small group of 6.3 per cent offenders committed five or more offences, yet the researchers were unable to predict at any stage who would become a serious repeat offender. Another US study of a cohort with at least one arrest for a violent crime concluded that 'our research is only one of many studies leading to the same conclusion. . . . the power to predict is too weak a basis for decision-making' (Hamparian et al. 1978: 133). A similar critique has been mounted against the promises of Australian legislation on repeat offenders. According to Broadhurst and Loh (1993), we know that a few offenders account for a large proportion of offending, but these young people are identified retrospectively, not prospectively. We cannot predict who will be in the high-risk group. When it comes to introducing legislation, there is simply no logic to setting periods like eighteen months for the offences to accumulate or setting thresholds at four convictions or more.

Some of the general problems in prediction of repeat offenders have been explained by Lundman (1994). The following discussion is based on the data in the New South Wales report by Coumarelos (1994) referred to in Chapter 5. Logically, if we want to stop re-offending we could incarcerate all first offenders before the court. Yet we know that incarceration would be unnecessary for about 70 per cent of these young people because they will not reappear in any case. We know that the remaining 30 per cent of young offenders will go on to contribute about 62 per cent of all court appearances, but we are unable to predict who the 30 per cent are on the basis of their first appearance. Perhaps, then, we could contemplate incarcerating all young people who appear for a second time. However, only half of those young people will go on to reappear in court for further offences. In effect, we are unnecessarily incarcerating twice the number of young people. The same problem remains as we go through the continuum of repeat offenders. The further we go along the scale of re-offending, the fewer potential offences we prevent. Based on similar research in South Australia, Morgan (1993) has argued that a focus on repeat offenders will not provide a panacea for juvenile offending.

Deterrence theorists have argued that incarceration deters further offending, either specifically through direct experience, or generally through knowledge of punitive consequences (specific and general deterrence). However, Thomas and Bishop (1984: 1242–43) found no support for the hypothesis that sanctions increase the perceptions of risk or diminish the likelihood of offending. In Australia, Kraus (1977) used a control group of school attenders and an experimental group of institutional inmates. He found that the use of penalties did not necessarily change offending behaviour, because the offender's fear of being caught and punished was not raised to the same level as that of the non-offender. Rutter and Giller (1983) have also argued that deterrence requires consistency in the detection of the offender and the sentence imposed in order to have an effect on behaviour. Our earlier discussion on clear-up rates, apprehension and unreported crime question consistency in detection.

Community protection is another reason given for detention. Yet the offences which are most commonly associated with detention orders are not crimes of violence but property crimes. This raises the ethical question of whether incarceration is a suitable response for the commission of these types of offences. It also raises questions of the link between property crimes, political economy and social class. Is it the most economically marginalised group of youth who are being sentenced to detention?

Finally we must consider whether detention actually works in terms of rehabilitation. There have been several empirical studies on aspects of effectiveness. Kraus (1974) examined a group of probationers and a group of juveniles in a detention centre, and generally found greater recidivism after institutionalisation. Another Australian study found that young people who were committed to a detention centre were about four and a half times more likely to be charged with a serious offence as adults than young people who were convicted of offences but not committed (Kraus 1981: 162). An overseas study by Benda (1987) of status offenders and criminal offenders found that 80 per cent had contact with police after their first release from an institution, and 63 per cent returned to a custodial facility.

There have been similar criticisms of the use of remand in custody. Kraus (1978) found that significantly more juveniles re-offended after being remanded in custody. Frazier and Cochran (1986) found young people remanded in custody received more severe judicial outcomes, even with controls for legal and socio-demographic variables.

In summary, the evaluations of the effect of detention have not been positive. At best, there seems to be little difference in outcomes in terms of recidivism. And in some cases it appears that non-custodial options have better results. Incarceration has been criticised on many grounds: ineffective; criminogenic; stigmatising; expensive; and inhumane (Cohen 1979; Murray 1985). It is also important to consider the effects of gathering often already marginalised young people into segregated groups (Erikson 1964). Such policies are likely to increase resentment and alienation.

To some extent these views are reflected in young people's perceptions of detention, as shown in a poem by a young person in South Australia.

Hate

I hate being told what to do
I hate being told what food to eat
I hate being told what time to go to bed
I hate being told what channel on TV to watch
I hate being told if I can read at night
 or not
I hate being told when I can play sport
 what sport
I hate being told what clothes to wear
I hate asking if I can go to the toilet
I hate being told what I can and can't say
I hate being told to do my work at school
I hate the fact that if you don't do what your told that you get into shit
I hate how the staff always have the last say in everything.

(C.B., in Searles and Goodfellow 1994: 13)

The Youth Justice Coalition (1990: 297) found in its interviews with young people in detention in New South Wales that detainees saw themselves as being punished. They did not see rehabilitation as the reason for their incarceration. They did view training in skills as useful, but it should be noted that some of these skills were related to crime. Similarly, interviews with young people in detention in Queensland noted that detention did little to assist young people to return to the community with income, housing or skills. Instead, it seemed to increase a young person's knowledge about crime and established a peer group from within the detention centre which extended to the outside on release—'you meet others you can do jobs with' (Youth Advocacy Centre 1993: 47).

The most negative aspects of detention related to loss of freedom, isolation, and loss of contact with family and friends. Boredom was also seen as an issue in some detention centres. More generally, these criticisms relate to the negative effects of lack of privacy, restriction of creativity, a tense atmosphere, and resentment of a disciplinary regime.

DETENTION CENTRES

If detention centres are the sanction of last resort, it is appropriate that we question what happens behind the walls of these institutions. The range of issues that arises from the administration and regulation of detention centres covers costs, staffing, location, and treatment of young people. For the purposes of this discussion, we will indicate the important points.

The detention of young people is expensive. The costs of incarcerating young people far exceed the costs of the adult system. In late 1989, the average cost per year for a young person in detention was approximately $54,000 (Youth Justice Coalition 1990: 307). Smaller units with better staff–inmate ratios were, of course, more expensive than the average. The cheaper centres were old-style reformatories, with large dormitories, large numbers of young people, few programs, and less staff.

The operational costs of detention centres account for a huge proportion of the juvenile justice budget. For example, over 80 per cent of the juvenile justice budget in New South Wales is expended on detention centres. This expenditure directly affects the amount of money which is available for the supervision and organisation of non-custodial sentencing options. Considered in another light, about 7 per cent of court outcomes are detention orders, yet the bulk of departmental resources are directed into this area. In some jurisdictions there have been moves to establish detention centres which are simply small versions of modern adult prisons. Kariong detention centre in New South Wales, built at the cost of several million dollars, is one example.

Detention centres are usually located in capital cities. As a result, enormous distances separate many young people from their families, friends and communities. In States like Western Australia and Queensland, the distance between detention and home can be thousands of kilometres. Even in the smaller States, the distance can effectively prevent a young person from receiving any family visits.

Staff recruitment has been a major problem in detention centres, partly because of low pay, poor working conditions, and lack of career structure. Some detention centres recorded that 50 per cent of their staff were casual (Youth Justice Coalition 1990: 307). There has been almost no training of youth workers in detention centres. A person starting as a casual youth worker might get less than 20 hours' training, but is expected to assist in the implementation of programs.

Contact between young people who are incarcerated and the outside world has been recognised as important in preventing further isolation and marginalisation. The importance of maintaining contact with family is often recognised in legislation. Yet in practice, contact is often determined by the political whims of senior bureaucrats and politicians. Visiting rights can be restricted, the number of phone calls reduced. These are important issues for young people who already identify loneliness as a key feature of institutional life. Similarly, the induction process into an institution can be a frightening experience (Youth Justice Coalition 1990: 319–320). A booklet of twenty or thirty pages is of little assistance to young people in understanding the day-to-day rules and procedures of a particular centre.

The use of segregation or solitary confinement is still a feature of detention centres throughout Australia. Rules governing segregation vary from State to State, but normally stipulate the reasons for segregation and the length of time for which it can be used. From the staff's perspective, it is a tool for managing disruptive inmates; but from the point of view of young people, the effect is very different.

> I was there for 12 hours. It's just a little cell, with carpet, a brick bench, with the floor coming up like that. No mattress or pillow or nothing. Just looking at the colour of the brick—makes you, starts to get you crazy after a while . . . at night time you think someone's going to come in and shoot you or something—it's just the colour of the wall—it sends you crazy. Then you start to get um . . . schizophrenic . . . When I was little I got shut in a washing machine. This bloke put me in a washing machine when I was little . . . (Youth Justice Coalition 1990: 324).

Other young people in solitary confinement were described as 'mad' because they 'kicked and screamed' when placed in the holding cells. Given the acute range of potential social, medical and psychological problems facing young people in detention centres, the use of isolation cells can be highly damaging.

A related issue is the problem of disturbances or riots. Riots have been a feature of the operation of juvenile institutions since the first reformatories were established in the nineteenth century, and they have occurred in both male and female sections of detention centres. We should acknowledge the point of desperation that is reached when prisoners (young or old) decide to rebel in a situation where they are largely without power. Riots are first and foremost rebellions against conditions of incarceration. They usually occur under regimes which manifest petty authoritarianism combined with a lack of programs. Certainly, young people interviewed after one New South Wales disturbance identified boredom, strictness and poor staff attitudes as central (Youth Justice Coalition 1990: 325). Similarly, a major disturbance in Queensland was, according to an official inquiry, partly associated with the failure to provide for the well-being and development of the inmates, and poor staff–inmate relations including verbal and physical abuse (Ryan & Smith 1994).

Finally we need to consider what is offered to the young person on release. How effectively do governments which have responsibility for incarcerating young people equip young people for life after release? Consider the following points.

- Young people in detention centres are likely to have a poor level of education which may not have significantly improved during time in the detention centre.
- Young people on release from detention are likely to face employment difficulties even though they want to work. Post-release employment programs for young people who have been institutionalised are rare.
- Inadequate income support can be another major problem facing young people on leaving detention, especially if they are under sixteen years of age and have to rely on the Young Homeless Allowance.
- If young people were living marginalised and possibly self-destructive lives prior to detention, how successfully has the detention centre improved their self-esteem and social skills? There appears to be little consistency or evaluation in the provision of these types of services.
- Many young people who have been institutionalised have had problems with substance abuse prior to detention. The level of services provided in drug and alcohol programs has come under criticism in many States.
- Young people need accommodation services upon their release from detention. There is a recognised lack of suitable accommodation for young people who will not return to their families and face the types of multiple disadvantages outlined above.

Finally, what level of personal support is offered to young people before and after leaving a period of incarceration? Support programs are generally far less common than those provided for adult offenders, and where available they are not consistent (Youth Advocacy Centre 1993: 12–24).

CONCLUSION

We began this chapter by considering the jurisdiction of the Children's Court and noted that one of its central features is that it is a mechanism for imposing penalties rather than determining guilt or innocence. It is therefore critical to assess how the courts go about sentencing. We did this first of all by looking at sentencing options and the hierarchy of sentences, and then discussed sentencing principles and the use of presentence reports. Most court outcomes involve dismissal, bond, probation or a fine. However, for some young people the court imposes a custodial sentence.

Most young people who are sentenced to detention have committed an offence related to property theft, particularly break, enter and steal. Most young people in detention are male and have a prior record. While there has been considerable controversy surrounding the incarceration of repeat offenders, it is apparent that it is impossible to predict who will be a repeat offender. In addition, the evaluations of incarceration of young people show that it does not prevent recidivism. In that sense, incarceration does not work—young people who have been institutionalised still go on to commit offences after release. There is also a range of other problems with incarceration, including both its expense and its isolating and marginalising effects.

In the following chapter we consider the alternatives to incarceration, looking at community and non-custodial sanctions.

12 diversion, community programs and informalism

The criminal justice system has a wide range of formal and informal ways of dealing with young people who have engaged in some type of offending behaviour. Public debate often centres on how best to intervene in the lives of young people. The arguments stem from different viewpoints, such as those which emphasise:

- 'just deserts' and individual responsibility (classical theory)
- early diagnosis and treatment or rehabilitation (positivist theory)
- negative labelling, stigmatisation, and the processes which underpin the criminal career (interactionist theory)
- reintegrative shaming and restoration of personal and community dominion (republican theory)
- class, ethnic, 'race' and gender biases in apprehension, official responses and punishment (Marxist and feminist theories)
- adoption of proactive strategies to reduce crime opportunities (conservative and strain theories).

The aim of this chapter is briefly to review those institutions, programs and strategies which operate at the *community* level and which have been designed to improve youth crime rates, and the activities and behaviour of the young offender. The different types of community-based programs reflect the diverse theoretical positions within criminology. Generally speaking, the idea which underpins these kinds of intervention is that the best way to deal with potential offending and with young offenders is to develop structures which operate in an unintrusive manner and/or which are locally based. Generally, it is felt that an appropriate 'solution' to youth crime is linked to the development of informal, user-friendly programs and services, which allow the young person to remain in or be part of a particular community.

An important concept behind these types of intervention is that of **diversion**. This refers to efforts to divert young people away from the formal

240

criminal justice system, or else to divert them to alternative institutions within the criminal justice system or the wider social system as a whole. Such strategies aim to forestall the movement of the young offender deeper into the juvenile justice system, and thus to reduce the possibility of stigmatisation, engagement with a criminal culture, alienation from mainstream social institutions, and so on. For young people who go through the court system and receive sanctioned penalties of some kind, the concern is to ensure that they benefit from the experience in a positive way, gaining new skills and having opportunities to change certain aspects of their behaviour.

The emphasis in this chapter is on those programs and strategies which attempt to deal with juvenile crime and the young offender at the community level. Such interventions reflect different ideological or theoretical concerns about the nature of juvenile behaviour and responses to it. The programs vary in their reliance on *formal or informal* procedures, rules, and professional expertise. They also place different emphasis on *direct or indirect* intervention in the lives of young people, although each approach has implications for the nature and types of activities engaged in by young people.

For ease of presentation, we have organised the discussion into three broad areas: preventive intervention; diversion from formal adjudication; and community corrections, including post-release programs. Each of these areas represents a particular decision point in the ways in which the criminal justice system, and allied institutions such as welfare, intervene to prevent or control juvenile offending.

PREVENTIVE INTERVENTION

Our concern here is with community-based strategies and programs which attempt to stop offending behaviour before it begins. In abstract terms, we can identify three broad approaches to issues of community-based crime control (see, for example, Iadicola 1986). These are not aimed specifically at preventing juvenile crime. Nevertheless, each approach affects young people in some way at the local community level.

Opportunity Reduction

This approach reduces opportunities for criminal behaviour in the belief that crime is ultimately a question of choice and calculation. It relies on a classical notion of criminality in which crime is said to be the result of rational choices, made on a calculated perception of the costs and benefits of particular courses of action. The solution to crime, therefore, is to increase the costs and reduce the opportunities for the commission of crime, and to increase the likelihood of detection.

The specific attributes of offenders (e.g., psychological profile, social background) and their circumstances (e.g., employment, accommodation) are deemed to be irrelevant, insofar as criminality is squarely located within individuals and the range of choices available to them. Strategically, this approach focuses on ways to limit or reduce the opportunities for offending behaviour. This can be done in several ways: by changing the physical setting of the neighbourhood; by encouraging residents and businesses to use various protective devices; and by increasing surveillance at the local community level.

In terms of specific programs, opportunity reduction has been associated with several distinct models or perspectives within criminology. For example, part of the concern is to alter the physical environment to increase surveillance and to transform what is seen to be an unsafe situation into a safe one. One approach is called **crime prevention through environmental design** (CPTED); it seeks to change the physical aspects of the built environment, using a range of social, architectural and planning techniques (Geason & Wilson 1989). The first phase of the CPTED model consists of identifying unsafe city sites, such as public spaces where there is a lot of pedestrian movement and locations where people tend to congregate. The second phase examines basic planning regulations, construction design and civic developments in order to modify potentially unsafe areas. The remedies are often surprisingly simple: for instance, fencing the bottom level of a tiered carpark, planting low shrubs rather than tall trees in front of buildings, or improving the lighting in particular street sites and around transport routes.

A related approach is **situational prevention**. This approach is tightly focused, dealing with specific problem areas or issues (Clarke 1992; Felson 1994). It incorporates some of the elements of the CPTED model, but does so in a very particularistic manner. In summary, situational prevention attempts to reduce crime opportunities by concentrating on three strategies (see Clarke 1992).

- *Increasing the effort required to commit crime:* for example, using locked gates to control access to property, installing bandit screens in banks.
- *Increasing the risks of crime detection:* for example, increasing police patrols in a local area, using anti-theft tags in shops or bar codes on books in libraries.
- *Reducing the rewards of crime:* for example, identifying property with secret markers, ensuring that pizza delivery drivers carry no more than $20 at any one time.

A third way of reducing opportunities is the use of **auxiliary justice** (McNamara 1992). These programs call upon local residents to play a supporting or auxiliary role alongside the formal institutions of criminal justice. Examples of this strategy include Neighbourhood Watch, Safety Houses, Crime

Stoppers and Business Watch. The main focus of such programs is early detection of unusual people or events, together with close co-operation with the authorities, especially the police, in reporting potential criminal activity.

In practice, all these approaches to reducing opportunities for crime often implicitly or explicitly target young people as the main potential culprits or as threats to private property and personal safety. These approaches are often premised upon **social exclusion** (see White & Sutton 1995). That is, they are designed to exclude certain categories or types of people from particular social spaces, geographical areas or economic resources. They operate in a climate of suspicion and fear, and it is usually young people who are deemed to be outside the community and who require the most surveillance, control and discipline.

Opportunity Enhancement

This approach sees crime as stemming from a variety of social factors, often linked to local economic conditions. The difference between a criminal and non-criminal is not the exercise of choice—it is directly related to individual differences based upon biological, psychological and sociological factors. Crime is seen in essentially positivistic terms, that is, as pertaining to some kind of deficit in the individual or in local community circumstances. It is symptomatic of either personal or social pathology of some type.

The prevention of crime is accordingly directed at remedying a situation before it flares up in offending behaviour. It is felt that we can correct individual deficits by establishing early intervention programs, in schools for example, to identify those young people who are at risk and most likely to offend (Semmens 1990). These juveniles can then be placed into contact with appropriate professionals—social workers, counsellors, educational specialists, or trained therapists—at the local community level.

Similarly, from the point of view of strain theory (e.g., social disorganisation, subcultures, differential association), the idea is to promote social integration in order to overcome youth disconnection from mainstream institutions and youth alienation. This approach favours positive, youth-oriented programs such as educational, recreational and training facilities. In program terms, the focus is not so much on reducing opportunities for crime, but on providing young people with enhanced choices and activities. It is argued that the provision of greater leisure outlets, recreational spaces, and job and educational opportunities will provide interesting and positive diversions for young people, and hence fewer of them will engage in crime (see Lundman 1984; Coventry & Walters 1993).

Specific programs include structured activities provided through police youth clubs, Blue Light Discos and the scouting movement, and less formal services and facilities provided by youth and community workers, such as drop-in centres. It is felt that these agencies, networks and activities provide young people with healthy and conventional alternatives to the beliefs and behaviours of deviant youth subcultures and delinquent groups.

In some cases, programs target specific populations. Targets are selected on the basis of statistical indicators showing particular regions as high crime areas, and according to common perceptions regarding which specific communities and localities are most likely to be at risk and in need of assistance (Hil 1994). This notion of crime prevention maximises the opportunities for young people to participate in activities which are seen to be healthy and positive (e.g., organised camps, alcohol-free events), and ensures that young people in 'disadvantaged' areas gain access to services and facilities.

In practice, the proponents of opportunity enhancement tend not to question the nature of the 'deficiencies' and 'disadvantages'; nor do they ask why these pertain to particular groups of young people, such as those from low-income backgrounds. They offer a 'helping hand' within the context of existing structural inequalities. The underlying premise is that the general social institutions and social values are acceptable, and it is the young person who must be given the opportunity to change in order to conform and take full advantage of what these institutions have to offer. It has also been suggested that the specific targeting of these programs (toward so-called at-risk individuals, groups and communities) puts a liberal face on what is, in reality, the imposition of even greater control and regulation by the state in the lives of certain young people (see Hil 1994).

Social Empowerment

This approach views youth crime as the consequence of wider social problems, and in particular as being linked to inequality, oppression and social alienation. It is critical of the notion that youth crime can somehow be overcome or reduced by focusing on the individual offender or by reducing the scope for involvement in criminal acts. In either of these cases, it is young people themselves who are seen as the problem. As Coventry, Muncie and Walters (1992: 21) point out:

'Crime prevention', by current definition, is about rectifying troublesome behaviour. By default, it has a disturbing tendency to establish the boundaries of policy for all young people. What seems needed is a shift in policy focus that de-emphasises the troublesome behaviour of particular young people and instead accentuates the positive and creative citizenship of all young people. This shift necessitates institutional changes and not behavioural management.

Those who support broad-based institutional changes tend to adopt a 'social development' approach to issues of juvenile justice. There is some ambiguity, however, as to the specific content of this approach. For example, one formulation appears simply to expand the scope of opportunity enhancement discussed above, so that whole communities, rather than individuals or specific groups, are seen as the object to be improved. In this view, intervention should be directed at improving the community as a whole, with programs to assist communities to use their own resources to improve their social and economic conditions (Lincoln & Wilson 1994). In essence, the emphasis is on self-help and 'participation'.

Another perspective argues that social development should aim to connect all young people to at least one of the major social institutions. Fundamentally, effective change is not seen simply in terms of people helping themselves; it requires structural transformations in the nature of existing social institutions, such as schools. This approach supports, for example, teaching styles that are co-operative and inclusive, and active negotiation between students and teachers on the relevant curriculum. Developments such as full employment and industrial democracy are seen as essential to any sort of lasting change in the area of juvenile justice (Semmens 1990). This view of social development aligns crime prevention with significant changes, and challenges, to present institutional arrangements.

In political terms, social empowerment tackles these issues by acknowledging the central place of power in both analysis and action. The problem is certainly not seen as one of bad choices or deficient people or neighbourhoods. Rather, the creation and presence of the young offender is seen as symptomatic of deep structural problems such as class division, gender inequality and racism. From a Marxist or feminist perspective, the solution does not lie in treating individuals or in socialising them to conform to mainstream norms and institutions—a strategy of social change is necessary, one which will transform basic social relations at the community level.

Accordingly, the response to youth crime does not include either increasing the costs of crime, or making individuals readjust to society. The community itself, as defined by common class, gender, and ethnic interests, is seen as an essential vehicle for wider social transformations which involve young people, but do not target them as potential or actual offenders. Crime is conceptualised in a much wider sense, to include victimisation of young people and other community members at the hands of the state and by capitalist businesses, and includes violations of human rights. Insofar as this is the case, this kind of community-based approach necessarily requires the linking of many different types of political and action campaigns which together challenge the logic and practices of an unequal system (Coventry & Walters 1993).

In strategic terms, the emphasis on social empowerment and general community participation is realised in action on issues such as allocation of resources and democratic control (Iadicola, 1986). Practical attempts are made to provide opportunities for individuals to meet their needs at the local level, with self-help measures regarding basic living necessities—housing, food, clothing. In the political sphere, attention is directed to achieving full employment, reducing the number of working poor, and redistributing community resources by reallocating wealth in society.

Young people are encouraged to be part of this process of social change. Their immediate physical needs are acknowledged, but they are also treated as active players in moulding and shaping their future as members of the community. Part of the strategic concern is to assert greater communal control over local activities and resources. In some cases, such as Aboriginal and Torres Strait Islander communities, this means self-determination over all facets of life, including the justice system. This approach is founded on a belief that people at the grassroots level should have an active say in how their lives are run, and that the community has the ability to make decisions about people who live in it. Social empowerment means giving power to the people, and this includes young people.

In practice, radical community action encounters problems with local power structures, and with popular attitudes and beliefs. The focus on local actions can be undercut by State and federal political processes which allocate grants and services at the neighbourhood level. It is difficult to raise consciousness of issues and of the importance of active engagement in community life in a general media context which tends to marginalise, trivialise and exclude young people from decision-making forums. Importantly, community action based upon ideals of community control may, in the specific case of trying to deal with juvenile crime, inadvertently be perceived as antagonistic to and by the young people themselves.

The unifying notion in preventive intervention is that something can be done now and at the local community level to prevent young people from engaging in criminal or offending behaviour. The approaches vary in political orientation, from conservative to liberal and radical. They also vary in their perceptions of the problem, their definitions of the causes and nature of crime, and their recommendations for preventing crime. They share similar concerns, however, in that they aim to deal with the possibility of youth crime before it becomes an actuality.

DIVERSION FROM FORMAL ADJUDICATION

Young people who do offend, and who are apprehended for (allegedly) doing so, are subject to a range of state sanctions. As explained in the previous chapter, they may have to attend court, and may be sentenced to a wide range of dispositions. However, not all young people end up in court, and of those that do, not all of them have the case adjudicated or decided upon in the formal court setting.

This is where 'diversion' is employed as a key concept within the juvenile justice system. The term generally refers to instances where young people are turned away from the more formal processes, procedures and sanctions of the criminal justice system. The rationale for diversion is twofold. First, from an interactionist perspective, concerns have long been raised regarding the harmful effects of the stigmatisation which may accompany the formal court and detention process. Young people are seen to be particularly vulnerable to the social effects of negative labelling, and if labelled 'bad' or 'criminal' by the courts, may take on the behaviours and attitudes described in the label. Labelling is seen to be harsh and unforgiving, affecting the opportunities and life chances of young people beyond the period of sanction.

The second rationale for diversion is provided by consideration of the needs of both victim and offender. The republican perspective, for instance, argues that young people know that they have done wrong—that they have harmed another human being in some way—but that they should be encouraged to make the situation right again through discussions with the victim. The method here is reintegrative shaming, a process which expresses reprobation for the act, not the actor, and which ultimately restores 'dominion' to both victim and offender. For young offenders, this theory suggests that the most positive and constructive approach is one which brings victim and offender together, under particular conditions, and which allows some kind of reconciliation and restitution to occur.

Actual program developments tend to reflect varying emphasis on these two rationales. Diversion in a strong or traditional sense means to divert the young person from the system as a whole. At a policy level this is manifest in statements which see diversion as a form of non-intervention, or at best minimal intervention.

Police Cautions

The use of an **informal police caution** is one example of the practical application of such an approach. This is where a police officer advises the young person directly, and on the spot, that they have done or are doing something wrong and will suffer bad consequences if they persist in the offending behaviour. In other words, it usually consists of police on the beat telling young people to move on or to desist from certain behaviour. No further action against the young person is taken.

Similarly, a **formal police caution** usually aims to divert the young person from the formal court system. This process involves an admission by the juvenile and a warning by the police officer, often in the presence of the young person's family. This normally takes place at the police station, and is officially recorded. No further action is taken, although the fact of having received a caution is likely to affect later police interactions with the young person.

There are important legal and administrative differences between the States in relation to police cautions. For example, in New South Wales cautioning programs are the result of administrative policy decisions, whereas in Queensland the rules guiding the cautioning program are stipulated in legislation which sets out the purpose of the caution and the procedures involved.

The actual use of the formal police caution also varies considerably between jurisdictions. In Queensland, cautions have represented up to 40 per cent of juvenile matters. In New South Wales, the figure has generally been closer to 10 per cent (Cunneen & Morrow 1994). In Victoria in 1990, some 10,000 young people were cautioned while only some 5500 went to court (Carroll 1994). In commenting on the Victorian statistics, the same author cites police responses which indicate that only about 15 per cent of those cautioned come to police attention again, and goes on to say: 'Advantages of this police cautioning program include its immediacy (it occurs soon after questioning), its simplicity (the criteria and process are well understood by police and others), the low level of resource requirement (no other professionals or costly processes are required) and its high level of success' (Carroll 1994: 170). Again it needs to be reiterated that such cautions are premised upon minimal intervention in the affairs of the young people who have been apprehended.

A further type of police caution involves a much higher degree of police intervention and youth engagement with criminal justice officials. An example is an experiment undertaken in 1991 in Wagga Wagga, New South Wales (O'Connell 1993). This was a cautioning program initiated by the police, which directly involved the young offender and their family (and significant others), and the victim and their family, with the police officer taking an active part in discussions.

This style of police cautioning makes use of models of conflict resolution which emphasise victim–offender relations. It incorporates many of the philosophical principles of the republican theory. Thus, for example, one of the initiators of the program in Wagga Wagga described it as follows:

> It only involves those people who are stakeholders or who can add some meaning to the process of resolving conflict. It challenges police to consider juvenile offending in a more appropriate light. It requires police to become facilitators and mediators, by ensuring that the best possible outcome is achieved for all involved in a cautioning conference. Juvenile offenders are no longer automatically charged unless they have committed a serious indictable offence, have been refused bail or have had onerous bail conditions placed upon them. (O'Connell, 1993: 226).

One of the apparent attractions of this model of police cautioning is that it demands more active intervention by the police in directly dealing with young people who have engaged in unacceptable behaviour. Although young offenders are diverted from formal court proceedings, they are nevertheless subject to sanctions as defined in the police cautioning process.

Indeed, the tacit extension of police involvement and police powers implied in the model have been recently entrenched in new South Australian legislation. Under the revamped *Young Offenders Act 1993*, the police now have three courses open to them for relatively minor or trivial offences: they can give the young person an informal caution; they can give a formal caution, accompanied by a range of specified requirements; or they can refer the young person to a family conference (which will be considered in greater depth shortly). Significantly, the new legislation grants the police themselves considerable leeway in the use of sanctions:

> When issuing a formal caution, a police officer may require the offender to do any or all of the following things:
>
> • apologize to the victim for what he/she did;
> • compensate the victim for the damage he/she caused or the goods they stole;
> • carry out up to 75 hours (i.e., 10 days) of community work;
> • anything else that may be appropriate.
>
> The youth will be required to sign an undertaking to do everything that is agreed to (South Australian Government 1993).

The role of the police has been extended significantly to include not only apprehension, but also adjudication (determination of guilt) and punishment (allocation of appropriate sanction).

From the point of view of diversion, a significant question is whether the use of such schemes as the Wagga Wagga experiment or South Australia's legislation represents anything other than a major increase in state intervention. The crucial area of change is that more cases can be dealt with on an informal basis, without referral to courts or legal assistance. Hence, it is diversion *to* other parts of the criminal justice system, rather than diversion *from* the system itself. It is also an intensification of state intrusion, insofar as immediate imposition of penalty is now possible at the very earliest stages of the process.

Panels

The treatment of juveniles charged with minor offences has generally been framed in terms of finding ways to divert them from formal court proceedings and sanctions. As we have seen, there are moves in several Australian jurisdictions to increase the role and powers of the police to deal with such cases. In addition to these cautionary measures, there are also a variety of diversionary panels, the focus of which is to deal with young people in an informal manner for minor offences.

In New South Wales, for example, **Community Aid Panels** began operating in 1987 for young people and adults. The panels, which were established by local police officers, hear minor cases or first offences where participants enter a plea of guilty. Normally, the court adjourns the matter for approximately three months before sentence is imposed, and meanwhile, the offender (and parents, where possible) attends a panel session to discuss the offence and the circumstances surrounding it. The panel consists of a police officer, a solicitor and one or two respected members of the community as well as the young person and their family. After discussion of the nature of the offence, suggestions are made for the person to undertake some kind of community-oriented activities (see Bargen 1992).

In some jurisdictions there are panels designed specifically for Aboriginal and Torres Strait Islander people. In Victoria, for instance, **Community Justice Panels** and **Koori Justice Programs** were established from 1991 to develop culturally sensitive approaches within the community to both adult and juvenile Koori offenders. Since their inception, there has been a decline in the number of Kooris in the juvenile justice system, and in particular in the number of Kooris in detention and those placed under community-based supervision programs (Carroll 1994).

The South Australian and Western Australian jurisdictions have had panel systems as an alternative to court for many years. For example, in South Australia the majority of matters used to go before a **Children's Aid Panel** rather than the Children's Court. In over 80 per cent of the matters before the Aid Panel, the child was warned and counselled (Cunneen & Morrow 1994). Recent changes to young offender legislation in both States, however, have seen the panels superseded by Family Conferences or Juvenile Justice Teams. These forms of interventions are much more intensive in nature than the previous panels, and involve a larger number of people in their operation. The introduction of these particular alternatives to panels reflects a major shift in thinking, away from a narrowly defined concern about the negative effects of labelling young offenders, toward making them responsible for their actions within a wider communal framework.

Family Group Conferences

The impetus for the adoption of Family Group Conferences for dealing with young offenders stems from varying pressures, depending upon jurisdiction. In some cases, it is linked to grassroots developments among indigenous people (Maxwell & Morris 1994; Morris & Maxwell 1993), in others, to police initiatives (O'Connell 1993); and more generally, new thinking at a theoretical level about juvenile justice (Braithwaite 1989, 1993). Certainly the rhetoric of this approach has caught on in most jurisdictions within Australia, although it is highly questionable whether the philosophical basis of the model is indeed being adhered to in practical programs.

In terms of actual program development, the leading example of the Family Group Conference (FGC) has been provided by New Zealand. The new approach to juvenile justice adopted there emphasises the need to keep children and young people with their families and in their communities. The model emphasises a number of key elements (see Maxwell & Morris 1994: 15–17).

- *Justice:* in the sense of making young offenders accountable for their offences, and doing so in the legal context of proportionality of punishment and respect for due process.
- *Diversion, decarceration and destigmatisation:* as means to avoid the negative labelling of young people.
- *Enhancing well-being and strengthening families:* by providing support for young people and their families.
- *Victim involvement, mediation, reparation and reconciliation:* reflecting wider trends to cater better for the needs of victims and to see 'justice' in terms of conflict resolution.
- *Family participation and consensus decision-making:* so that people are empowered by the process itself.
- *Cultural appropriateness:* wherein services and procedures are appropriate to the background of the people involved.

At a theoretical level, the FGC is perceived to be a form of reintegrative shaming which is designed to heal social relationships (see Braithwaite 1989). It is premised upon the ideals of respect by each of the participants for the other. It is intended to right a wrong in a meaningful, engaging manner for all concerned.

The practical elements of the FGC model have been described as follows (Braithwaite 1993: 40).

- Convene a conference of the offender, the people who are most supportive of the offender (usually the family), the victim, and people to support the victim.
- Give all the participants an opportunity to explain how the offence affected their lives and to put forward proposals for a plan of action.
- After the offender and their family have listened to the other speakers, empower them to propose plans until they come up with one that is agreeable to all participants in the conference (including the police).
- Monitor implementation of the plan, particularly those elements involving compensation to victims and community work.

In New Zealand, the FGC program is highly systematic and set within a legislative framework which clearly outlines the young person's rights, what precisely the roles of the police are to be, and the operation of the conference from start to finish. The administrative responsibility for the model is located within the Department of Social Welfare, and the key figure in the process is the Youth Justice Co-ordinator who has responsibility for ensuring that the objects and principles of the relevant legislation are met. A FGC is convened either as a result of direct referral by the police to a Youth Justice Co-ordinator or, when there has been an arrest and charges have been laid, as a result of referral from the Youth Court. Importantly, in New Zealand there has been an increased use of police diversion through warnings and the use of cautions. It has been estimated that this kind of low-level police diversion now accounts for 62 per cent of police–offender contact (Maxwell 1993). The FGC is seen as a new method of diversion which is available primarily for the persistent offender and for those who commit serious offences.

By way of contrast, Australian jurisdictions tend to utilise the FGC as a means of first resort. This is evident, for example, in the way in which the FGC has been incorporated into the police cautioning program in New South Wales. It is also evident in jurisdictions such as South Australia, that the FGC is being linked to the sanctioning of minor offences and is available for use at a very early stage in the processing of juvenile offenders. Further differences between the New Zealand model and Australian versions is that the latter grant the police a pivotal role in the proceedings, and generally the administration is through traditional criminal justice agencies rather than through social welfare departments.

Programs and strategies designed to divert the young offender from formal court proceedings are generally characterised by a degree of *informalism* in terms of their structures, operations and records. From a theoretical perspective, the trend toward informalism and community-based programs has been conceptualised as an expansion of regulation. While, superficially, power is transferred to the community level, and into the hands of members of the community or individual police officers, the overall tendency is for the state to retain control over the process and for social control to be maintained in fairly conventional ways.

For example, Cohen (1985: 44) argues that such moves, while defended on the basis on being less intrusive and less coercive than formal court-based systems, serve as a form of **net-widening**. Specifically, Cohen argues that we need to evaluate the impacts of apparently benign community-based programs like those described above. Accordingly, we need to inquire into the size of the net which is being constructed to process the young offender, and whether those now in the net would have been processed previously (wider nets). We need to examine the level of intervention, and whether it is in fact more intense than it was in the past (denser nets). Thirdly, we need to evaluate whether the new agencies and strategies are supplementing rather than replacing the original, formal mechanisms of social control (different nets).

In practical terms, there are likewise a number of issues which require attention and debate. For example, in some cases it has been shown that community aid panels hand out penalties which are actually harsher than those provided by the court (Bargen 1992). Concerns have been raised regarding the systematic denial of young people's legal rights due to the informal nature of some community-based schemes and the prior guilty plea demanded of young people (Warner 1994). More generally, evaluations of diversionary programs have tended to be mixed: net-widening is a persistent problem, and there are gender discrepancies in the use of such mechanisms (see Alder & Polk 1985). Similarly, the use of diversionary measures has tended to be biased against Aboriginal and Torres Strait Islander people, who are quickly drawn deeper and deeper into the criminal justice system with fewer diversionary options (Gale et al. 1990; Cunneen 1994). Thus, community-based programs may not only be unequal in application to specific groups of young people, but they may serve to channel young people into a system which otherwise they might have avoided.

COMMUNITY CORRECTIONS AND POST-RELEASE PROGRAMS

The establishment of sanctions via community involvement, in the form of Family Group Conferences or panels or police cautioning programs, represents a concerted effort to keep young people within some kind of local participatory context, to address the needs of victims, and to divert offenders from the formal aspects of the criminal justice system. Similar trends can be observed with respect to the actual punishment or treatment deemed to be appropriate for young people who have appeared before the Children's Court and have been convicted of an offence.

In particular, the concepts of deinstitutionalisation and decarceration gained substantial support throughout the 1970s and continue to influence court dispositions. The main impetus for the adoption of so-called community corrections as a method of dealing with young people is, at a theoretical level, to prevent stigmatisation as far as possible and, at a practical level, to manage the overall costs of juvenile punishment by allowing for options that are cheaper than incarceration. A third rationale for keeping young people out of prison is that detention centres are known to function as 'universities of crime', where offenders trade knowledge about criminal techniques and activities and are socialised into a criminal culture.

Deinstitutionalisation refers to the use of alternatives to traditional institutional care or imprisonment. Typically, programs do not lock up young people but keep them under some kind of control and surveillance in the community. **Decarceration** refers to attempts to remove individuals from the prison environment by minimising the time they have to spend there. While deinstitutionalisation diverts young people from prison, decarceration removes them from prison.

We begin this section by considering the range of sanctions available to the court beyond that of detention, and which can be seen as community-based measures.

Probation

An individual placed on **probation** is ordered by the court to be of good behaviour for the duration of the sentence. Further conditions generally attach to the order, such as supervision and regular meetings with a probation officer. A similar type of scheme is the **recognisance** or **bond** whereby the offender is likewise required to be of good behaviour for a specified time; if they breach the order, they may be fined or imprisoned. The court may impose conditions such as paying compensation to the victim or attending a drug rehabilitation clinic.

A **good-behaviour bond** is similar to these measures but does not have the consequence of imprisonment on breach, or the requirement that the bond be supervised. The conditions of the bond are generally that the offender keep the peace, and be of good behaviour.

Closely related to probationary sentencing options is the **suspended or deferred sentence**. The court defers passing a sentence (which might include imprisonment) for a designated period, during which certain conditions may be stipulated. At the end of that period, and with the satisfactory completion of the conditions, the sentence lapses. In New South Wales, deferred sentences are sometimes referred to as 'Griffith Bonds' or 'Griffith Remands', where the magistrate requests that an offender undertake specified activities during an adjournment of court proceedings, prior to a sentence being imposed. The activities do not constitute part of the formal sentence, but may reduce the sentence that is imposed.

Another type of diversionary program which is designed to channel young offenders away from offending behaviour is the **Day-in-prison** scheme. Based upon the American 'scared straight' model, this program is for young repeat offenders who are assessed as likely to receive a custodial sentence. Operating in several States, including New South Wales and Victoria, the program is aimed at discouraging juveniles from future offending by obliging them to spend a day in prison, during which they are subject to a body search by prison officers, spend time alone in a cell, and attend an encounter session with a panel of prisoners (see Hil & Moyle 1992). Evaluation of such programs in both Australia and the United States, however, suggests that they do not affect the rate of recidivism among participants; moreover, they traumatise some of the young people involved (Hil & Moyle 1992; O'Malley, Coventry & Walters 1993; Lundman 1984).

Attendance Centre and Community Service Orders

Community-based programs which stand midway between probation and prison provide more extensive intervention while still keeping juveniles out of detention. A **youth** or **community attendance centre order** requires that the young offender attend an activity centre with specialist programs as an alternative to detention. Such programs include individual counselling, group work, employment skills, life skills, and specialist drug and alcohol counselling. Offenders can also be placed at an attendance centre in order to undertake a specified amount of unpaid community work. The sanction is punitive in that it deprives the young person of spare time, but it is also meant to provide positive alternatives which may help to rehabilitate the young person.

Placement at an attendance centre varies from State to State. In Victoria, offenders can be sentenced directly to community-based orders requiring a set number of hours of community work and educational or other programs. In New South Wales, offenders can be placed at an attendance centre through the courts, or through recognisance orders or referral from probation and parole officers. In the Australian Capital Territory, an order to attend an attendance centre is a sentencing option available to judges and magistrates. While there are community corrections centres in Western Australia, there are no attendance orders as such.

The biggest questions regarding youth attendance orders, in their various forms and legal frameworks, relate to the issues of eligibility, specific goals, and reduction of the use of custody (Muncie & Coventry 1989). Concern has been expressed over the specific offences and offender groups (e.g., 'less difficult' rather than persistent and serious offenders, young men rather than young women) that are subject to attendance centre orders. The quality of the tasks and programs to which a young person may be assigned also needs continual evaluation. Finally, it has been suggested that use of such orders may actually funnel young offenders towards custody rather than out of it, because the breach of such an order could lead to imprisonment even though the original offence did not warrant such a response (see Muncie & Coventry 1989).

Closely linked to the attendance centre order is the more broadly conceived **community service order.** This is a sentencing option which requires young offenders to perform a certain number of hours community work in a designated form and for a designated community organisation (or, in some situations, for the victim). Tasks assigned may include, for example, working in aged people's homes, hospitals or rehabilitation centres, and as part of the requirement the young offender may have to attend an attendance centre for a specified number of hours per week. Generally, the use of such orders is premised upon work being available in the offender's area, and limits are set on the total number of hours which the young offender is required to put into their community-based work. In Queensland, a community service order is undertaken only when the young offender has given formal consent to that order, and the order may contain other requirements such as restitution and compensation as well as a probationary order.

As with the use of attendance centre orders, concern has been raised regarding the purposes and consequences of community service orders. For instance, there is evidence in the case of Tasmania that community service orders have not been used directly as an alternative to imprisonment, but instead have replaced less intrusive options such as a bond or a fine (Warner 1991). More generally, the breach of a community service order may result in imprisonment, and thus an escalation in the punishment regardless of the seriousness of the original offence.

In recent years, several States have seen administrative shifts in the use of both attendance centre orders and community service orders. Specifically, a case-management approach has been adopted, with a systematic assessment of the needs and problems of each young offender. Case plans are drawn up with the participation of case-workers, the young person, their family or significant others, relevant community groups, and government departments. These plans outline both short-term and long-term goals, and are intended to provide the young offender with a range of options for employment, skills, education and personal development.

Importantly, case management is intended to make the case-worker a central player in the rehabilitation process, and also to make case-workers more accountable for carrying out the specific program order. This has a number of implications for finances, staffing and resources. It also raises questions regarding how the broad 'control' function of such personnel is to be merged in practice with a more finely mapped 'developmental' role. Again, the actual nature and extent of resources available at a local level determines the amount of assistance and service that can be provided.

Conditional Release Orders and Camps

In addition to measures which put young offenders into community-based institutions as part of their sentence (which are perceived to be part of a de-institutionalisation movement away from secure custody), there are programs designed to decarcerate young offenders who have spent some time in detention. These come in various forms, and are subject to varying conditions. **Parole** is where an offender ordered into detention can serve part of the sentence in the community under the supervision of parole officers and under certain restrictive behaviour conditions. Similarly, **day-leave** and special leave allow individuals to take advantage of educational or work-related activities while still serving the sentence in some type of secure custody. There are other means to foster the young offender's contact with the outside world.

In New South Wales, for example, a **conditional release order** is available for for those offenders already in detention who are deemed to be amenable to and who would benefit from a community-based program. Essentially, the conditional release order is seen as a transitional phase, wherein the young offender is granted leave from the detention centre in order to begin the process of reintegrating into the community. Offenders are assessed regarding potential danger to the community or themselves, and then 'Under close supervision and intensive counselling, conditional release permits the juvenile to live in the general community and participate in community-based educational and vocational programs' (Cain 1994b: 31). The intention of such orders is to provide young people with the opportunity to acquire skills and to participate fully in their community.

There are various **camps**, outdoor and wilderness programs for young offenders already in detention, and for those deemed to be at risk of detention. They vary greatly in terms of primary focus, target group and intended outcomes. Some wilderness programs are intended as early intervention to forestall potential future offending behaviour in certain identified populations of young people; others are designed to cater specifically for young offenders.

Evaluation has shown that non-voluntary intensive programs for offenders tend to fail both in prevention and in rehabilitation (Collis & Griffin 1993; Sveen 1993). These camps are oriented toward building self-esteem, co-operative attitudes and positive problem-solving skills. That is, they are intended to be rehabilitative in nature. After assessing the reasons for the failure of some programs, and analysing the elements of successful wilderness programs, Sveen (1993: 19) comments that 'It has been posited that a socially-based community response, a voluntary code of practise, a focus on maturation levels, and a recognition of experiential learning; rather than a segregated, legally-imposed and coerced homogeny, will achieve positive behavioural changes with our youth'.

A possible exception to these general findings regards programs designed specifically for young Aboriginal offenders which utilise indigenous skills in relation to the land. For example, the Lake Jasper Project in Western Australia (now closed) was designed for young Aboriginal offenders as an alternative to custody, and incorporated principles of the Royal Commission into Aboriginal Deaths in Custody regarding the use of extended family members to act as mentors and to teach the young people about their heritage and culture.

A type of camp promoted in Western Australia as an alternative to conventional detention is the boot camp. This kind of camp is clearly punitive in orientation, and costs as much as—or more than—programs such as the Lake Jasper Project. It is intended to provide young offenders with a 'short, sharp, shock' and to instil self-discipline and control (see Indermaur & White 1994). It involves a rigorous program of early-morning rising and hard physical labour. Four months' attendance at a boot camp reduces an offender's overall time in detention, and is followed up by an intensive supervision program in the community.

Boot camps have operated in the United States for a number of years, and the evidence indicates that they do not significantly affect post-release criminality. They are more likely to increase prison populations and total correctional costs rather than decrease them, and such camps neither reduce repeat offending nor reduce the number of young people in detention (Parent 1994). Furthermore, the location of the Western Australian boot camp in a remote area goes against the established evidence that close family and community contact are integral to any kind of rehabilitation.

A third kind of outback or wilderness camp is that intended for offenders after release, and aims to develop their skills, knowledge and confidence. These are few and far between, and are generally run by non-government agencies such as the Brosnan Centre in Victoria. The idea behind such programs is to provide young offenders with an opportunity to develop their personal and practical skills in order to improve their employment prospects. The location of the programs is in rural or outback areas, detaching the young person for a week or two from the social and economic context within which their offending behaviour occurred. The emphasis is on personal development, improved health, physical and emotional well-being, and learning of important social skills and vocational skills. The key problem with such programs (in addition to the perennial issues of resources, funding and staffing), is that when the young person returns to their previous environment, even though they might have changed and developed in some personal way, the general social conditions remain the same.

Generally speaking, the use of probation, community service orders, conditional release, and various types of wilderness program or camp have tended to focus on the twin issues of controlling offenders and treating individuals. In some cases, the emphasis is simply on how best to punish the young offender at the community level (broadly defined to include boot camps). The key questions regarding each of these alternatives are:

- to what extent do they prevent recidivism or repeat offending
- how successful are they in reintegrating the young person back into the community, and, given the communities they might come from, is this always desirable

- do programs centring on individual attributes and which are based upon case management principles address the structural causes of the offending behaviour
- do the competing aims of punishment—including, for example, treatment, retribution, community protection, and deterrence—actually preclude the possibility of a coherent and positive response on the part of the state and community to the young offender?

In other words, we still need to know whether or not the shift toward community-based strategies and programs really does make a difference in terms of dealing adequately with youth crime and with young people who offend.

CONCLUSION

This chapter has examined a wide range of formal and less formal programs which are designed to prevent youth crime, divert young offenders from the formal criminal justice system, and deal with young offenders through community-based sanctions. As can be seen, there has been a proliferation of programs at all levels of the criminal justice system. In specific terms, problem areas were identified in each of the three phases of intervention discussed: the issue of social exclusion as it relates to crime prevention programs; the issue of net-widening as it pertains to alternatives to formal adjudication; and the issue of recidivism as it extends to community-based sanctions. Likewise, processes such as diversion, deinstitutionalisation and decarceration have been shown to be subject to varying definitions and organisational implementation, some of which appear to contradict the theoretical propositions upon which they are based. Thus, for example, rather than system diversion, we often see programs actually expanding the intervention of state agencies in the lives of young people.

More generally, we argue that the rhetoric of 'community' has clouded the specific impacts, processes and institutional arrangements impinging upon young people who may or may not have offended. The term 'community' implies consensus, general social approval, and positive outcomes. However, we need to critically evaluate just who the community actually is, which members of the community are making the crucial decisions concerning juvenile justice, and whose interests are represented in general community-based programs. Furthermore, it is important to examine more closely the relationship of the state with community-based organisations and agencies.

For instance, far from being somehow more democratic or grassroots-oriented, most of the programs examined in this chapter are controlled directly, and through financial means, by the formal agents of the criminal justice system. If anything, 'community' has referred to low-cost ways of processing greater numbers of young people through the system of criminal justice, rather than to measures for increasing the well-being of people generally at the local level. Programs emphasise the individual offender, rather than the social conditions underpinning both youth crime and the process of criminalisation through specific policing policies and techniques. The overall concern is how best to control and manage the youth population, rather than how to change the general circumstances (e.g., low income, unemployment, racism, sexism) within which they live and develop as human beings.

Related to this is the fact that programs, even those apparently based upon skills training or social education, are invariably framed within a criminal justice agenda. That is, they are conceived and funded in terms of the institutions of coercive control, rather than developmental institutions (see Polk 1994). To put it differently, the primary goal of community-based measures derives from consideration of criminal justice, not social justice. This serves to individualise the problem (e.g., by highlighting the characteristics of the young offender) and to displace attention from wider issues of social inequality, the material effects of which are evident both in the lack of local community resources, and in specific population groups such as Aborigines and Torres Strait Islanders.

Conclusion

Juvenile justice is a complex area with many different and often competing ideas and institutions. In this book we have provided a broad overview of the main theoretical perspectives, institutional frameworks, and existing and new program developments in the field in Australia.

From our perspective, the crucial themes which ought to permeate any discussions of youth offending, the young offender and state intervention in the lives of the young are those of social justice and social empowerment. Issues surrounding juvenile justice cannot be separated from consideration of the overall directions and philosophies of a society generally. In other words, it is essential to locate discussion and analysis of juvenile justice in the context of a critical understanding of the nature of our society (society as it is), and of a vision which, for us, relates to the ideals of social equality and political emancipation (society as it ought to be). Ultimately, we would like to be part of a society in which human dignity is cherished and preserved. In such a society there would be a maximisation of individual choice in a societal framework of co-operation, democratic participation, and social and environmental responsibility. Such objectives necessarily require us actively to take the side of the most marginalised and least powerful sections of the population, including young people.

We would like to conclude the book, therefore, by mapping out three broad areas where we feel more investigation and thought needs to be devoted in future work of this nature. These topics not only require further empirical research, but demand a conscious commitment to a project of social emancipation—one oriented toward making society a better place for young people specifically, and for everyone generally, regardless of age or circumstance.

NATURE OF STATE INTERVENTION

One striking feature of most material written about juvenile justice, and indeed about criminology as a discipline, is that there has been little attempt to theorise the nature of the state in such discussions. Most of the analysis has assumed a particular form of the state, seeing it in liberal democratic terms as simply a neutral entity which stands above, and separate from, sectional interest groups, rather than exploring the relationship between the state and specific social interests (e.g., class, gender, ethnic, indigenous people).

The focus has been on particular concrete issues, such as youth crime rates or abusive police practices, or on mid-range analysis of how specific institutions operate in relation to young people at a practical level (e.g., the intersection of welfare, criminal justice and educational institutions as these impact upon young people).

We would argue that the role of the state is important both analytically and strategically in the development of juvenile justice interventions. Different conceptions of the state—as an interlocking set of bureaucratic institutions, as reflecting the 'general public', as the embodiment of class power—lead to different conclusions regarding what ought to be done to and with young people. The relationship between state power and specific social interests warrants much closer analysis and discussion in the juvenile justice field.

This is particularly so given recent developments in state intervention in the lives of young people. Here we wish to highlight two trends which appear to hold sway in Australia at the present time.

Intensification of Control

This is most noticeable in jurisdictions which are providing police with extensive proactive powers to intervene and stop young people on the street. For all the rhetoric about 'community policing' and doing things in 'the best interests of the child', the tendency in recent years has been for both Labor and conservative governments to respond to media panics relating to 'youth crime' by allowing or enacting tough measures to deal with young people.

In early 1994, for example, the police in Perth and Fremantle embarked upon Operation Sweep, an offensive designed to round up young people on the street from as early as 8 p.m. and take them to the police station. Under the guise of protecting their welfare, the campaign was clearly directed at 'cleaning up the streets', even though no crimes had been committed, and in many cases the young people were there with the full knowledge and consent of their parents.

Later in 1994, the New South Wales government passed the *Children (Parental Responsibility) Act 1994*, which likewise gives the police the power to return children under fifteen years of age to their homes (or to a designated place) if they are at risk of becoming involved in anti-social or criminal behaviour. Again, no actual offence needs to be committed before intervention. Community groups have refused to co-operate with the implementation of the legislation.

Meanwhile, in Victoria the police were granted new powers to search people, especially young people, suspected of carrying dangerous weapons in public places, such as entertainment venues, sporting events and the streets. Accompanied by a state-wide advertising campaign against carrying knives ('Blood and Guts One End, No Bloody Guts the Other'), the intervention reproduced the worst type of moral panic over youth misbehaviour and dangerousness, while greatly extending the powers of intrusion into young people's group activities.

The nature and extent of direct police intervention, and the expansion of powers to investigate and punish young people, are concerns which need close monitoring (see Sandor 1993). Policing is a fundamental part of the operation of juvenile justice. One of the major areas that needs attention is the nature of police discretion. Discretionary decisions by police can disadvantage some young people and lead to greater criminalisation. One example of this process is demonstrated in the research on Aboriginal and Torres Strait Islander young people, which shows that the inequitable use of discretionary decisions disadvantages indigenous young people. Police discretion also enables the intent of juvenile justice legislation to be circumvented, a point which must be taken into account in any reforms. The failure to use alternatives to arrest procedures in some jurisdictions is an example. In the broadest sense, the problem is clearly one of inadequate regulation of the policing of young people. One of the more disturbing features of current trends in juvenile justice is the increase in police powers which has occurred through the introduction of what are ostensibly community-based sanctions and diversionary alternatives to the court process, such as Family Group Conferences. Inadequate regulation and increased informal power is a dangerous combination.

Regardless of actual juvenile crime rates, the overwhelmingly trivial and minor nature of juvenile offending, the disproportionate focus on indigenous and unemployed young people, and the failures of tough measures to actually alleviate or remedy the situation, the fact is that State governments continue to regard youth behaviour as a problem and to introduce measures which intensify the levels of official contact between the criminal justice system and young people.

Extension of Control

In addition to increased measures at street-level, many governments have also embarked upon various crime prevention initiatives which are likely to widen the criminal net. Programs are often linked to increased surveillance of and intervention in groups and communities that are perceived to be at risk.

Such pre-emptive action tends to widen the scope of official involvement in the lives of young people, albeit usually on an informal basis. Here questions need to be asked regarding the assumptions guiding such programs (e.g., notions of deficiency in the young people and/or their families) and the penetration of state institutions into local neighbourhoods under the guise of 'community' rhetoric.

The sentencing options utilised by the courts also need to be rethought. In particular, we need to reconsider the modes of punishment being used against young people at the serious end of the sentencing scale. Strategies which were supposed to be alternatives to detention, such as community service orders, have become sentencing options in their own right. Meanwhile, young people continue to be sent to detention centres even though we are aware that the chances of rehabilitation are not high and the experience of incarceration is likely to result in further alienation and marginalisation. And why do we continue to use prison for young people? A small number of young people in Australia each year commit homicide and are imprisoned as a result of these serious crimes of violence. But hundreds of young people are sentenced to detention each year because they have violated laws relating to private property. Our society holds the right to private property in high esteem, yet simultaneously fosters profound inequalities. Many young people are never granted their right to work or to a liveable income, yet are imprisoned for failing to respect the laws of private ownership.

As with the intensification of intervention, the extension of various forms of social control is often presented as necessarily benign and benevolent. Yet when accountability and real participatory decision-making power are demanded by grassroots community members, the response tends to be in the negative. Further, such programs ultimately avoid the wider issue of how inequality is socially structured via the unequal distribution of community resources generally. As long as the deep structures of inequality remain intact, social divisions will remain, along with attendant pressures toward certain types of criminality and repressive state responses to these.

METHODOLOGICAL AND RESEARCH ISSUES

Conceptually, we see analysis of the state, both in general terms and in the specifics of institutional operation (e.g., police, courts), as a prime area for further discussion and debate. There are other, more specific issues which need investigation as well. The relationship of Aboriginal and Torres Strait Islander young people to juvenile justice will continue to be of fundamental importance. No matter what illusions Australia has of being a progressive liberal democracy, its gaols for young people are filled with indigenous Australians. Let us not forget that the majority of young people locked up in States like Western

Australia and in the Northern Territory are Aboriginal. The relationship between indigenous young people and juvenile justice demonstrates that the operation of the juvenile justice system can be fundamentally oppressive. Indigenous issues also have the possibility of destructuring the way the current juvenile justice system operates. The recognition of the right to self-determination may see the development of new modes of dealing with young people which come from, and are responsive to, the community.

Gender analysis will continue to influence debates in juvenile justice. There needs to be a greater theorisation of the ways in which types of femininity and masculinity relate to particular forms of criminal activity. There needs to be rigorous research on the relationship of gender to juvenile justice under specific political, economic and social conditions. A fruitful beginning has been made in considering the relationship between the survival strategies of young women and their contact with juvenile justice agencies. Further work needs to be done on the shift from welfare to criminalisation in terms of what this change will mean for young women. There also needs to be greater theorisation and evaluation of state responses to young women. What are the implications of the state agencies recognising young women as a 'special needs' group?

In writing this book, we were continually struck by dearth of research and scholarship relating to young people from other than English-speaking backgrounds. This is surprising in a society which is extensively polyethnic, in which large-scale immigration and a significant intake of refugees have continued for decades, and where general political support for multiculturalism has been evident for many years. There has been a burgeoning of interest in issues associated with Aboriginal and Torres Strait Island people, in part spurred by the Royal Commission into Aboriginal Deaths in Custody and the political activism of indigenous people's organisations, but little has been done on other non-Anglo sections of the youth population. Clearly, the social dynamic that operates in this area is not that of colonialism and post-colonialism. There is a critical need both to undertake empirical work in this area, and to develop conceptual tools whereby we can explain the position of young people of non-English-speaking background in Australian society and the processes of criminal justice in relation to these groups.

The urgency of this matter is apparent from frequent references in the media and by police and politicians to the threat posed by so-called ethnic youth gangs. Ideologically, groups of young people from national or cultural backgrounds such as Vietnam, Cambodia, China, and Laos are often lumped together into one social category ('Asians'), branded as threats to the Australian social fabric (having different ways of life), suspected of being dangerous (likely to carry knives), and associated with particular kinds of crimes (drug trade, organised criminal rings).

Clearly, more empirical work is needed to dispel the myths and stereotypes pertaining to the diverse cultural and national groups within Australia, and to separate actual social trends from perceived developments involving these young people. Additionally, we need to be aware that more young people from non-English-speaking backgrounds are now entering into contact with the juvenile justice system at all levels. This raises big issues relating to such topics as racism, the form and nature of police intervention, assumptions which underlie the court and sentencing process, and cultural sensitivities with regard to imposed sanctions, including the conditions of incarceration.

The multiple and different perceptions of young people, of the law, of the police and of behaviour are important in another sense as well. Specifically, there is a need for greater attention to be given to what young people themselves have to say about their contact with the criminal justice system. In particular, it would be of great value to have more in the way of ethnographic and qualitative research on the perceptions and experiences of young people. Much can be gained by interviewing young people, talking with them about issues they feel are important, and observing their activities as far as this is possible without being intrusive. This can lead to accounts of youth behaviour and attitudes that are often quite different from those provided by the media.

For example, a study of youth 'gangs' in Melbourne discovered that groups of young people did not in fact see the focus of the activity as being delinquent or criminal. Furthermore, there was little evidence that 'gangs'—in the organised, and violent, characterisation commonly associated with the term—were at all prevalent in the Australian context (Aumair & Warren 1994). The understandings which young people themselves bring to bear upon their activities should be central to the analysis of the dynamics of youth offending and the criminalisation process. Rather than simply being objects of study (or of reform or punishment), young people should be active participants in and contributors to the discussions on juvenile justice and other meaningful aspects of their lives.

YOUTH RIGHTS

State intervention in the lives of young people is coercive, particularly with regard to street policing and the general neglect of the rights of children once they have entered into sustained contact with the criminal justice system (including the courts, detention centres and community-based programs). Given this fact, it is pertinent to once again reaffirm the human rights of young people. How we portray, treat, interact with and respond to young people reflects something fundamental about our society. And a society which fails to maintain and enhance the material well-being of a great proportion of its young, and fails to offer them the protections and opportunities afforded in rights discourse, is a society which has its basic priorities wrong.

Youth rights are perhaps best seen in terms of a broad statement of principle, and with respect to specific spheres of acknowlegement. Raynor (1994: 60–1) explains that human rights presuppose 'the recognition of the inherent worth and dignity of every human being: that every person is inherently worthy, and is entitled to control their own destiny, and to the respect of others, and to self-respect, the ultimate primary good'. Does the evidence on what is happening in the field of juvenile justice suggest that young people are indeed being recognised as people with human rights? Again, as Raynor (1994: 66) points out, 'The interest of the community demands respect for the rights of *all*.' If the rights of young people are not respected, if young people themselves do not receive respect, then it is hard to see why young people would in turn respect the law and the institutions of the state.

The specific areas covered by the United Nations *Convention on the Rights of the Child* include those relating to the following rights (see Brownell 1989).

- *Civil rights:* protection from torture and maltreatment, special rules governing the circumstances and conditions under which children may be deprived of their liberty.
- *Economic rights:* right to benefit from social security, to a standard of living adequate to ensure proper development.
- *Social rights:* right to highest attainable standard of health and access to medical services, protection from sexual exploitation.
- *Cultural rights:* right to education, access to appropriate information, leisure and recreation, participation in artistic and cultural activities.

Given the profile of young people against whom the state has proceeded via the criminal justice system, it is clear that broad social, economic and cultural rights have not been translated into substantive practice. Evidence of high levels of youth unemployment, homelessness and poverty demonstrate the depth of the problem, and the woeful inadequacies of welfare and employment provision for these young people.

Similarly, in the case of juvenile justice *per se*, we see continual abuses of the civil rights of young people, abuses which have persisted even when they directly contradict the principles of the *Convention on the Rights of the Child*. These take the form of police operational practices and campaigns, as well as government legislation which allows for particularly punitive sanctions to be directed at young people. Ludbrook (1994: 5) has commented: 'Despite Australia's ratification of the Convention, state and territory governments have not changed their laws and policies to bring them into line with the Convention and

they continue to pass laws and develop policies which breach the Convention.'
Surely this too is another instance of the politics of denial, where for the sake of
dealing with a perceived problem, the solution is simply to find harsher ways of
punishing someone.

If history has taught us anything, it is that rights are indeed precious: they
must be fought over and defended as a matter of course. The challenge for all of
us as we enter the new millenium is to ensure that our children and young
people know their rights, that they can exercise these rights in practice, and that
they participate in any struggle to maintain and extend the rights which, in the
end, are central to their worth, dignity and self-respect.

We are entering a new era, characterised by global systems of production and
consumption, the advent of the so-called information highway, regional wars,
mass migration due to environmental and human-made catastrophe, and
increasing polarisation of wealth and poverty on a worldwide scale. In this
setting, the position of young people in general is increasingly precarious.
Practitioners, researchers and scholars in the field of juvenile justice carry much
responsibility in grappling with difficult issues, which ultimately are connected
to wider social and economic developments.

With regard to these responsibilities, our hope is that the reader will think
critically about the ideas and information presented here, and that this book will
be useful as a guide to practical interventions in juvenile justice issues. We have
written it to inform and to stimulate thought on the institutions and processes
of juvenile justice. In our view, the role of criminology is not divorced from
contemporary political and social debates but is integral to these debates. To
intervene practically and effectively in matters of policy and practice, and to
make constructive and critical assessment of the orientations and philosophies
of the existing system, an informed opinion is essential. It is to this that the
present work has been directed.

bibliography

Airo-Farulla, G. (1992) 'Community Policing and Self-Determination', *Aboriginal Law Bulletin*, 2(54): 8–9.

Alder, C. (1984) 'Gender Bias in Juvenile Diversion', *Crime and Delinquency*, 30(3) July.

—— (1985) 'Theories of Female Delinquency', in Borowski, A. and Murray, J. (eds) *Juvenile Delinquency in Australia*, Methuen, North Ryde.

—— (1986) ' "Unemployed Women Have Got It Heaps Worse": Exploring the Implications of Female Youth Unemployment', *Australian and New Zealand Journal of Criminology*, 19: 210–24.

—— (1991) 'Victims of Violence: The Case of Homeless Youth', *Australian and New Zealand Journal of Criminology*, 24(1): 1–14.

—— (1993) 'Services for Young Women: Future Directions', in Atkinson, L. and Gerull, S.-A. (eds) *National Conference on Juvenile Justice*, Australian Institute of Criminology, Canberra.

—— (1994) 'The Policing of Young Women', in White, R. and Alder, C. (eds) *The Police and Young People in Australia*, Cambridge University Press, Melbourne.

Alder, C., O'Connor, I., Warner, K. and White, R. (1992) *Perceptions of the Treatment of Juveniles in the Legal System*, National Youth Affairs Research Scheme, National Clearinghouse for Youth Studies, Hobart.

Alder, C. and Polk, K. (1985) 'Diversion Programmes', in Borowski, A. and Murray, J. (eds) *Juvenile Delinquency in Australia*, Methuen, Melbourne.

Alder, C. and Wundersitz, J. (eds) (1994) *Family Conferencing and Juvenile Justice*, Australian Institute of Criminology, Canberra.

Allen, J. (1990) ' "The Wild Ones": The Disavowal of Men in Criminology', in Graycar, R. (ed.) *Dissenting Opinions*, Allen & Unwin, Sydney.

Alston, P., Parker, S. and Seymour, J. (eds) (1992) *Children, Rights and the Law*, Clarendon Press, Oxford.

Anti-Discrimination Board (1982) *A Study of Street Offences by Aborigines*, NSW Anti-Discrimination Board, Sydney.

Asher, G. (1986) *Custody and Control: The Social Worlds of Imprisoned Youth*, Allen & Unwin, Sydney.

Atkinson, L. (1994) 'An Overview of Juvenile Detention in Australia', in Atkinson, L. and Gerull, S.-A. (eds) *National Conference on Juvenile Detention*, Australian Institute of Criminology, Canberra.

Attwood, B. (1989) *The Making of the Aborigines*, Allen & Unwin, Sydney.

Aumair, M. and Warren, I. (1994) 'Characteristics of Juvenile Gangs in Melbourne', *Youth Studies Australia*, 13(2): 40–4.

Australian Council of Social Services (1992) 'A Day of Action on Unemployment', special insert, *Social Welfare Impact*, 22(4).

Australian Council of Trade Unions (1989) *Youth Strategy*, ACTU, Melbourne.

Australian Youth Action and Policy Coalition (1992) *A Living Income: Income Support for Young People*, Youth Action and Policy Association (NSW), Sydney.

—— (1993) *A Living Wage: The Right of Young People in Employment and Training to a Living Income*, Youth Action and Policy Association (NSW), Sydney.

Bargen, J. (1992) 'Going to Court CAP in Hand: A Preliminary Evaluation of a Community Aid Panel', *Current Issues in Criminal Justice*, 4(2): 117–40.

—— (1994) 'In Need of Care: Delinquent Young Women in a Delinquent System', in Atkinson, L. and Gerull, S.-A. (eds) *National Conference on Juvenile Detention*, Australian Institute of Criminology, Canberra.

Bartollas, C. (1985) *Juvenile Delinquency*, John Wiley & Sons, New York.

Beccaria, C. (1767) *An Essay on Crimes and Punishments*, J. Almon, London.

Becker, H. (1963) *Outsiders: Studies in the Sociology of Deviance*, Free Press, New York.

Benda, B. (1987) 'Comparison Rates of Recidivism Among Status Offenders and Delinquents', *Adolescence*, 37(5): 31–4.

Benton, T. (1977) *Philosophical Foundations of the Three Sociologies*, Routledge & Kegan Paul, London.

Berger, P. and Luckmann, T. (1971) *The Social Construction of Reality*, Allen Lane, London.

Bernard, T. J. (1992) *The Cycle of Juvenile Justice*, Oxford University Press, New York.

Bessant, J. (1991) 'Described, Measured and Labelled: Eugenics, Youth Policy and Moral Panic in Victoria in the 1950s', in White, R. and Wilson, B. (eds) *For Your Own Good: Young People and State Intervention in Australia*, La Trobe University Press, Melbourne.

Beyer, L. (1993) *Community Policing: Lessons from Victoria*, Australian Institute of Criminology, Canberra.

Biondo, S. and Palmer, D. (1993) *Federation of Community Legal Centres Report into Mistreatment by Police, 1991–92*, FCLC, Melbourne.

Blacktown Youth Services Association and Holroyd/Parramatta Migrant Services (1992) *NESB Youth Needs in Blacktown and Parramatta: Strategic Plan Summary*, Blacktown Youth Services Association, Blacktown.

Boehringer, G., Brown, D., Edgeworth, B., Hogg, R. and Ramsay, I. (1983) ' "Law and Order" for Progressives? An Australian Response', *Crime and Social Justice*, 19: 2–12.

Bottomley, K. and Coleman, C. (1981) *Understanding Crime Rates*, Gower, Aldershot.

Box, S. (1987) *Recession, Crime and Punishment*, Macmillan, London.

Brady, M. (1985) 'Aboriginal Youth and the Juvenile Justice System', in Borowski, A. and Murray, J. (eds) *Juvenile Delinquency in Australia*, Methuen, North Ryde.

Braithwaite, J. (1989) *Crime, Shame and Reintegration*, Cambridge University Press, Cambridge.

—— (1991) 'Poverty, Power, White-Collar Crime and the Paradoxes of Criminological Theory', *Australian and New Zealand Journal of Criminology*, 24(1): 40–58.

—— (1993) 'Juvenile Offending: New Theory and Practice', in Atkinson, L. and Gerull, S.-A. (eds) *National Conference on Juvenile Justice: Conference Proceedings*, Australian Institute of Criminology, Canberra.

Braithwaite, J. and Chappell, D. (1994) 'The Job Compact and Crime: Submission to the Committee on Employment Opportunities', *Current Issues in Criminal Justice*, 5(3): 295–300.

Braithwaite, J. and Pettit, P. (1990) *Not Just Deserts: A Republican Theory of Criminal Justice*, Clarendon Press, Oxford.

Brake, M. (1985) *Comparative Youth Culture*, Routledge & Kegan Paul, London.

Brannigan, A. (1984) *Crimes, Courts and Corrections: An Introduction to Crime and Social Control in Canada*, Holt, Rinehart & Winston, Toronto.

Broadhurst, R. and Loh, N. (1993) 'Selective Incapacitation and the Phantom of Deterrence', in Harding, R. (ed.) *Juvenile Repeat Offenders*, Crime Research Centre, University of Western Australia, Perth.

Broadhurst, R., Ferrante, A. and Susilo, N. (1991) *Crime and Justice Statistics for Western Australia: 1990*, Crime Research Centre, University of Western Australia, Nedlands.

Brook, J. and Kohen, J. (1991) *The Parramatta Native Institution and the Black Town*, UNSW Press, Kensington.

Brown, C. (1979) *Understanding Society: An Introduction to Sociological Theory*, John Murray, London.

Brownell, M. (1989) 'The Impact of the Convention of the Rights of the Child', *Youth Studies*, 8(4): 48–53.

Bryett, K., Harrison, A. and Shaw, J. (1994) *The Role and Functions of Police in Australia*, Butterworths, Sydney.

Buchanan, C. and Hartley, P. (1992) *Criminal Choice: The Economic Theory of Crime and its Implications for Crime Control*, Centre for Independent Studies, Sydney.

Burdekin, B. (1989) *Our Homeless Children: Report of the National Inquiry into Homeless Children by the Human Rights and Equal Opportunity Commission*, Australian Government Publishing Service, Canberra.

Cain, M. (1989) 'Introduction: Feminists Transgress Criminology' in Cain, M. (ed.) *Growing Up Good*, Sage, London.

Cain, M. (1994a) *Juveniles in Detention. Special Needs Groups: Young Women, Aboriginal and Indo-Chinese Detainees*, Information and Evaluation Series No. 3, Department of Juvenile Justice, Sydney.

—— (1994b) 'Diversion from Custody and Rehabilitation of Juvenile Detainees: Management Philosophies of the NSW Department of Juvenile Justice', *Youth Studies Australia*, 13(1): 29–35.

—— (1994c) 'A Profile of Juveniles in NSW Juvenile Justice Centres', in Atkinson, L. and Gerull, S.-A. (eds) *National Conference on Juvenile Justice: Conference Proceedings*, Australian Institute of Criminology, Canberra.

Campbell, A. (1984) *The Girls in the Gang*, Basil Blackwell, Oxford.

Carrington, K. (1989) 'Girls and Graffiti', *Cultural Studies*, 3(1): 89–100.

—— (1990a) 'Youth: The Right Police?', *Arena*, 91: 18–24.

—— (1990b) 'Aboriginal Girls and Juvenile Justice: What Justice? White Justice', *Journal for Studies in Social Justice*, 3: 1–17.

—— (1993) *Offending Girls*, Allen & Unwin, Sydney.

Carroll, M. (1994) 'Implementational Issues: Considering the Conferencing Options for Victoria', in Alder, C. and Wundersitz, J. (eds) *Family Conferencing and Juvenile Justice*, Australian Institute of Criminology, Canberra.

Carter, J. (ed.) (1991) *Measuring Child Poverty*, Brotherhood of St Laurence, Melbourne.

Casburn, M. (1979) *Girls Will be Girls*, Explorations in Feminism, WRRC, London.

Chambliss, W. (1975) 'The Political Economy of Crime: A Comparative Study of Nigeria and USA', in Taylor, I., Walton, P. and Young, J. (eds) *Critical Criminology*, Routledge & Kegan Paul, London.

Chambliss, W. and Mankoff, M. (1976) *Whose Law, What Order? A Conflict Approach to Criminology*, John Wiley & Sons, Toronto.

Chan, J. (1994) 'Policing Youth in Ethnic Communities: Is Community Policing the Answer?', in White, R., and Alder, C., *The Police and Young People in Australia*, Cambridge University Press, Melbourne.

Chappell, D. (1989) 'Opening Remarks', in Vernon, J. and Bracey, D. (eds) *Police Resources and Effectiveness*, Australian Institute of Criminology, Canberra.

Charikar, K. and Seiffert, J. (1994) *On the Scrapheap? The Costs of School Closures*, Victorian Council of Social Services, Melbourne.

Chesney-Lind, M. (1974) 'Juvenile Delinquency and the Sexualisation of Female Crime', *Psychology Today*, July: 4–7.

Chesney-Lind, M. and Shelden, R. (1992) *Girls, Delinquency and Juvenile Justice*, Brooks/Cole Publishing, California.

Chisholm, R. (1984) 'Aborigines and the Juvenile Justice System' (unpublished paper), Law School, University of New South Wales.

—— (1988) 'Towards an Aboriginal Child Placement Principle: A View from New South Wales' in Morse, B. and Woodman, G. (eds) *Indigenous Law and the State*, Foris Publications, Dordrecht.

Cicourel A. (1976) *The Social Organisation of Juvenile Justice*, Heinemann, London.

Clarke, J. (1985) 'Whose Justice? The Politics of Juvenile Control', *International Journal of the Sociology of Law*, 13: 407–21.

Clarke, J., Hall, S., Jefferson, T. and Roberts, B. (1976) 'Subcultures, Cultures and Class: A Theoretical Overview', in Hall, S. and Jefferson, T. (eds) *Resistance Through Rituals: Youth Subcultures in Post-War Britain*, Hutchinson, London.

Clarke, R. (ed.) (1992) *Situational Crime Prevention: Successful Case Studies*, Harrow & Heston, New York.

Clinard, B. (1974) *The Sociology of Deviant Behaviour*, Holt, Rinehart & Winston, New York.

Cloward, R. and Ohlin, L. (1960) *Delinquency and Opportunity: A Theory of Delinquent Gangs*, Free Press, Chicago.

Cohen, A. (1955) *Delinquent Boys: The Culture of the Gang*, Free Press, Chicago.

Cohen, P. (1979) 'Policing the Working-Class City', in Fine et al. (eds) *Capitalism and the Rule of Law*, Hutchinson, London.

Cohen, S. (1973) *Folk Devils and Moral Panics*, Paladin, London.

—— (1979) 'The Punitive City: Notes on the Dispersal of Social Control', *Contemporary Crises*, 3: 339–63.

—— (1985) *Visions of Social Control*, Polity Press, Cambridge.

Collis, M. and Griffin, M. (1993) 'Developing a Course for Young Offenders', *Youth Studies Australia*, 12(3): 25–8.

Comstock, G. D. (1991) *Violence Against Lesbians and Gay Men*, Columbia University Press, New York.

Connell, R.W. (1987) *Gender and Power*, Allen & Unwin, Sydney.

Considine, M. (1988) 'The Costs of Increased Control: Corporate Management and Australian Community Organisation', *Australian Social Work*, 14(3): 17–25.

Conway, E. (1992) 'Digging into Disorder: Some Initial Reflections on the Tyneside Riots', *Youth and Policy*, 37: 4–14.

Cornforth, M. (1987) *Historical Materialism* (vol. 2 of *Dialectical Materialism: An Introduction*), Lawrence & Wishart, London.

Corrigan, P. (1979) *Schooling the Smash Street Kids*, Macmillan, London.

Coumarelos, C. (1994) *Juvenile Offending: Predicting Persisitence and Determining Cost-Effectiveness of Interventions*, NSW Bureau of Crime Statistics and Research, Sydney.

Coventry, G., Muncie, J., and Walters, R. (1992) *Rethinking Social Policy for Young People and Crime Prevention*, Discussion Paper No. 1, National Centre for Socio-Legal Studies, La Trobe University, Melbourne.

Coventry, G. and Polk, K. (1985) 'Theoretical Perspectives on Juvenile Delinquency', in Borowski, A. and Murray, J. (eds) *Juvenile Delinquency in Australia*, Methuen, Sydney.

Coventry, G. and Walters, R. (1993) 'Towards a National Perspective on Australian Youth Crime Prevention', in Atkinson, L. and Gerull, S.-A. (eds) *National Conference on Juvenile Justice: Conference Proceedings*, Australian Institute of Criminology, Canberra.

Cowlishaw, G. (1988) *Black, White or Brindle*, Cambridge University Press, Cambridge.

Cozens, M. (1993) 'Ensuring Detention is a Last Resort for Young Women', paper presented to *Youth 93: The Regeneration Conference*, Hobart, 3–5 November 1993.

Crane, P. (1993) 'The United Nations and Juvenile Justice: An Overview', *Transitions*, 3(3): 41–7.

Crawford, J. (1982) *Australian Courts of Law*, Oxford University Press, Melbourne.

Crawford-Maher, E. (1993) 'Developing Community Initiatives in Juvenile Justice', in McKillop, S. (ed.) *Aboriginal Justice Issues*, Australian Institute of Criminology, Canberra.

Cunneen, C. (1985) 'Working Class Boys and Crime: Theorising the Class/Gender Mix', in Patton, P. and Poole, R. (eds) *War/Masculinity*, Intervention Publications, Sydney.

—— (1987) 'Newspaper Reporting of Crime, Law and Order in North-west NSW', *Journal for Social Justice Studies*, 2: 14–32.

—— (1988) 'The Policing of Public Order: Some Thoughts on Culture, Space and Political Economy', in Findlay, M. and Hogg, R. (eds) *Understanding Crime and Criminal Justice*, Law Book Company, Sydney.

—— (1989) 'Constructing a Law and Order Agenda: Conservative Populism and Aboriginal People in North-west New South Wales', *Aboriginal Law Bulletin*, 2(38): 6–9.

—— (1990a) 'Aborigines and Law and Order Regimes', *Journal for Social Justice Studies*, Special Edition Series, Contemporary Race Relations, 3: 37–50.

—— (1990b) *A Study of Aboriginal Juveniles and Police Violence*, Human Rights and Equal Opportunity Commission, Sydney.

—— (1993) 'Juvenile Justice Compromise in NSW', *Alternative Law Journal*, 18(4): 186–7.

—— (1994) 'Enforcing Genocide? Aboriginal Young People and the Police', in White, R. and Alder, C. (eds) *The Police and Young People in Australia*, Cambridge University Press, Melbourne.

Cunneen, C., Findlay, M., Lynch, R. and Tupper, V. (1989) *Dynamics of Collective Conflict. Riots at the Bathurst Motorcycle Races*, Law Book Company, North Ryde.

Cunneen, C. and Morrow, J. (1994) 'Alternative Penal Sanctions', in Tay, A. and Leung, C. (eds) *Australian Law and Legal Thinking in the 1990s*, Faculty of Law, University of Sydney.

Cunneen, C. and Robb, T. (1987) *Criminal Justice in North-west New South Wales*, NSW Bureau of Crime Statistics and Research, Sydney.

Datesman, S. and Scarpitti, F. (1980) 'Unequal Protection for Males and Females in the Juvenile Court', in Datesman, S. and Scarpitti, F. (eds) *Women, Crime and Justice*, Oxford University Press, Oxford.

Davis, M. (1990) *City of Quartz: Excavating the Future in Los Angeles*, Verso, London.

Dodson, M. (1993) *First Report Aboriginal and Torres Strait Islander Social Justice Commission*, AGPS, Canberra.

Donzelot, J. (1979) *The Policing of Families*, Hutchinson, London.

Downes, D. (1966) *The Delinquent Solution*, Routledge & Kegan Paul, London.

D'Souza, N. (1990) 'Aboriginal Children and the Juvenile Justice System', *Aboriginal Law Bulletin*, 2(44): 4–5.

Easteal, P. (1989) *Vietnamese Refugees: Crime Rates of Minors and Youths in NSW*, Australian Institute of Criminology, Canberra.

Eaton, M. and Stilwell, F. (1993) 'Ten Years Hard Labor', *Journal of Australian Political Economy*, 31: 89–105.

Edgar, D., Kean, D. and McDonald, P. (eds) (1989) *Child Poverty*, Allen & Unwin, Sydney.

Edwards, C. and Read, P. (1988) *The Lost Children*, Doubleday, Moorebank.

Eisenstein, H. (1984) *Contemporary Feminist Thought*, Unwin Paperbacks, London.

Elder, B. (1988) *Blood on the Wattle*, Child & Associates, Frenchs Forest.

Empey, L. (1982) *American Delinquency: Its Meaning and Construction*, The Dorsey Press, Chicago.

Erikson, K. (1964) 'Notes on the Sociology of Deviance', in Becker, H. (ed.) *The Other Side: Perspectives in Deviance*, Free Press, New York.

Ethnic Affairs Commission of NSW (1986) *Not a Single Problem: Not a Single Solution*, Ethnic Affairs Commission of NSW, Sydney.

Eysenck, H. (1984) 'Crime and Personality', in Muller, D., Blackmann, D. and Chapmann, A. (eds) *Psychology and Law*, John Wiley & Sons, New York.

Fanon, F. (1967) *The Wretched of the Earth*, Penguin, London.

Farrell, A. (1992) *Crime, Class and Corruption: The Politics of the Police*, Bookmarks, London.

Federation of Ethnic Communities' Councils of Australia (FECCA) (1991) *Background Paper on Ethnic Youth*, paper prepared for FECCA's Multicultural Youth Conference, Sydney.

Felson, M. (1994) *Crime and Everyday Life: Insights and Implications for Society*, Pine Forge Press, London.

Ferdinand, T. N. (1989) 'Juvenile Delinquency or Juvenile Justice: Which Came First?', *Criminology*, 27(1): 79–106.

Fine, B. (1984) *Democracy and the Rule of Law: Liberal Ideals and Marxist Critiques*, Pluto, London.

Finkenhauer, J. (1982) *Scared Straight and the Panacea Phenomenon*, Engle Cliffs, Prentice Hall.

Finnane, M. (1994) 'Larrikins, Delinquents and Cops: Police and Young People in Australian History', in White, R. and Alder, C. (eds) *The Police and Young People in Australia*, Cambridge University Press, Melbourne.

Fishbein, D. (1990) 'Biological Perspectives in Criminology', *Criminology*, 28(1): 27–72.

Fitzgerald, G. (1989) *Report of the Commission of Possible Illegal Activities and Associated Police Misconduct*, Queensland Government Printer, Brisbane.

Foucault, M. (1977) *Discipline and Punish: The Birth of the Prison*, Penguin, London.

Frazier, C. and Cochran, J. (1986) 'Detention of Juveniles: Its Effects on Subsequent Juvenile Court Processing', *Youth and Society*, 17(1): 286–305.

Freiberg, A., Fox, R. and Hogan, M. (1988) *Sentencing Young Offenders*, Australian Law Reform Commission, Sentencing Research Paper 11, Sydney.

Freund, J. (1969) *The Sociology of Max Weber*, Vintage Books, New York.

Gale, F., Bailey-Harris, R. and Wundersitz, J. (1990) *Aboriginal Youth and the Criminal Justice System*, Cambridge University Press, Cambridge.

Gale, F., Naffine, N. and Wundersitz, J. (eds) (1993) *Juvenile Justice: Debating the Issues*, Allen & Unwin, Sydney.

Garland, D. (1985) *Punishment and Welfare: A History of Penal Sanctions*, Gower, Aldershot.

Geason, S. and Wilson, P. (1989) *Designing Out Crime: Crime Prevention Through Environmental Design*, Australian Institute of Criminology, Canberra.

Gelsthorpe, L. (1989) *Sexism and the Female Offender*, Gower, Aldershot.

Gelsthorpe, L. and Morris, A. (eds) (1990) *Feminist Perspectives in Criminology*, Open University Press, Milton Keynes.

Gendreau, P. and Ross, R. (1983–4) 'Correctional Treatment: Some Recommendations for Effective Intervention', *Juvenile and Family Court Journal*, Winter: 31–7.

Ghys, P. (1994) 'Aboriginals and the Juvenile Justice System. The Victorian Koori Justice Project', paper presented to the Australian Institute of Criminology, Aboriginal Justice Issues II Conference, Townsville, 14–17 June 1994.

Gibbons, D. (1977) *Society, Crime and Criminal Careers*, Prentice Hall, New Jersey.

—— (1979) *The Criminological Enterprise: Theories and Perspectives*, Prentice Hall, New Jersey.

Gillis, J. R. (1975) 'The Evolution of Juvenile Delinquency in England 1890–1914', *Past and Present*, 65: 96–126.

—— (1981) *Youth and History*, Academic Press, New York.

GLAD (Gay Men and Lesbians Against Discrimination) (1994) *Not A Day Goes By*, GLAD, Melbourne.

Goodhall, H. (1982) 'A History of Aboriginal Communities in NSW, 1909–1939', Ph.D. thesis, Sydney University.

—— (1990a) 'Saving the Children', *Aboriginal Law Bulletin*, 2(44): 6–9.

—— (1990b) 'Policing in Whose Interest?', *Journal for Social Justice Studies*, 3: 19–36.

Gottfredson, M. and Hirschi, T. (1990) *A General Theory of Crime*, Stanford University Press, Stanford.

Grabosky, P. and Wilson, P. (1989) *Journalism and Justice: How Crime is Reported*, Pluto Press, Leichhardt.

Graycar, A. and Jamrozik, A. (1989) *How Australians Live: Social Policy in Theory and Practice*, Macmillan, Melbourne.

Graycar, R. and Morgan, J. (1990) *The Hidden Gender of Law*, Federation Press, Sydney.

Greenberg, D. (ed.) (1993) *Crime and Capitalism: Readings in Marxist Criminology*, Temple University Press, Philadelphia.

Hall, S. (1980) 'Popular-Democratic vs. Authoritarian Populism: Two Ways of "Taking Democracy Seriously" ', in Hunt, A. (ed.) *Marxism and Democracy*, Lawrence & Wishart, London.

—— (1994) 'Reform and Change: An Agenda for the 1990s', in White, R. and Alder, C. (eds) *The Police and Young People in Australia*, Cambridge University Press, Melbourne.

Hall, S. and Jefferson, T. (eds) (1976) *Resistance Through Rituals: Youth Subcultures in Post-War Britain*, Hutchinson, London.

Hall, S., Jefferson, T., Critcher, C., and Roberts, B. (1978) *Policing the Crisis: Mugging, the State, and Law and Order*, Macmillan, London.

Hall, S. and Scraton, P. (1981) 'Law, Class and Control', in Fitzgerald, M., McLennan, G. and Pawson, J. (eds) *Crime and Society: Readings in History and Theory*, Routledge & Kegan Paul and Open University Press, London.

Hamparian, D., Schuster, R., Dinitz, S. and Conrad, J. (1978) *The Violent Few: A Study of Dangerous Juvenile Offenders*, Lexington Books, Lexington.

Hancock, L. (1980) 'The Myth that Females are Treated More Leniently than Males in the Juvenile Justice System', *Australian and New Zealand Journal of Sociology*, 63: 4–13.

Hancock, L. and Chesney-Lind, M. (1982) 'Female Status Offenders and Justice Reforms: An International Perspective', *Australian and New Zealand Journal Of Criminology*, 15: 109–23.

—— (1985) 'Juvenile Justice Legislation and Gender Discrimination', in Borowski, A. and Murray, J. (eds) *Juvenile Delinquency in Australia*, Methuen, North Ryde.

Hancock, L. and Hiller, A. (1981) 'The Processing of Juveniles in Victoria', in Mukherjee, S.K. and Scutt, J. (eds) *Women and Crime*, Allen & Unwin, Sydney.

Harris, R. and Webb, D. (1987) *Welfare, Power and Juvenile Justice*, Tavistock.

Hearn, R. (1993) 'Policing or Serving? The Role of Police in the Criminalisation of Young People with Mental Health Problems', *Youth Studies Australia*, 12(1): 40–4.

Herek, G. M. and Berrill, K. T. (eds) (1992) *Hate Crimes: Confronting Violence Against Lesbians and Gay Men*, Sage, London.

Hil, R. (1994) ' "Targetting" and Control: Unmasking the Rhetoric of Queensland's Juvenile Crime Prevention Strategy', *Transitions*, 3(3): 16–23.

Hil, R. and Moyle, P. (1992) 'A Day in Prison: A Solution to Reducing Juvenile Recidivism Rates?', *Alternative Law Journal*, 17(5): 224–7.

Hirschi, T. (1969) *Causes of Delinquency*, University of California Press, Berkeley and Los Angeles.

Hirschi, T. and Gottfredson, M. (1983) 'Age and the Explanation of Crime', *American Journal of Sociology*, 89(3): 552–84.

Hogan, M. (1991) 'Youth Crime Prevention and the New Federalism: The Role of Governments', in Halstead, B. (ed.) *Youth Crime Prevention*, Australian Institute of Criminology, Canberra.

Hogg, R. (1988) 'Taking Crime Seriously: Left Realism and Australian Criminology', in Findlay, M. and Hogg, R. (eds) *Understanding Crime and Criminal Justice*, Law Book Company, Sydney.

Howe, A. (1990) 'Sweet Dreams: Deinstitutionalising Young Women' in Graycar, R. (ed.) *Dissenting Opinions*, Allen & Unwin, Sydney.

Human Rights and Equal Opportunity Commission (1993) *State of the Nation Report on People of Non-English Speaking Background*, AGPS, Canberra.

Humphries, S. (1981) *Hooligans or Rebels?*, Basil Blackwell, Oxford.

Hutchings, S. (1995) 'The Great Shoe Store Robbery', in Cowlinshaw, G. and Morris, B. (eds) *Racism Today*, AIATSI Press, Canberra (forthcoming).

Iadicola, P. (1986) 'Community Crime Control Strategies', *Crime and Social Justice*, 25: 140–65.

Indermaur, D. and White, R. (1994) 'Juvenile Rights Given the Boot in Western Australia', *Civil Liberty*, 10(2): 12–14.

Inverarity, J., Lauderdale, P. and Feld, B. (1983) *Law and Society: Sociological Perspectives on Criminal Law*, Little, Brown & Company, Boston.

Jackomos, M. (1994) 'Community and Culture Integration Program for Aboriginal and Torres Strait Islander Young People in Detention (Queensland)', paper presented to the Australian Institute of Criminology, Aboriginal Justice Issues II Conference, Townsville, 14–17 June 1994.

Jackson, H. (1994) 'Youth: Western Australian Legislation and Practice', paper presented to the Australian Institute of Criminology, Aboriginal Justice Issues II Conference, Townsville, 14–17 June 1994.

Jaggs, D. (1986) *Neglected and Criminal: Foundations of Child Welfare Legislation in Victoria*, Phillip Institute of Technology, Melbourne.

James, S. (1994) 'Contemporary Programs with Young People: Beyond Traditional Law Enforcement?', in White, R. and Alder, C. (eds) *The Police and Young People in Australia*, Cambridge University Press, Melbourne.

James, S. and Polk, K. (1989) 'Policing Youth: Themes and Directions', in Chappell, D. and Wilson, P. (eds) *Australian Policing: Contemporary Issues*, Butterworths, Sydney.

Jamrozik, A. (1984) 'Community Resources as a Component of the Social Wage: Implications for Youth Services', paper presented at a conference on community-based care, Adelaide.

—— (1987) 'Winners and Losers in the Welfare State: Recent Trends and Pointers to the Future', in Saunders, P. and Jamrozik, A. (eds) *Social Welfare in the Late 1980s: Reform, Progress or Retreat?*, Social Welfare Research Centre, University of New South Wales, Sydney.

Johnston, E. (1991) *National Report, 5 vols, Royal Commission into Aboriginal Deaths in Custody*, AGPS, Canberra.

Jowett, T. (1993) 'Aboriginal Children Stolen by the State. Williams v. State of New South Wales', *On the Record*, 28: 1–3.

Juvenile Justice Advisory Council (1993) *Green Paper Future Directions for Juvenile Justice in NSW*, Juvenile Justice Advisory Council, Sydney.

Kersten, J. (1989) 'The Institutional Control of Boys and Girls', in Cain, M. (ed.) *Growing Up Good*, Sage, London.

Kraus, J. (1974) 'A Comparison of Corrective Effects of Probation and Detention on Male Juvenile Offenders', *British Journal of Criminology*, 8(1): 49–62.

—— (1977) 'Do Exisiting Penal Measures Reform Juvenile Offenders', *Australian and New Zealand Journal of Criminology*, 10: 217–22.

—— (1978) 'Remand in Custody as a Deterrent in the Juvenile Jurisdiction', *British Journal of Criminology*, 18(3): 285–92.

—— (1981) 'On the Adult Criminality of Male Juvenile Delinquents', *Australian and New Zealand Journal Of Criminology*, 14: 157.

Kraus, J. and Bowmaker, S. (1982) 'How Delinquent are the Delinquents? A Study of Self-Reported Offences', *Australian and New Zealand Journal of Criminology*, 15: 163–9.

Larwill, K. (1992) *Unemployed Australia: A Resource Book*, Brotherhood of St Laurence, Melbourne.

Lea, J. and Young, J. (1984) *What is to be Done about Law and Order?*, Penguin, London.

Lemert, E. (1969) 'Primary and Secondary Deviation', in Cressy, D. and Ward, D. (eds) *Delinquency, Crime and Social Process*, Harper & Row, New York.

Lesbian and Gay Anti-Violence Project (1992) *The Off Our Backs Report: A Study into Anti-Lesbian Violence*, Gay and Lesbian Rights Lobby, Sydney.

Lincoln, R. and Wilson, P. (1994) 'Questioning Crime Prevention: Towards a Social Development Approach', *Transitions*, 3(3): 7–11.

Ludbrook, R. (1994) 'Why Australia Needs A Commissioner for Children', Discussion Paper No. 2, National Children's and Youth Law Centre, Sydney.

Luke, G. (1988) 'Gaol as a Last Resort: The Situation for Juveniles', in Findlay, M. and Hogg, R. (eds) *Understanding Crime and Criminal Justice*, Law Book Company, Sydney.

—— (1993) 'Theory vs Practice: A Case Study', in Gale, F., Naffine, N. and Wundersitz, J. (eds) *Juvenile Justice: Debating the Issues*, Allen & Unwin, Sydney.

Luke, G. and Cunneen, C. (1993) 'Aboriginal Juveniles and the Juvenile Justice System in NSW', in Atkinson, L. and Gerull, S.-A. (eds) *National Conference on Juvenile Justice*, Australian Institute of Criminology, Canberra.

Lukes, S. (1973) *Emile Durkheim: His Life and Work*, Penguin, London.

Lundman, R. (1994) *Prevention and Control of Juvenile Delinquency*, Oxford University Press, Oxford.

Maas, F. (1990) 'Shifting Responsibility: A Decade of Youth Policy', *Family Matters*, 26: 19–24.

McCulloch, J. and Schetzer, L. (1993) *Brute Force: The Need for Affirmative Action in the Victoria Police Force*, Federation of Community Legal Centres (Victoria), Melbourne.

McDonald, B. (1992) 'Unemployment Statistics—Figure it Out', *Social Welfare Impact*, May: 10–12.

McDonald, J. (1991) 'The New South Wales Police Service and Youth Crime Prevention', in Halstead, B. (ed.) *Youth Crime Prevention*, Australian Institute of Criminology, Canberra.

McDonald, P. (1991) 'Youth Wages and Poverty', *Family Matters*, 28: 38–41.

McKillop, S. and Vernon, J. (1991) *The Police and the Community*, Australian Institute of Criminology, Canberra.

McNamara, L. (1992) 'Retrieving the Law and Order Issue from the Right: Alternative Strategies and Community Crime Prevention', *Law In Context*, 10(1): 91–122.

McRobbie, A. and Garber, J. (1976) 'Girls and Subcultures', in Hall, S. and Jefferson, T. (eds) *Resistance through Rituals: Youth Subcultures in Post-War Britain*, Hutchinson, London.

McRobbie, A. and Nava, M. (1984) (eds) *Gender and Generation*, Macmillan, London.

Markus, A. (1990) *Governing Savages*, Allen & Unwin, Sydney.

Martinson, R. (1974) 'What Works? Questions and Answers About Prison Reform', *The Public Interest*, 10: 22–54.

Matza, D. (1964) *Delinquency and Drift*, John Wiley & Sons, New York.

Maunders, D. (1984) *Keeping Them Off The Streets: A History of Voluntary Youth Organisations in Australia 1850–1980*, Phillip Institute of Technology, Melbourne.

Maxwell, G. (1993) 'Family Decision-Making in Youth Justice: The New Zealand Model', in Atkinson, L., and Gerull, S.-A. (eds) *National Conference on Juvenile Justice: Conference Proceedings*, Australian Institute of Criminology, Canberra.

Maxwell, G. and Morris, A. (1994) 'The New Zealand Model of Family Group Conferences', in Alder, C. and Wundersitz, J. (eds) *Family Conferencing and Juvenile Justice*, Australian Institute of Criminology, Canberra.

May, M. (1981) 'Innocence and Experience: The Evolution of the Concept of Juvenile

Delinquency in the Mid-Nineteenth Century', in Dale, R. (ed.), *Education and the State*, vol. 2, Falmer Press, Lewes.

Merton, R. (1957) *Social Theory and Social Structure*, Free Press, New York.

Miller, J. B. (1958) 'Lower Class Culture as a Milieu of Gang Delinquency', *Journal of Social Issues*, 14: 3.

Miller, L. (1983) *Runaway Girls: Uncontrollable or Unsupported*, Marrickville Legal Centre, Marrickville.

Milne, C. and Munro, L. Jnr. (1981) 'Who is Unresponsive: Negative Assessments of Aboriginal Children', Discussion Paper No. 1, Aboriginal Children's Research Project, Family and Children's Services Agency, Sydney.

Moore, E. (1994) 'Alternatives to Secure Detention for Girls', in Atkinson, L. and Gerull, S.-A. (eds) *National Conference on Juvenile Detention*, Australian Institute of Criminology, Canberra.

Morgan, F. (1993) 'Contact with the Justice System over the Juvenile Years', in Atkinson, L. and Gerull, S.-A. (eds) *National Conference on Juvenile Justice*, Australian Institute of Criminology, Canberra.

Morris, A. (1987) *Women, Crime and Criminal Justice*, Basil Blackwell, Oxford.

Morris, A. and Giller, H. (1987) *Understanding Juvenile Justice*, Croom Helm, London.

Morris, A. and Maxwell, G. (1993) 'Juvenile Justice in New Zealand: A New Paradigm', *Australian and New Zealand Journal of Criminology*, 26(1): 72–90.

Morris, L. and Irwin, S. (1992) 'Employment Histories and the Concept of the Underclass', *Sociology: The Journal of the British Sociological Association*, 26(3): 401–20.

Mukherjee, S. K. (1983) *Age and Crime*, Australian Institute of Criminology, Canberra.

—— (1985) 'Juvenile Delinquency: Dimensions of the Problem', in Borowski, A. and Murray, J. (eds) *Juvenile Delinquency in Australia*, Methuen, North Ryde.

Mukherjee, S. K. and Dagger, D. (1990) *The Size of the Crime Problem in Australia*, Australian Insitute of Criminology, Canberra.

Muncie, J. and Coventry, G. (1989) 'Punishment in the Community and the Victorian Youth Attendance Order: A Look into the Future', *Australian and New Zealand Journal of Criminology*, 22(2): 179–90.

Murray, M. (1985) 'The Development of Contemporary Juvenile Justice and Correctional Policy', in Borowski, A. and Murray, J. (eds) *Juvenile Delinquency in Australia*, Methuen, North Ryde.

Naffine, N. (1987) *Female Crime: The Construction of Women in Criminology*, Allen & Unwin, Sydney.

—— (1990) *Law and the Sexes: Explorations in Feminist Jurisprudence*, Allen & Unwin, Sydney.

—— (1993) 'Philosophies of Juvenile Justice', in Gale, F., Naffine, N. and Wundersitz, J. (eds) *Juvenile Justice: Debating the Issues*, Allen & Unwin, Sydney.

Naffine, N. and Gale, F. (1989) 'Testing the Nexus: Gender, Crime and Unemployment', *British Journal of Criminology*, 29: 144.

Naffine, N., Wundersitz, J. and Gale, F. (1990) 'Back to Justice for Juveniles: The Rhetoric or Reality of Law Reform', *Australian and New Zealand Journal of Criminology*, 23(3): 192–205.

National Youth Affairs Research Scheme/Australian Bureau of Statistics (NYARS/ABS) (1993) *Australia's Young People: A Statistical Profile*, National Clearinghouse for Youth Studies, Hobart.

Nava, M. (1984) 'Youth Service Provision, Social Order and the Question of Girls', in McRobbie, A. and Nava, M. (eds) *Gender and Generation*, Macmillan, London.

Nettler, G. (1984) *Explaining Crime*, McGraw-Hill, New York.

New South Wales Bureau of Crime Statistics and Research (1990) *NSW Lower Criminal Courts and Children's Courts Statistics*, Sydney.

New South Wales Department of Family and Community Services (1988) *Report from the Working Party on Services to Young People with Intellectual Disabilities in the Juvenile Justice System*, NSW Department of Family and Community Services, Sydney.

New South Wales Department of Juvenile Justice (1992) *Annual Report 1991–92*, NSW Department of Juvenile Justice, Sydney.

—— (1993) *Annual Children's Court Statistics Criminal Matters 1992–93*, NSW Department of Juvenile Justice, Sydney.

New South Wales Office of the Ombudsman (1994) *Race Relations and Our Police*, Office of the Ombudsman, Sydney.

O'Connell, T. (1993) 'Wagga Wagga Juvenile Cautioning Program: "It May Be The Way To Go!" ', in Atkinson, L. and Gerull, S.-A. (eds) *National Conference on Juvenile Justice: Conference Proceedings*, Australian Institute of Criminology, Canberra.

O'Connor, I. (1994) 'Young People and their Rights', in White, R. and Alder, C. (eds) *The Police and Young People in Australia*, Cambridge University Press, Melbourne.

O'Connor, I. and Sweetapple, P. (1988) *Children in Justice*, Longman Cheshire, Melbourne.

O'Grady, C. (1992) 'A Rising Star in the Prosecution of Juveniles in Victoria', *Youth Studies Australia*, 11(4): 35–40.

Ohlin, L., Miller A. and Coates R. (1976) *Juvenile Correctional Reform in Massachusetts*, National Institute for Juvenile Justice and Delinquency Prevention, US Government Printing Office, Washington.

O'Malley, P. (1983) *Law, Capitalism and Democracy*, Allen & Unwin, Sydney.

O'Malley, P., Coventry, G. and Walters, R. (1993) 'Victoria's "Day in Prison Program": An Evaluation and Critique', *Australian and New Zealand Journal of Criminology*, 26(2): 171–83.

Ozols, E. (1994) 'Pre-Sentence Reports on Aboriginal and Islander People: Overcoming the Myths and Providing Culturally Appropriate Information', paper presented to the Australian Institute of Criminology, Aboriginal Justice Issues II Conference, Townsville, 14–17 June 1994.

Palmer, D. and Collard, L. (1993) ' "Aboriginal Youth" as "Watjela" Artifacts: Aboriginalism in Youth Studies', paper presented at Youth 93: The Regeneration Conference, National Clearinghouse for Youth Studies, Hobart, 3–5 November 1993.

Parent, D. (1994) 'Boot Camps Failing to Achieve Goals', *Overcrowded Times*, 5(4): 8–11.

Parker, H., Casburn, M. and Turnbull, D. (1981) *Receiving Juvenile Justice*, Basil Blackwell, Oxford.

Pearce, F. (1976) *Crimes of the Powerful: Marxism, Crime and Deviance*, Pluto, London.

Pearson, G. (1983) *Hooligan: A History of Respectable Fears*, Macmillan, London.

Pettit, P. and Braithwaite, J. (1993) 'Not Just Deserts, Even in Sentencing', *Current Issues in Criminal Justice*, 4(3): 225–39.

Pitts, J. (1988) *The Politics of Juvenile Crime*, Sage, London.

Pixley, J. (1993) *Citizenship and Employment: Investigating Post-Industrial Options*, Cambridge University Press, Melbourne.

Platt, A. (1977) *The Child Savers*, University of Chicago, Chicago.

Plummer, K. (1979) 'Misunderstanding Labelling Perspectives', in Downes, D. and Rock, P. (eds) *Deviant Interpretations*, Martin Robertson, Oxford.

Polk, K. (1988) 'Education, Youth Unemployment and Student Resistance', in Slee, R. (ed.) *Discipline and Schools: A Curriculum Perspective*, Macmillan, Melbourne.

—— (1993) 'Jobs, Not Gaols: A New Agenda for Youth', in Atkinson, L. and Gerull, S.-A. (eds) *National Conference on Juvenile Justice: Conference Proceedings*, Australian Institute of Criminology, Canberra.

—— (1994) 'Family Conferencing: Theoretical and Evaluative Questions', in Alder, C. and Wundersitz, J. (eds) *Family Conferencing and Juvenile Justice*, Australian Institute of Criminology, Canberra.

Polk, K. and Tait, D. (1990) 'Changing Youth Labour Markets and Youth Lifestyles', *Youth Studies*, 9(1): 17–23.

Potas, I., Vining, A. and Wilson, P. (1990) *Young People and Crime: Costs and Prevention*, Australian Institute of Criminology, Canberra.

Pratt, J. (1989) 'Corporatism: The Third Model of Juvenile Justice', *British Journal of Criminology*, 29(3): 236–54.

Pusey, M. (1991) *Economic Rationalism in Canberra: A Nation-Building State Changes its Mind*, Cambridge University Press, Melbourne.

Quinney, R. (1970) *The Social Reality of Crime*, Little Brown, Boston.

—— (ed.) (1974) *Crime and Justice in America: A Critical Understanding*, Little Brown, Boston.

Raynor, M. (1994) 'Human Rights, Families and Community Interests', *Family Matters*, 37: 60–6.

Read, P. (1982) *The Stolen Generations*, NSW Ministry of Aboriginal Affairs, Sydney.

Roach Anleu, S. (1991) *Deviance, Conformity and Control*, Longman Cheshire, Melbourne.

Rodger, J. (1992) 'The Welfare State and Social Closure: Social Division and the "Underclass" ', *Critical Social Policy*, 35: 45–63.

Rose, N. (1989) *Governing the Soul: The Shaping of the Private Self*, Routledge, London.

Rubington, E. and Weinberg, M. (eds) (1978) *Deviance: The Interactionist Perspective*, Macmillan, New York.

Rutherford, A. (1986) *Growing Out of Crime*, Penguin, Harmondsworth.

Rutter, M. and Giller, M. (1983) *Juvenile Delinquency: Trends and Perspectives*, Penguin, Harmondsworth.

Ryan, M. and Smith, D. (1994) *Investigation of the Circumstances Surrounding Incidents at Westbrook Youth Detention Centre*, Department of Family Services and Aboriginal and Islander Affairs, Brisbane.

Sandor, D. (1993) 'The Thickening Blue Wedge: Juvenile Justice', *Alternative Law Journal*, 18(3): 104–8.

Sansom, B. and Baines, P. (1988) 'Aboriginal Child Placement in the Urban Context', in Morse, B. and Woodman, G. (eds) *Indigenous Law and the State*, Foris Publications, Dordrecht.

Sarri, R. (1983) 'Gender Issues in Juvenile Justice', *Crime and Delinquency*, 29(3): 381.

Saville, L. (1993) 'Future Directions for Girls in Custody', in Atkinson, L. and Gerull, S.-A. (eds) *National Conference on Juvenile Justice*, Australian Institute of Criminology, Canberra.

Schlossman, S. and Wallace, S. (1978) 'The Crime of Precocious Sexuality: Female Juvenile Delinquency in the Progressive Era', *Harvard Educational Review*, 48(1): 65–94.

Schur, E. (1973) *Radical Non-Intervention: Rethinking the Delinquency Problem*, Prentice Hall, New Jersey.

Schwendinger, H. and Schwendinger, J. (1975) 'Defenders of Order or Guardians of Human Rights', in Taylor, I., Walton, P. and Young, J. (eds) *Critical Criminology*, Routledge & Kegan Paul, London.

Scutt, J. (1990) *Women and the Law*, Law Book Company, Sydney.

Searles, M. and Goodfellow, G. (eds) (1994) *Heroes and Villains: An Anthology of Poems by Young People in Detention*, South Australian Youth Participation Arts Project, Adelaide.

Segal, L. (1987) *Is The Future Female? Troubled Thoughts on Contemporary Feminism*, Virago Press, London.

—— (1990) *Slow Motion: Changing Masculinities, Changing Men*, Virago Press, London.

Semmens, R. (1990) 'Individual Control or Social Development', *Youth Studies*, 9(3): 23–9.

Senate Standing Committee on Employment, Education and Training (1992) *Wanted: Our Future*, Australian Government Publishing Service, Canberra.

Sercombe, H. (1993) 'Easy Pickings: The Children's Court and the Economy of News Production', paper presented to *Youth 93: The Regeneration Conference*, Hobart, 3–5 November 1993.

Seymour, J. (1988) *Dealing With Young Offenders*, Law Book Company, North Ryde.

Shacklady-Smith, L. (1978) 'Sexist Assumptions and Female Delinquency: An Empricial Investigation', in Smart, C. and Smart, B. (eds) *Women, Sexuality and Social Control*, Routledge & Kegan Paul, London.

Shaw, C. and McKay, H. (1942) *Juvenile Delinquency and Urban Areas*, Chicago University Press, Chicago.

Sheen, V. and Trethewey, J. (1991) *Unemployment in the Recession: Policies for Reform*, Brotherhood of St Laurence, Melbourne.

Sheldon, W. (1940) *Varieties of Human Physique*, Harper & Row, New York.

Shoemaker, D. (1984) *Theories of Delinquency*, Oxford University Press, New York.

Simpson, B. (1994) '. . . And The Judge Wore Blue', *Alternative Law Journal*, 19(5): 207–10.

Simpson, B. and Simpson, C. (1993) 'The Use of Curfews to Control Juvenile Offending in Australia: Managing Crime or Wasting Time?', *Current Issues in Criminal Justice*, 5(2): 184–99.

Smart, C. (1976) *Women, Crime and Criminology: A Feminist Critique*, Routledge & Kegan Paul, London.

Smith, A. (1776; 1974) *The Wealth of Nations*, Books I–III, Penguin, London.

Smith, G. (1975) 'Kids and Coppers', *Australian and New Zealand Journal of Criminology*, 8(2): 221–30.

SNAICC (1994) 'Aboriginal Children—Still in Terra Nullius', paper presented to the Australian Institute of Criminology, *Aboriginal Justice Issues II Conference*, Townsville, 14–17 June 1994.

Sommerlad, E. (1977) *Aboriginal Juveniles in Custody*, Department of Aboriginal Affairs, Canberra.

South Australian Government (1993) *South Australia's New Juvenile Justice System: Resource & Information Kit*, Adelaide.

Sparkes, R.F., Genn, H.G. and Dodd, D.J. (1977) *Surveying Victims*, Wiley, UK.

Spitzer, S. (1975) 'Toward a Marxian Theory of Deviance', *Social Problems*, 22: 638–51.

Standing Committee on Social Issues (1992) *Juvenile Justice in New South Wales*, Parliament of New South Wales, Legislative Council, Sydney.

Stokes, I. (1992) 'Juvenile Justice in Tasmania', *Criminology Australia*, 4(1): 11–13.

Stratton, J. (1992) *The Young Ones: Working Class Culture, Consumption and the Category of Youth*, Black Swan Press, Perth.

Sumner, C. (1990) 'Foucault, Gender and the Censure of Deviance', in Gelsthorpe, L. and Morris, A. (eds) *Feminist Perspectives in Criminology*, Open University Press, Milton Keynes.

Sutherland, E. and Cressy, D. (1974) *Criminology*, Lippincott Company, New York.

Sutton, A. (1994) 'Crime Prevention: Promise or Threat?', *Australian and New Zealand Journal of Criminology*, 27(1): 5–20.

Sveen, R. (1993) 'Travelling in the Wilderness: Experiential Learning and Youth-at-Risk', *Youth Studies Australia*, 12(3): 14–20.

Sweet, R. (1987) *The Youth Labour Market: A Twenty-Year Perspective*, Curriculum Development Centre, Canberra.

Sykes, G. and Matza, D. (1957) 'Techniques of Neutralization: A Theory of Delinquency', *American Sociological Review*, 22: 664–70.

Tait, D. (1994) 'Cautions and Appearances: Statistics About Youth and Police', in White, R. and Alder, C. (eds) *The Police and Young People in Australia*, Cambridge University Press, Melbourne.

Tait, G. (1993) 'Re-assessing Street Kids: A Critique of Subculture Theory', in White, R. (ed.) *Youth Subcultures: Theory, History and the Australian Experience*, National Clearinghouse for Youth Studies, Hobart.

Tame, C. (1991) 'Freedom, Responsibility and Justice: The Criminology of the "New Right" ', in Stenson, K. and Cowell, D. (eds) *The Politics of Crime Control*, Sage, London.

Taylor, I. (1981) *Law and Order: Arguments for Socialism*, Macmillan, London.

Taylor, I., Walton, P. and Young, J. (1973) *The New Criminology*, Routledge & Kegan Paul, London.

—— (eds) (1975) *Critical Criminology*, Routledge & Kegan Paul, London.

Thomas, C. and Bishop, D. (1984) 'The Effect of Formal and Informal Sanctions on Delinquency: A Longitudinal comparison of Labelling and Deterrence Theories', *The Journal of Criminal Law and Criminology*, 75(4): 1222–45

Thomas, M. (1993) 'A Report of Aboriginal and Torres Strait Islander Children and Young People in the Child Welfare and Juvenile Justice System', unpublished paper, Criminology Department, Melbourne University.

Tong, R. (1989) *Feminist Thought: A Comprehensive Introduction*, Unwin Hyman, London.

Tucker, M. (1977) *If Everyone Cared*, Ure Smith, Sydney.

Underwood, R., White, R. and Omelczuk, S. (1993) *Young People, Youth Services and Legal Issues*, Edith Cowan University, Joondalup.

Van Krieken, R. (1991) *Children and the State*, Allen & Unwin, North Sydney.

Vernon, J. and Bracey, D. (eds) (1989) *Police Resources and Effectiveness*, Australian Institute of Criminology, Canberra.

Venables, P (1988) 'Petford Training Farm', *Aboriginal Law Bulletin*, 1(30).

Walker, L. (1993) 'Girls, Schooling and Subcultures of Resistance', in White, R. (ed.)

Youth Subcultures: Theory, History and the Australian Experience, National Clearinghouse for Youth Studies, Hobart.

Walton, P. (1993) 'Youth Subcultures, Deviancy and the Media', in White, R. (ed.) *Youth Subcultures: Theory, History and the Australian Experience*, National Clearinghouse for Youth Studies, Hobart.

Warner, C. (1982) 'A Study of Self-reported Crime of a Group of Male and Female High School Students', *Australian and New Zealand Journal of Criminology*, 15: 255–73.

Warner, K. (1991) *Sentencing in Tasmania*, Federation Press, Sydney.

—— (1994) 'The Legal Framework of Juvenile Justice', in White, R. and Alder, C. (eds) *The Police and Young People in Australia*, Cambridge University Press, Melbourne.

Watkins, J. (1992) *Youth and the Law*, Discussion Paper No. 3, Select Committee into Youth Affairs, Western Australian Government Printer, Perth.

Watson, L. (1988) 'Our Children: Part of the Past, Present, and Providing a Vison for the Future. A Murri Perspective', *Australian Child and Family Welfare*, August.

Watts, R. (1987) *The Foundations of the National Welfare State*, Allen & Unwin, Sydney.

West, D. (1982) *Delinquency: Its Roots, Careers and Prospects*, Heinneman, London.

White, R. (1989) 'Making Ends Meet: Young People, Work and the Criminal Economy', *Australian and New Zealand Journal of Criminology*, 22(2): 136–50.

—— (1990) *No Space of Their Own: Young People and Social Control in Australia*, Cambridge University Press, Melbourne.

—— (1991) 'Taking Custody to the Community: The Dynamics of Social Control and Social Integration', *Current Issues in Criminal Justice*, 3(2): 171–84.

—— (1992) 'Tough Laws for Hard-Core Politicians', *Alternative Law Journal*, 17(2): 58–60.

—— (ed) (1993a) *Youth Subcultures: Theory, History and the Australian Experience*, National Clearinghouse for Youth Studies, Hobart.

—— (1993b) 'Young People and the Policing of Community Space', *Australian and New Zealand Journal of Criminology*, 26(3): 207–18.

—— (1993c) 'Police Vidiots', *Alternative Law Journal*, 18(3): 109–12.

—— (1994a) 'The Problem of Theory in Australian Youth Studies', *Discourse: The Australian Journal of Educational Studies*, 14(2): 79–91.

—— (1994b) 'Young People, Unemployment and Health', in Waddell, C. and Petersen, A. (eds) *Just Health: Inequality in Illness, Care and Prevention*, Churchill Livingstone, Melbourne.

—— (1994c) 'Shaming and Reintegrative Strategies: Individuals, State Power and Social Interests', in Alder, C. and Wundersitz, J. (eds) *Family Conferencing and Juvenile Justice*, Australian Institute of Criminology, Canberra.

—— (1995 in press) 'The Poverty of the Welfare State: Managing the Underclass', in Emy, H. and James, P. (eds) *The State in Question*, Allen & Unwin, Sydney.

White, R. and Alder, C. (eds) (1994) *The Police and Young People in Australia*, Cambridge University Press, Melbourne.

White, R. and Haines, F. (forthcoming) *Crime and Criminology: An Introduction to Concepts and Explanations*, Oxford University Press, Melbourne.

White, R. and Richards, C. (1992) 'Police Unions and Police Powers', *Current Issues in Criminal Justice*, 4(2): 157–76.

White, R. and Sutton, A. (1995) 'Crime Prevention, Urban Space and Social Exclusion', *Australian and New Zealand Journal of Sociology*, 31(1): 82–99.

Wilkie, M. (1991) *Aboriginal Justice Programs in Western Australia*, Research Report No. 5, Crime Research Centre, University of Western Australia.

—— (1992) 'WA's Draconian New Juvenile Offender Sentencing Laws', *Aboriginal Law Bulletin*, 2(55): 15–17.

Willis, S. (1980) 'Made To Be Moral—At Parramatta Girl's School, 1898–1923', in Roe, J. (ed.) *Twentieth Century Sydney*, Hale and Iremonger, Sydney.

Wilson, P. and Lincoln, R. (1992) 'Young People, Economic Crisis, Social Control and Crime', *Current Issues in Criminal Justice*, 4(2): 110–16.

Wolfgang, M. E., Figlio, R. M. and Sellin, T. (1972) *Delinquency in a Birth Cohort*, University of Chicago Press, Chicago.

Women's Co-ordination Unit (1986) *Girls at Risk Report*, Women's Co-ordination Unit, NSW Premier's Office, Sydney.

Wootten, H. (1989) *Report of the Inquiry into the Death of Malcolm Charles Smith*, Royal Commission into Aboriginal Deaths in Custody, AGPS, Canberra.

—— (1991) *Regional Report of Inquiry in New South Wales, Victoria and Tasmania*, Royal Commission into Aboriginal Deaths in Custody, AGPS, Canberra.

Wundersitz, J. (1993) 'Some Statistics on Youth Offending', in Gale, F., Naffine, N. and Wundersitz, J. (eds) *Juvenile Justice: Debating the Issues*, Allen & Unwin, North Sydney.

Wundersitz, J., Naffine, N. and Gale, F. (1988) 'Chivalry, Justice or Paternalism? The Female Offender in the Juvenile Justice System', *Australian and New Zealand Journal of Criminology*, 24(3): 359–76.

Yasmar Juvenile Justice Centre (1994) *Mission and the Philosophy, Objectives and Key Outcomes for the Young Women in Custody Program*, Yasmar Juvenile Justice Centre, Sydney.

Young, J. (1971) 'The Role of the Police as Amplifiers of Deviancy, Negotiators of Reality and Translators of Fantasy: Some Consequences of Our Present System of Drug Control as Seen in Notting Hill', in Cohen, S. (ed.) *Images of Deviance*, Penguin, London.

—— (1981) 'Thinking Seriously About Crime: Some Models of Criminology', in Fitzgerald, M., McLennon, G. and Pawson, J. (eds) *Crime and Society: Readings in History and Theory*, Routledge & Kegan Paul, London.

—— (1986) 'The Failure of Criminology: The Need for a Radical Realism', in Matthews, R. and Young, J. (eds) *Confronting Crime*, Sage, London.

—— (1991) 'Left Realism and the Priorities of Crime Control', in Stenson, K. and Cowell, D. (eds) *The Politics of Crime Control*, Sage, London.

Youth Advocacy Centre (1993) *Juvenile Justice: Rhetoric or Reality?*, Youth Advocacy Centre, Brisbane.

Youth Justice Coalition (1990) *Kids in Justice. A Blueprint for the 90s*, Youth Justice Coalition, Sydney.

Youth Justice Coalition, Western Sydney Juvenile Justice Interest Group and Youth Action and Policy Association (NSW) (1994) *Nobody Listens. The Experience of Contact Between Young People and Police*, Youth Justice Coalition, Sydney.

index